Contemporary Models in Liaison Psychiatry

Contemporary Models in Liaison Psychiatry

Edited by

Robert A. Faguet
Fawzy I. Fawzy
David K. Wellisch
Robert O. Pasnau

UCLA School of Medicine
Los Angeles, California

SP MEDICAL & SCIENTIFIC BOOKS
a division of Spectrum Publications, Inc.
New York • London

SPECTRUM PUBLICATIONS, INC.
175-20 Wexford Terrace, Jamaica, N.Y. 11432

Library of Congress Cataloging in Publication Data

Main entry under title:

Contemporary models in liaison psychiatry.

   Includes index.
   1. Psychiatric consultation. 2. Sick--
Psychology. I. Faguet, Robert Andrew.
RC455.2.C65F33   616.8'91·   77-22528
 ISBN 0-89335-031-1

DEDICATION

To Our Families

Acknowledgments

Sincere thanks to Susan Crow for her invaluable editorial assistance; to Jan I. Perlstein for his help during long Saturday afternoons; and to Betty Romero, Melody Norris, and Mary J. Bersheid for their kind and cheerful cooperation in the preparation of this volume. And special thanks to Kay R. Jamison, Ph.D. and Kay F. Rowland, Ph.D. for their constant support and encouragement.

Contributors

Daniel B. Auerbach, M.D.
Department of Psychiatry
University of California at Los Angeles
School of Medicine
Los Angeles, California
Department of Consultation-Liaison
    Psychiatry
Veteran's Administration Hospital
Sepulveda, California

Susan D. Diskin, M.A.
Department of Psychology
University of California at Los Angeles
Los Angeles, California

Robert Andrew Faguet, M.D.
Department of Psychiatry
University of California at Los Angeles
School of Medicine
Southern California Psychoanalytic
    Institute
Los Angeles, California

Fawzy I. Fawzy, M.D.
Department of Psychiatry
Psychiatric Consultation-Liaison Service
University of California at Los Angeles
School of Medicine
Los Angeles, California

Gregory J. Firman, M.D.
Department of Psychiatry
University of California at Los Angeles
School of Medicine
Los Angeles, California

Craig Fischer, M.D.
Department of Psychiatry
University of California at Los Angeles
School of Medicine
UCLA Family Planning Clinic
Los Angeles, California

Claude T. H. Friedmann, M.D.
Department of Psychiatry
University of California at Los Angeles
School of Medicine
Department of Adult Psychiatry
Harbor General Hospital
Torrance, California

Susan Fukushima, M.D.
Department of Psychiatry
University of California at Los Angeles
School of Medicine
Los Angeles, California

Charles Hollingsworth, M.D.
Department of Psychiatry
University of California at Los Angeles
School of Medicine
Los Angeles, California

Martha Bates Jura, Ph.D.
Department of Psychiatry
University of California at Los Angeles
School of Medicine
Los Angeles, California

Walter Kaye, M.D.
Department of Psychiatry
University of California at Los Angeles
School of Medicine
Los Angeles, California

Ellen E. Linn, R.N., E.T.
Department of Nursing
Center for the Health Sciences
University of California at Los Angeles
Los Angeles, California

Z.J. Lipowski, M.D.
Department of Psychiatry
Dartmouth Medical School
Hanover, New Hampshire

Richard G. Ness, M.D.
Department of Psychiatry
University of California at Los Angeles
School of Medicine
Los Angeles, California

Regina Pally, M.D.
Department of Psychiatry
University of California at Los Angeles
School of Medicine
Los Angeles, California

Robert O. Pasnau, M.D.
Department of Psychiatry
Psychiatric Consultation-Liaison Service
University of California at Los Angeles
School of Medicine
Los Angeles, California

Betty Pfefferbaum, M.D.
Department of Psychiatry
University of California at Los Angeles
School of Medicine
Los Angeles, California

Nicholas H. Putnam, M.D.
Department of Psychiatry
University of California at Los Angeles
School of Medicine
Los Angeles, California

S. Charles Schulz, M.D.
Department of Psychiatry
University of California at Los Angeles
School of Medicine
Los Angeles, California

Gordon D. Strauss, M.D.
Department of Psychiatry
University of California at Los Angeles
School of Medicine
Los Angeles, California

David K. Wellisch, Ph.D.
Department of Psychiatry
University of California at Los Angeles
School of Medicine
Los Angeles, California

Jeffery N. Wilkins, M.D.
Department of Psychiatry
University of California at Los Angeles
School of Medicine
Los Angeles, California

Joel Yager, M.D.
Department of Psychiatry
University of California at Los Angeles
School of Medicine
Los Angeles, California

Foreword

Liaison psychiatry has been practiced in this country for about 40 years, but has emerged as a special area of interest within psychiatry only in the last decade. Its broadening clinical applications, growing theoretical base, and rising popularity are reflected in the increase of published works related to these aspects. The quality of this literature has been quite uneven. We have seen more than a fair share of clinical anecdotes, plain exhortations, and wooly verbiage. This is beginning to change. More scholarly and sophisticated publications are gradually setting the tone for the literature in this relatively new area of psychiatry.

The present book exemplifies this welcome trend. It should help establish more exacting standards of excellence for aspiring writers in the field. It offers a blend of clinical observations, practical guidelines, and provocative questions for future research. Dr. Faguet and his colleagues, mostly members of the youngest generation of liaison psychiatrists, have approached their task with enthusiasm tempered by critical reason. Their main and novel contribution is to expand the boundaries of the field. Most of the chapters deal with clinical problems and situations that have not usually been associated with liaison psychiatry. By focusing on these new frontiers for consultation-liaison activities, the editors and contributors have performed a valuable service to all of us working in this area.

The book starts appropriately with a description of liaison with a service for the neonates—an important area for primary prevention. The last chapter focuses on the borderlands between neurology and psychiatry, brain and behavior. The remaining chapters deal with the liaison aspects of clinical issues revolving around some of the universals of human experience and medical practice: the dilemmas of conception, the quest for more attractive appearance through surgery, the vicissitudes of dependence on chemicals for excitement or oblivion, the anguish of the rape victim and of the dying, and the effects of body chemistry on mood.

The volume is well written and referenced. The style is free of the strident pitch of the salesman or the missionary that mars some of the liaison literature. The approach is generally eclectic, as befits liaison psychiatrists: this is not a hunting ground for captive minds that view people and ideas from only one theoretical vantage point.

Both the editors and the contributors have done their share in producing a practically useful and valuable book. If others follow their exacting standards, then liaison psychiatry will survive its recent popularity.

Z.J. Lipowski, M.D.

Introduction

> Words are at best only an outline of form
> and motion while emotional expression is
> what color and texture are to creative paint-
> ing. Understanding and interpretation of
> this intensely personal, unique, and dynamic
> language is essential to a Healing Art.
>
> Benjamin B. Faguet, M.D.,
> *The Healing Art*

Ogden and Richards[1] introduce their study of language, *The Meaning of Meaning,* with this idea: "Let us get nearer to the fire, so that we can see what we are saying" (p. 1). These words may serve to describe the liaison psychiatrist's task: to understand and interpret the multiple meanings and consequences of an individual's "dis-ease" in light of his current circumstances and personal history.

Clinical experience has heightened our awareness of the psychological threat of illness and hospitalization. Sickness challenges an individual's productivity and life goals, prestige, social roles, family equilibrium, physical and emotional autonomy, as well as his body image and sensorium. There may be a disruption in his usual coping and defensive styles, resulting in a variety of responses, in both the patient and those who attend him, which may be inimical to optimal care and recovery.

The liaison psychiatrist therefore works on many fronts. Lipowski[2] has summarized a number of essential functions:

(1) provision of expert diagnostic consultations and advice on the psychological aspects of the care of the physically ill; (2) early identification of psychiatric morbidity as well as its prevention in the "medical" patient population; (3) management of the psychopathological reactions to and complications of physical illness and injury; (4) prevention and management of deviant illness behaviour and psychological invalidism, which often follow in the wake of catastrophic illness, such as myocardial infarction, or complicate a chronic disease, such as epilepsy or rheumatoid arthritis; (5) work with the patient's family in an attempt to prevent psychiatric morbidity precipitated by reactions to the illness of a family member and to avoid a tendency of some families to promote deviant illness behaviour, such as excessive dependence, gross denial of illness, noncompliance with medical management, etc.; (6) teaching the medical staff at all levels how to identify and deal with the patient's abnormal reactions to illness and hospitalization; (7) drawing attention to the importance of a medical ward as a therapeutic milieu involving both the attitudes of the clinical staff and the physical features of the hospital environment, such as sensory deprivation or overload; (8) maintenance of adequate communication between patients and staff to avoid disruptive interpersonal conflicts, emotional over-reactions, and emergence of attitudes interfering with optimal patient care[p. 16].

To each consultation the liaison psychiatrist brings certain attitudes and working principles. First, illness represents a crisis with individual implications and meanings. It is therefore important to remember that the patient's psychological and physical responses may be influenced by multiple factors, which Lipowski[3] has enumerated:

(1) Personality structure and unconscious conflicts; (2) the meaning and importance for the patients of the affected organ, lesion, actual bodily change, changed proprioceptive sensations, and body image; (3) the degree and nature of the inclusion of Item 2 into unconscious conflicts; (4) psychodynamic effect of the beliefs about the cause of disease; (5) cultural and educational factors; (6) the state of the patient's current interpersonal relationships; (7) the actual extent of mutilation and loss of function and their socioeconomic consequences for the patient; (8) previous experience with disease; (9) the patient's state of awareness and cognitive functioning; (10) degree of acceptance by him of the "sick role;" (11) the doctor-patient relationship [p. 213].

Second, there are aspects of hospitalization that make it a particularly difficult experience: the loss of personal identity and privacy; the unfamiliarity of the surroundings; the separation from usual roles, special status, and comforting contact with family and friends; the pain and embarrassment of medical manipulation. Wahl[4] has stated this pointedly: "All of these stresses are not easy to identify, first, because most patients are ashamed of them and conceal their reactions, and also because we physicians, through long habituation, are blinded to their import. To medical personnel, hospitals represent security and comfortable loci of learning and working. An empathy with the patient's point of view, in which the hospital is often frightening and alien, is difficult"(pp. 1005-1006).

Third, one must be mindful of the special kinds of relationships in a therapeutic community and their vulnerability on all sides to interpersonal conflict, distortion, and imbalance. Miller[5] reminds us that while the liaison psychiatrist needs to remain an observer and consultant, it may simultaneously be important for him to become a temporary or partial member of the therapeutic system. He may have to assume limited responsibilities for the members of the working unit and concurrently collect, synthesize, and impart information to repair the disrupted system and approximate the wound edges of the therapeutic community.

The selections included in this book originated in Consultation Liaison Grand Rounds organized by the Department of Psychiatry at the UCLA School of Medicine as a response to intriguing psychiatric consultations requested by the medical-surgical staff of the UCLA Medical Center. They delineate the psychiatrist's effort to understand each consultation within the patient's unique psychosocial milieu.

As editors, we faced the inevitable problem of reviewing many clinicians' papers on liaison psychiatry. Our dilemma was how to present a wide variety of models and at the same time avoid anecdotal accounts without significant educational value. As Hawkins[6] has stated: "We are interested in new conceptual approaches to psychosomatic medicine, and in reports about well-tested techniques for enriching the medical curriculum with the knowledge gained in the systematic study of human behavior and psychosocial response. We are interested in ways of training the physician to be a psychosocial force in the practice of medicine, and we are anxious to contribute to his technical ability to employ for the benefit of his patients all of the therapeutic potential of the doctor-patient relationship" (pp. 477-478). Even though the chapters in this volume are written by individuals with differing backgrounds and experiences, the common, primary focus is on their educational value for the reader.

This volume also illustrates the expanding frontiers of liaison psychiatry. If it is true, as West[7] and others believe it to be, that liaison psychiatry represents a major direction for psychiatry in the future, it is clear that the previous definitions and limitations of its scope of operation are too circumscribed to permit the kind of growth necessary. The chapters in this volume clearly demonstrate (1) the multidisciplinary character of the new liaison psychiatry, (2) the community and family orientation of the treatment methodologies, and (3) the liaison psychiatrist's unique role in serving the traditional physician's functions of personal, comprehensive, and continuous care through the course of the patient's illness.

January, 1978, Los Angeles

Robert Andrew Faguet, M.D.
Fawzy I. Fawzy, M.D.
David K. Wellisch, Ph.D.
Robert O. Pasnau, M.D.

REFERENCES

1. Ogden, C.K., and Richards, I.A. *The Meaning of Meaning*. New York: Harcourt, Brace & World, 1923.
2. Lipowski, Z.J. Psychosomatic medicine: An overview. In: *Modern Trends in Psychosomatic Medicine*, 3, ed. O. Hill. London: Butterworths, 1976, pp. 1-20.
3. Lipowski, Z.J. Review of consultation psychiatry and psychosomatic medicine. II. *Psychosom. Med.*, 29:201-225, 1967.
4. Wahl, C.W. (Mod.) The UCLA interdepartmental conference: Toxic and functional psychoses: Diagnosis and treatment in a medical setting. *Ann. Intern. Med.*, 66:989-1007, 1967.
5. Miller, W.B. Psychiatric consultation in the general hospital. In: *Psychiatric Treatment: Crisis, Clinic, Consultation*, ed. C.P. Rosenbaum and J.E. Beebe. New York: McGraw-Hill, 1975, pp. 496-504.
6. Hawkins, D.R. Editorial. *Psychosom. Med.*, 37:477-478, 1975.
7. West, L.J. The future of psychiatric education. *Am. J. Psychiat.*, 130:521-528, 1973.

Contents

CHAPTER 1

The Earliest Intervention: Consultation to the High-Risk Parent and Professional in the Neonatal Intensive Care Unit

MARTHA BATES JURA
ROBERT ANDREW FAGUET

> My mother groan'd! my father wept.
> Into the dangerous world I leapt:
> Helpless, naked, piping loud:
> Like a fiend hid in a cloud.
>
> Struggling in my father's hands,
> Striving against my swadling bands,
> Bound and weary I thought best
> To sulk upon my mother's breast.
>
> William Blake,
> *Infant Sorrow*

The ultimate aim of consultation liaison psychiatry has been described as the optimal care of the sick.[1] This goal is usually attained by tending to those personal and interpersonal issues involving the patient, family, and staff that interfere with medical treatment and management.

In the case of the UCLA Neonatal Intensive Care Unit, the patient is frequently under five pounds, nonverbal, immobilized in an open bed or isolated in a plastic box, and connected to solutions and machinery by tubes and wires. What is worse, he is often indifferent and ungrateful. As a result, the consultation we describe here is directed to the patient's caretakers: his parents and members of the medical staff.

1

There is another reason for addressing the parents and professionals: the infant is at risk in part because his caretakers and caretaking are "at risk." In large measure the risk is related to the hazards of dealing with a very sick infant—not only because of the concerns he engenders in his caretakers regarding damage and death, but also because of specific behaviors associated with immaturity and illness. In relating to the sick infant, both parents and professionals seem subject to similar forces, which work both for detachment and attachment. Just as the infant may influence his own maternal care, he may possibly influence his own medical care. As a result, the infant's health may be affected by his early interactions with his physicians and nurses, as well as his parents.

THE RISKS

The infants in an ICU are at risk for a number of distortions in their interpersonal relations, as well as in their perceptual, motor, and cognitive development.[2] Many investigators have found the overlapping populations of low-birthweight and critically ill infants overrepresented in the (in turn) overlapping populations of battered and failure-to-thrive children.[3] Kennell and Klaus[4] and their colleagues at Case Western Reserve University point out that these immature and sick infants have been separated from their mothers shortly after birth; they emphasize this fact as an explanation for later differences and disruptions in mother-infant interaction.[4] The best evidence, however, for the disruptive influence of separation on mother-infant relations comes from studies of healthy full-term infants and their mothers. Klaus et al.[5] found that mothers who had an additional 16 hours of contact with their full-term newborns during the first days of life showed greater soothing behavior and engaged in more eye-to-eye contact and fondling one month later than did those control mothers without the opportunity for extra handling. At one year the investigators found that differences persisted.[6]

The evidence for the disruptive influence of the separation of mothers from their premature and sick infants is more equivocal. Although the Case Western Reserve group reports some suggestive differences in the interpersonal behaviors and later cognitive development of two groups having early and late contact with their relatively healthy prematures,[7] other results are mixed. For example, another study[8] noted no differences between contact groups in maternal visiting patterns to an ICU, though the authors feel their sample was too small to evaluate the influence of contact. On other occasions investigators[9,10] have found the differences in contact groups to be short-lived. While Leifer et al.[11] found differences between contact groups in later maternal and family adjustment, the greatest differences in mother-infant interaction were not between mothers with early and late contact with their prematures, but between mothers and their preterm and full-term infants. Furthermore, because the authors did not control for gestational age in comparing preterm and full-term infants, it is unclear whether the differences in maternal behavior reflect differences in the mothers or babies.

Although the issue of separation is an important one, its recent emphasis has caused us to overlook what we all know: the high-risk infant is immature or sick. Even though the Case Western Reserve group[12] acknowledges the importance of the infant's illness in interpersonal disruptions, they[4] focus on separation as "one of the simplest variables to manipulate" (p. 105). However, since it is not only hospital procedure, but the infant himself who contributes to separation, it is in fact neither a simple variable nor easy to manipulate. Despite the fact that it is important to allow and encourage mothers to visit their infants in the ICU, they will not have the same experiences as mothers of healthy full-term babies. Furthermore, the medical staff is susceptible to the same factors associated with the infants' immaturity and illness that cause the parents to approach or avoid their infants.

Although illness, like separation. interacts in complex ways with other interpersonal events, its impact on caretakers can be explored, and is worth making explicit. When the issue of illness has been addressed, the focus has been on the parents' concerns about damage and death,[13] rather than on the way the infant's caretaking is shaped by his being a different "kind" of baby, strikingly unlike the healthy full-term baby in appearance and behavior.

The specific behaviors of the very ill child have not been well documented, but the behaviors of the immature infant are beginning to be studied. Investigations suggest that the preterm's visual,[14] state regulation,[15] reflexive,[16] and other systems which might have an effect on caregiving are different. Although the premature's gross development will lag only temporarily, this is meager consolation for the distressed staff and parents who must care for him for ten to 15 weeks, instead of six to eight, before he smiles.

To professionals as well as parents, the high-risk infant's appearance and behavior may be unusual, disappointing, or frightening, and their ambivalence may partly determine their care. The suggestion that infants may affect their own medical care is not a new one. It has often been observed that the staff is more apt to be engaged with certain institutionalized[17] or hospitalized children than others. The suggestion that infants may contribute to their own medical care is a variation of the argument that children influence the way others respond to them,[18] including possibly inducing their own neglect[19] and malnutrition.[20]

Although we have some understanding of how parents' experiences with their infants may alter parenting, we are only beginning to understand how physicians' and nurses' experiences may alter future decisions regarding similar babies or their perception of themselves as caring people and professionals. The literature about stress on the professional in critical care has emphasized not the very human concerns that affect the staff, but rather the professional pressures they experience. Vreeland and Ellis[21] describe the nature of these stresses. Furthermore, just as the parental literature emphasizes mothers, the professional literature emphasizes nurses. Apparently, doctors, like fathers, are "strong and reasonable" and do not have emotional reactions to the pressures, decisions, and disappointments they face in all intensive care units. This idealized image is placed in doubt by evidence that doctors have very troubled, but unarticulated feelings about human loss and medical failure in the case of stillbirths. Bourne[22] attempted to study mothers' reactions to such loss through questionnaires addressed to their physicians. The physicians reported that they felt there was no difference in the anxiety level of mothers who had unsuccessfully or successfully borne a previous pregnancy as they approached a new delivery. Further, it also became apparent that many more physicians attending stillbirths failed to return the questionnaire, and, on the forms returned, many more of the physicians attending stillbirths failed to give the asked-for information. Two of these physicians wrote long letters explaining they did not have time for questionnaires. The author concluded: "The doctor whose patient has had a stillbirth does not want to know, he does not want to notice and he does not want to remember anything about it. This must mean doctors under strain and a group of patients in danger of neglect" (p. 334).

Concerns of physicians and nurses in critical care facilities have begun to emerge in highly intellectualized and controlled discussion of the ethical[23-25] and legal[26] dilemmas faced in such units. Yet one suspects that these ethical and legal issues are essentially a variation of the emotional dilemma confronting the parent. However, while the parent asks, "*How* am I going to take care of this very sick infant who might die or be damaged?;" the professional asks in addition, "*Should* I take care of this very sick infant who might die or be damaged?"

One physician, for example, was greatly troubled by a baby in his care. He was following a case of meningomyelocele and hydrocephalus which had been previously seen in the ICU. The neurosurgical staff had decided against operating on this baby because of the severity of his difficulties, so the doctor was essentially presiding over the baby's death. The doctor became uncomfortable with this role and called several other hospitals to reassure himself that in fact there was nothing to be done. He was still distressed. He understood, however, that making a heroic effort to save every baby's life was not necessarily best for the infant or the parents. He had worked in another hospital where the religious climate directed that every life be saved. In one case he had worked extra shifts and exhausted himself saving a baby's life. Everyone in the unit told him, "If it had not been for you that baby would have died." He was later alarmed, however, to see the extent of the baby's damage and the way his parents cried over him. At this point, he felt "damned if he did, and damned if he didn't."

THE CONSULTATION

Mindful of these stresses on parents and professionals and desirous of contributing to the infant's long-term as well as short-term health and development, we undertook our consultation. There is a paucity of literature on psychological and psychiatric services to neonatal intensive care units. There have been some reports on the provision of services to adult and pediatric, as well as neonatal, intensive care facilities; these include a description of types of problems encountered,[27] types of special techniques that might be used (theme interference,[28] group-oriented,[29,30] systems-based,[31] crisis intervention,[32,33] and infant stimulation[34]), as well as other services provided to parents by professionals.[35]

Our consultation contained features of many of these techniques; group as well as individual and direct as well as indirect services were provided to professionals and parents. The consulting psychologist originally waited for referrals from the unit, but after the identification of certain high-risk populations (the critically ill or low-birthweight babies who tended to have long hospitalizations), she began to see several sets of parents routinely. As a result, the consultation took on a preventitive as well as remedial aspect. In many cases the decision to intervene was based not on the symptomatic behavior of the parents, but rather on the difficult circumstances in which the parents found themselves.

The parents were originally referred for one of two reasons: they seemed to be overly anxious, often to the point of disrupting the unit, or they appeared to have "attachment" difficulties. In both cases it became evident that the parents were ambivalent about caring for and becoming attached to the infant.

One mother was referred for consultation when she became very disruptive to the unit. She was determined to breast-feed her jaundiced baby despite the staff's opinion that it was medically inadvisable. She contacted physicians at other hospitals for support of her view that breast-feeding was no hazard to the infant's health. A nurse, concerned about the baby, became impatient with the mother and said that it seemed she would breast-feed the baby "whether it killed the baby or not." Conversations with the mother revealed that she had been beaten by her father, who had been beaten by his. It became apparent that this mother hoped that strong feelings of attachment would keep her from abusing this baby. However, she had never beaten either of her other two children, even when she was under considerable stress. One of the reasons the staff probably became impatient with her was because they sensed her behavior was determined by *her* need, not that of the baby.

Another mother was not referred to the consultant, but was seen as a matter of routine because her premature baby appeared to be a long-term admission.

This mother had aborted several times before delivering a premature, but healthy baby girl. Despite the fact this infant did not develop any serious complications, the mother was clearly concerned about her. She denied any worry, but responded to any comment on how well the baby was doing by "knocking on wood." She soon refused to enter the ICU for fear of introducing germs and insisted that her husband wear a mask in the unit to protect the baby. She stood watching at the window of the unit, critical of the nurses' "rough" handling and fearful someone would drop the infant. The mother's fears had not abated at discharge, so consultation continued in weekly home visits. At home the mother feared the baby would choke or stop breathing. During the course of counseling, the mother acknowledged she had been surprised to find herself pregnant and to have delivered the baby. When asked at what point she had accepted that she would be able to "have" this infant, she said, "I don't believe that I have it yet." Her history revealed she was the daughter of an alcoholic and had been deprived and disappointed throughout her life. She had never believed she would be able to "have" anything.

In another case the staff thought the mother behaved somewhat artificially toward her baby. Observations indicated there was some truth to their perception: the mother would smile and speak to the baby regardless of the infant's cues, even when his eyes were closed. The mother mentioned at one point that after she took the infant home, she would "flick" the baby on the feet every five minutes to make sure he was still alive. She acknowledged she was afraid the baby would die in her arms. She denied she was afraid there was something wrong with the baby, but she said she would worry about him until he "went to school." The consultant suggested that this was a "long time to wait." The mother, however, refused both individual and group therapy because after six weeks the "worst" (the fear of death) was over.

Intervention in these cases took a number of forms. The consultant spoke with the medical staff regarding possible reasons for difficulties and solutions to them. For example, in the case of the mother with the jaundiced infant, the consultant shared the mother's fears with the staff and encouraged them to acquiesce to her wishes when medically feasible and to approach her through her desire to be a "good mother." With the mother of the healthy premature, the staff discovered early that she responded well to modeling and direction, which increased her sense of control. The head nurse responded to the mother's inability to enter the unit for fear of introducing germs by taking the isolette to the mother's room, opening the door, and calmly handing the baby to her. Her concern that the baby might stop breathing was met by clear information about the periodic breathing of preterms and how to handle situations in which she felt the baby had stopped breathing. She was urged to contact the unit, day or night, for advice.

The work with the ICU staff was often supplemented by the consultant's direct intervention with the parents. The consultant met with the parents of the jaundiced baby on several occasions, responding to the mother's anxieties and emphasizing the fact she had not beaten her older children. The consultant saw the parents of the healthy premature in the hospital and in the home. Because this mother's anxieties did not abate and threatened to become a serious obstacle to her rearing of the child, she was later referred for psychotherapy. Of course, as with the mother who seemed artificial with her baby, there are times when the parents will not accept any intervention at all. One can only hope that if the mother or child have problems in the future, the difficulty will be identified and treated by another medical or educational facility.

A special word about separation: often when a mother's "attachment difficulty" was identified from her failure to visit her baby, some staff members wanted to urge the mother to do so. These members often saw the mother's failure to visit as her failure to love the baby and believed her attachment would be enhanced by proximity. Yet this interpretation of the mother's behavior must be amended. First, the fact that a mother avoids visiting need not mean she does not love her baby. The mother's inability to visit may be due to the baby's failure to engage her, her need to stay away from a very deviant or disturbing baby, or her fear of becoming attached to an infant who might be damaged or die. Second, the fact that the mother is separated from the infant in meaningful ways cannot be changed. Our unit, like many in the country, appropriately encourages a mother to participate as much as possible in her own baby's care. Nothing can alter the reality, however, that the mother cannot take her baby home and assume complete care herself. One mother lamented as she stood next to her infant in its warmer, "She doesn't even know I'm here; the people she really knows and needs are the nurses." Third, equal in importance to the separation is how it is interpreted. Separation, like illness, cannot be completely eliminated, but it can be discussed. Many mothers, particularly primipara,[36] do lose confidence in themselves as mothers when they see others caring for their babies, and this may influence later care. The baby's immediate, but limited need for the staff and his current and ongoing need for mother must be clarified. Fourth, failure to visit is a sign that the parents are distressed; the solution is not to "make them visit," but to help them with their distress.

Interestingly, we found that the staff responded to the babies in ways reminiscent of those of the parents. One mother, for example, was having difficulty visiting her baby. Early in the hospitalization she related this difficulty to her fear that the baby would die, a fear strengthened by the fact she had lost a previous baby at six months in another ICU. The staff became concerned and in some cases critical about her failure to visit. Often in such units the staff members may become convinced that in a similar position they would be "good mothers" and visit unfailingly. However, in this case the nurse who was critical of the mother for not visiting recognized that the usually patient nurses had to "draw straws" to determine who would care for the very sick and irritable baby. Furthermore, the nurses were discouraged by the situation because the baby was a "bottomless pit." Staff, like the parents, need some response to their efforts, some sign that the baby is coming along. There was much speculation, particularly among those who dealt with her every day, that the baby would not grow because she did not have enough intestine to absorb sufficient nutriment and that perhaps the infant's life-support machinery would have to be turned off. However, the anxieties about her prognosis seemed to disappear when the infant began to look and smile at the staff. The nurses began to bring in bonnets and toys from home; at the same time, the mother resumed her visits. This change in behavior on the part of the staff and the mother occurred despite the fact the infant's medical condition did not change: the baby continued to fail, and she finally weakened and died. Tragically, the mother lost this baby as she had lost the previous one, in the sixth month of life.

In another case, a very alert nurse was concerned about parents she considered overly anxious about their baby. This infant had symptoms of his mother's myasthenia gravis, which caused him to appear neurologically abnormal, although it was understood that this medical problem, and the resulting abnormal neurological status, were temporary. Nothing anyone said seemed to reduce the parents' anxiety and reassure them. Conversation with the nurse, however, revealed that she herself was very anxious about the baby and fearful for his future. She too was convinced that despite what she had been told, the infant would be damaged. When she was asked how she knew this, she gave as evidence the awkward way he held his hand and then demonstrated with hers. This gesture reminded her of the way older spastics held their hands. It seemed that certain features of the baby were so striking that they contradicted what the physician said. Faced with the contradictory messages received from the baby and from the physician, the nurse—and very likely the parents—believed the baby.

These examples illustrate that although the feelings of the staff may interfere with the management of the parents and the baby, if properly understood, they may serve as important tools. In the first case, the nurse was better able to understand the mother's feelings and to tolerate her own once she realized how the caretakers—mother and staff—were withdrawing from this difficult, anxiety-provoking baby. In the second case, after the nurse had clarified the source of the confusion, she was able to speak to the parents about it. Just as the consultant helped the nurse to notice minor changes in the baby's behavior, so the nurse helped the parents to focus on these signs of progress.

Because of the anxieties engendered by the babies, there is always the danger that the staff will deal with the stress at the expense of themselves or the child. A highly skilled nurse, for instance, was leaving the unit after 16 years in the critical care facility. On her last day before transferring to a well-baby nursery, she passed a portable isolette being wheeled in from a transport helicopter. She knew that the baby would be introduced to the currently calm nursery and the pace would quicken and the pressure mount. She thought, "Thank God I don't have to go in there." She mentioned that she had functioned from the "eyebrows up" in the unit, and that her feelings had been subordinated to pure thinking. When the consultant pointed out that her detachment might have been helpful for the patients, but costly to her, she said, "Maybe it wasn't so good for the babies or families either." She wondered whether one could become genuinely involved with the babies or talk to the families if one functioned only "from the eyebrows up."

In another instance, a physician was saddened after the loss of two very small, sick babies. However, he was also disturbed because he felt the deaths had been predictable, since he knew that infants with certain illnesses and certain weights die if they also require respirators; those who do not need respirators have some chance of survival. The conviction that this subset of babies will die is so great that some intensive care units do not even put them on respirators. This physician wondered whether such a policy in the UCLA ICU would have avoided needless emotional and financial wear on the staff and the parents. But then he wondered how one could learn to keep such babies alive if one did not make the attempt. And he knew how hard it was for everyone concerned to either withhold or terminate care, even when the medical situation was considered hopeless.

When two physicians discussed the expenditure of resources in hopeless cases, they both agreed that useless expense was less important than the frustration of trying to save a baby who could not survive. Like parents who are afraid of loving a baby they may lose, medical staff members have trouble making a gigantic effort without some assurance that they are going to save a baby. One physician felt that the staff members who succeeded in keeping the most babies alive were those able to provide care regardless of their beliefs that the baby would die.

The losses and disappointments in such units are difficult to accept personally and professionally. There is the danger that the stressed staff members, like the stressed parents, may withdraw not only from the babies, but also from their roles. One doctor was depressed by the babies who died and by those who survived but were damaged. He mentioned that sometimes he "doubted his specialty." He said he had never talked with the attending physicians about his doubts and wondered if they had ever felt this way.

One would assume that because of the large numbers of parents and staff members who shared common concerns in the ICU, group discussions would have been welcomed. This was not the case. Two groups were offered to the parents by the consultant and the unit social worker—one for parents whose babies were living and one for parents whose babies had died on the unit. Neither parent group was successful, although individual sessions were well received. There were a number of reasons for the failure. The most important was probably the withdrawal associated with grieving experienced by both sets of parents. Indeed, one study found that parents whose babies were admitted to a regional ICU were already grieving for their babies, regardless of the severity of the baby's illness.[37] Another reason for the failure may have been the imcompatibility of parents in different stages of reaction to their baby's hospitalization or death. Among the parents of the surviving, but sick babies, the extensive use of denial was also a major impediment to the formation of a group. One mother told the consultant that she would join the group as long as Mrs. H did not. She believed that Mrs. H's baby was dying in contrast, she hoped, to her own, and she could not tolerate the other woman's "pain." Another stated that she was too busy with her own problems to take on anyone else's.

Although the staff members, primarily the nurses, met in a group, they preferred individual discussions. Like the parents who wanted to be good mothers and fathers, the professionals wanted to be good doctors and nurses; they may have been ashamed of confusing, contradictory, and threatening feelings, which they may have regarded as a betrayal of their commitment to the parents and their own standards. Staff members may also have been afraid that they would be asked to relinquish the intellectualization and isolation that serve them so well in most medical situations. There is, moreover, the possibility that just as the parents experience a grief process, so does the medical staff. But unlike that of the parents, the staff's grief is constantly reinstated, and its lost love objects are constantly replaced, to be lost once again.

When staff members say, "Why didn't they let this baby die," they are acting toward the baby with the same intensity and distress as the parents. In fact, they are acting "like parents." Although professionals share the concerns of the parents, they may not always be in a position to help them, in part because the professionals' time frame differs from the parents'. The nurse or physician has to react over and over again to infants at the height of their immaturity and sickness; consequently, the staff's assumptions about a baby's future or his parents' adaptation may be erroneous. The baby will not always appear as he does in the ICU. As his behavior matures, others' responses to him may change. Beckwith[38] found that after correcting for gestational age in preterms, many of the differences in mother-infant interaction between preterm and full-term infants disappear. Even in cases where the baby cannot change, the parents' reaction may. Roskies[39] found that even Thalidomide babies were integrated in surprising ways into normal families. The staff found mental rather than physical deficiencies disturbing, and certainly the same is true for most families. Staffs can take heart from evidence that the incidence of mental subnormality in low-birthweight populations has dropped dramatically in the past 15 years,[40] while the number of infants saved has been increasing. Because of the staff's need to expand its time frame, followup becomes as important to the staff as it is to the babies. Some neonatal intensive care units organize reunions or keep photographs of growing alumni to remind them of their successes.

Because of the inevitable and necessary involvement of staff members with the infants, it may sometimes be difficult for them to make the decision to restrict or terminate an infant's care. The use of committees can serve as protection for both the baby and the staff, and there has been a movement in recent years toward making such decisions through committees.[41]

SUMMARY AND CONCLUSIONS

Caring for vulnerable infants is a difficult task for both parents and professionals. The successes and failures of our consultation have given us some idea of the kinds of services that such a facility, working with the psychiatric liaison service, might offer if it is to interpret its role as fostering all aspects of its patients' health—long-term as well as short-term, emotional as well as physical.

Certain parents of critically ill infants were seen as a matter of routine rather than referral. They were identified not on the basis of the "pathology of their behavior," but rather on the basis of the "pathology of the circumstance." We cannot yet know the long-range effect of this intervention in diminishing those distortions of parent-infant interactions recognized by such labels as "vulnerable child" and "battered-child syndrome." One can only hope that one important result would be to alleviate the parents' anxiety and enhance their ability to confront their child's illness as realistically as possible. It is not clear that a psychiatric consultation liaison service could or should single-handedly undertake such extensive work on a routine basis. But certainly it can be helpful in identifying this need and formulating ways of meeting it.

In our ICU, the consultant and nursing staff discussed the possibility of a primary nursing concept, in which a nurse, along with a physician, would be assigned to each baby to monitor parental reactions and to either provide or obtain intervention. The unit has also introduced a clinical nurse specialist to work primarily with families and offer supportive services to other nurses. Because of the conflicts accompanying a dual emotional involvement with both the parents and the baby, the services of a person with no responsibility for the baby's medical care is helpful in dealing with the parents, either as a consultant, counselor, or caseworker.

In view of the numbers of parents and staff members who share similar concerns, it is tempting to try to organize groups, but it has been our experience that both parents and professionals resist this effort. We felt that the withdrawal associated with the parents' grieving was the main obstacle to their participation. Although the staff members also grieved, their grief should not have been a barrier to group discussion because they shared the same lost objects; the difficulty in forming a staff group was probably more related to their reluctance to suspend the isolation and intellectualization they habitually rely on in medical situations. Those who were able to discuss their feelings did so in the informal ward setting. Since not everyone can use either the informal or formal group, our unit has instituted a weekly case conference in which all babies and their families are discussed. This setting may provide the combination of distance and assistance some staff members need.

During our consultation, we began to consider more intently the possibility that just as the infant affects his own maternal care, he may affect his own medical care. Often we observed the alarm with which some staff members seemed to respond to some ill or damaged babies. Their reaction was similar to that of the parents: Who could take care of or love this baby? Because of the decisions that must be made about babies in intensive care units, it is particularly important that we become alert to the stresses on staff and parents and support them in the difficult task of caring for these sick infants. This will ensure the best care for the infant while it diminishes the "risk" for all of the members of the neonatal intensive care unit.

We would like to give special thanks to Michael Jura, Ph.D. and Irene Faguet who were kind enough to read and comment on the manuscript.

REFERENCES

1. Lipowski, Z.J. Psychiatric liaison: Past, present, and future. In: *Consultation-Liaison Psychiatry,* ed. R. Pasnau. New York:Grune & Stratton, 1975, pp. 1-28.
2. Sameroff, A.J., and Chandler, M.J. Reproductive risk and the continuum of caretaking casualty. In: *Review of Child Development Research,* Vol. 4, F.D. Horowitz et al. Chicago:University of Chicago Press, 1975, pp. 187-244.
3. Elmer, E., and Gregg, G.S. Developmental characteristics of abused children. *Pediatrics,* 40:596-602, 1967.
4. Klaus, M., and Kennell, J. Care of the mother. In: *Care of the High-risk Neonate,* M. Klaus and A.A. Fanaroff. Philadelphia:Saunders, 1973, pp. 98-118.
5. Klaus, M.H., Jerauld, R., Kreger, N., McAlpine, W., Steffa, M., and Kennell, J.H. Maternal attachment: Importance of the first post-partum days. *New Eng. J. Med.,* 286:460-463, 1972.
6. Kennell, J.H., Jerauld, R., Wolfe, H., Chesler, D., Kreger, N.C., McAlpine, W., Steffa, M., and Klaus, M.H. Maternal behavior one year after early and extended post-partum contact. *Dev. Med. Child Neurol.,* 16:172-179, 1974.
7. Klaus, M.H., and Kennell, J.H. *Maternal-Infant Bonding: The Impact of Early Separation or Loss on Family Development.* St. Louis:C.V. Mosby, 1976.
8. Fanaroff, A.A., Kennell, J.H., and Klaus, M.H. Follow-up of low-birth-weight infants—the predictive value of maternal visiting patterns. *Pediatrics,* 49:287-290, 1972.
9. Kennell, J.H., Gordon, D., and Klaus, M.H. The effects of early mother-infant separation on later maternal performance. *Pediat. Res.,* 4:273-274, 1970.
10. Leiderman, P.H., and Seashore, M.J. Mother-infant neonatal separation: Some delayed consequences. In: *Parent-Infant Interaction,* Ciba Foundation Symposium 33. Amsterdam:Elsevier, 1975, pp. 213-239.
11. Leifer, A.D., Leiderman, P.H., Barnett, C.R., and Williams, J.A. The effects of mother-infant separation on maternal attachment behavior. *Child Dev.,* 43:1203-1218, 1972.
12. Kennell, J.H., and Rolnick, A.R. Discussing problems in newborn babies with their parents. *Pediatrics,* 26:832-838, 1960.
13. Green, M., and Solnit, A.J. Reactions to the threatened loss of a child: A vulnerable child syndrome. *Pediatrics,* 34:58-66, 1964.
14. Sigman, M., and Parmelee, A.H. Visual preference of four month old premature and full-term infants. *Child Dev.,* 45:959-965, 1974.

15. Michaelis, R., Parmelee, A.H., Sterm, E., and Haber, A. Activity states in premature and term infants. *Dev. Psychobiol.*, 6:209-215, 1973.
16. Johnson, S.H., and Grubbs, J.P. The premature infant's reflex behaviors effect on the maternal-child relationship. *JOGN*, 4:15-21, 1975.
17. Provence, S.A., and Lipton, R.C. *Infants in Institutions.* New York:International Universities Press, 1962.
18. Thoman, E. How a rejecting baby effects mother-infant synchrony. In: *Parent-Infant Interaction,* Ciba Foundation Symposium 33. Amsterdam:Elsevier, 1975, pp. 177-191.
19. Milowe, I.D., and Lourie, R.S. The child's role in the battered child syndrome. *J. Pediatrics,* 65:1079-1081, 1964.
20. Pollitt, E. Behavior of infant in causation of nutritional marasmus. *Am. J. Clin. Nutrition,* 26:264-270, 1973.
21. Vreeland, R., and Ellis, G.L. Stresses on the nurse in an intensive care unit. *JAMA,* 208:332-334, 1969.
22. Bourne, S. The psychological effects of stillbirths on the doctor. In: Psychosomatic Medicine in Obstetrics and Gynaecology, 3rd International Congress, ed. N. Morris. London:Basel:Karger, 1972, pp. 333-334.
23. Duff, R.S., and Campbell, A.G.M. Moral and ethical dilemmas in the special-care nursery. *New Eng. J. Med.,* 289:890-894, 1974.
24. Hauerwas, S. The demands and limits of care—ethical reflections on the moral dilemma of neonatal intensive care. *Am. J. Med. Sci.,* 269:222-236, 1975.
25. Waldman, A.M. Medical ethics and the hopelessly ill child. *J. Pediatrics,* 88:890-892, 1976.
26. Robertson, J.A., and Fost, N. Passive euthanasia of defective newborn infants: Legal considerations. *J. Pediatrics,* 88:883-889, 1976.
27. Kornfeld, D.S. Psychiatric view of the intensive care unit. *Br. Med. J.,* 11:108-110, 1969.
28. May, J.G. A psychiatric study of a pediatric intensive care unit. *Clin. Pediatrics,* 11: 76-82, 1972.
29. Drotar, D. Consultation in the intensive care nursery. *Int. J. Psychiat. Med.,* 7:69-81, 1976.
30. Rosini, L.A., Howell, M.C., Todres, I.D., and Dorman, J. Group Meetings in a pediatric intensive care unit. *Pediatrics,* 53:371-374, 1974.
31. Koumans, A.J.R. A psychiatric consultation in an intensive care unit. *JAMA,* 194: 163-167, 1965.
32. Baldridge, A.E. Crisis intervention in the neonatal intensive care unit. *J. Pract. Nursing,* 26:22-23, 38, 1976.
33. Hancock, E. Crisis intervention in a newborn intensive care unit. *Soc. Work Health Care,* 1:421-432, 1976.
34. Brown, J., and Hepler, R. Stimulation—a corollary to physical care. *Am. J. Nursing,* 76:578-581, 1976.
35. Littman, B., and Wooldridge, P. Caring for families of high-risk infants. *Western J. Med.,* 124:429-433, 1976.
36. Seashore, M.J., Leifer, A.D., Barnett, C.R., and Leiderman, P.H. The effects of denial of early mother-infant interaction on maternal self-confidence. *J. Pers. Soc. Psychol.,* 26:369-378, 1973.
37. Benfield, D.G., Leib, S.A., and Reuter, J. Grief response of parents after referral of the critically ill newborn to a regional center. *New Eng. J. Med.,* 294:975-978, 1976.
38. Beckwith, L. A comparison of care-giver-infant interaction in preterm and term infants. UCLA Department of Pediatrics, 1977 (Unpublished).
39. Roskies, E. *Abnormality and Normality: The Mothering of Thalidomide Children.* Ithaca:Cornell University Press, 1972.

40. Kopp, C., and Parmelee, A.H. Prenatal and perinatal influences on infant behavior. In: *Handbook of Infancy,* ed. J. Osofsky. New York:Wiley (In press).
41. Pontoppidan, H. Special article: Optimum care for hopelessly ill patients, a report of the clinical care committee of the Massachusetts General Hospital. *New Eng. J. Med.,* 295:362-364, 1976.

CHAPTER 2

Liaison to Medically Ill Heroin Addicts: The Mental Health Professional as a Tightrope Walker

DAVID K. WELLISCH
DANIEL B. AUERBACH

> All of them, all except Phineas, constructed at infinite cost to themselves these Maginot Lines against this enemy they thought they saw across the frontier, this enemy who never attacked that way—if he ever attacked at all; if he was indeed the enemy.
> —John Knowles,
> *A Separate Peace*

The management of the heroin addict in a university-based general hospital almost always creates a severe strain on both the health service delivery system and the addict patient with a physical illness. The inevitable conflict between the patient and the system often leads to a disastrous outcome for the patient, including inadequate care of his illness in order to expedite discharge, avoidance by the health care professional, and sometimes his expulsion from the hospital. This engenders in the patient resentment of the hospital system and results in reluctance (with some realistic justification) to seek future medical care.[1,2]

Our thesis is that this problem may be minimized or avoided if it is conceptualized in terms of a "systems" model (the system including the addict patient, nursing staff, house staff, and attending senior physicians) in which all elements are seen to perpetuate conflict in a "closed-loop" fashion, no one element can be blamed for the inception of this social-systems problem, and no one can be released from responsibility for its maintenance. This chapter will examine the genesis of the potential conflict from the perspective of both the addicted patient and the medical personnel. It will next move to three case histories, which illustrate the dynamics and realities of the problem, and finally will offer a group of suggestions to health care professionals on the treatment of such a problem when it arises.

GENESIS OF THE PROBLEM

The Perspective of the Medical System

Medical practice and health care delivery within the modern setting is a complex interaction among many—and at times conflicting—forces. The holistic ideal of patient care, which is acknowledged by every health care professional, is threatened in everyday practice by several factors.[3]

Every hospitalized patient is part of an operational group made up of physicians, nursing staff, family, and others significant to him.[4] What each member of this group brings to the interaction will determine the vicissitudes of the patient's course; thus, the patient's personality, past history, coping styles, assumptions about illness, as well as those of his family, friends, and caretakers in the hospital, will have an important influence on his treatment, response, and eventual recovery. For the professional, however, there are other extremely significant variables that affect his role: professional training, postgraduate medical education, and current attitudes about illness and how "things ought to be"— that is, the working ethic—on a medical or surgical service.

At times, though, the capacity of the professional team to deliver comprehensive care is impaired: certain kinds of patients and certain kinds of problems may put an intolerable strain on the system. When this point is reached, the patient is seen as the problem, and the group often mobilizes to define the "solution" as the removal of the patient from the system.

There are several types of patients who frequently surpass the tolerance of the operational group: dying persons, the chronically ill, those with chronic pain—but none more often than the seriously ill, addicted patient. What is it, then, about the preparation of health professionals that makes the addict patient such a source of irritation? In such cases the complex nature of the disturbing situation is not recognized, and pointing it out is one of the most essential and difficult tasks of the mental health consultant.

One way to understand the problem is to examine the early training the young physician or nurse receives. The student is taught that illness is caused by forces for which the patient is not responsible (for example, the infectious agent, a malignancy) and against which the patient wages a valiant struggle in cooperation with the medical team. Yet this model patient is the antithesis of the addicted ill person, who outwardly has induced his own illness and almost always fights, frustrates, and derogates the attempts of the medical team to treat and cure.

Moreover, the young health care professional frequently has had a minimum of psychiatric training and little practical instruction on how to understand people who inflict serious disease upon themselves. Most important, the young professional is rarely taught to monitor or understand uncomfortable affects generated in himself by such patients. Thus, frustrating situations with difficult patients are often seen as created, maintained, and escalated by the patient alone.

The Reluctant Protagonists

The addict patients who become the central figures in these dramatic struggles enter the scene with a massive load of conflictual preconceptions, anxieties, hostilities, and psychic scars. In many cases poor parenting experiences have led them to abandon the idea of receiving nurturance and relief from people and to switch instead to the more dependable "old lady" (addict jargon for heroin; the symbolism is evident).[5-7] Thus, the addict presents the physician with a "no win" set of options. If the physician performs poorly and is a hostile authoritarian, he is only a predictable reinforcement of the addict's expectations. If the physician is empathic, supportive, and involved, the addict scornfully labels him a "chump." This attitude is the last line of defense for the addict, who feels extraordinarily threatened by the presence of an available, caring figure, upon whom years of pent-up rage and disappointment can be displaced. Thus, the addict must often behave outrageously in an attempt to allay his anxiety.

The anxiety endured by the hospitalized addict is exacerbated by the enforced limitation of his movements. The world of the addict turns on a perpetual cycle of obtaining cash to obtain drugs. This movement also serves to help the addict avoid all sustained interpersonal contacts. In the hospital, however, this situation is totally reversed: severe restrictions in the addict's motion are attended with feelings of vulnerability, entrapment, and submission to a system perceived as judgmental and persecutory.

CASE EXAMPLES

The following case histories illustrate the ways in which the addict patient— often with the unconscious collusion of medical personnel—attempts to manipulate the hospital system.

Case 1

M.W., a 23-year-old, white, single male, admitted to the UCLA Medical Center with a diagnosis of subacute bacterial endocarditis (SBE), gave a history detailing use of intravenous cocaine, but not heroin. M.W. had experienced a severely deprived life, marked by his father's abandonment of his addict mother during his infancy and the death of his mother during his early childhood. His primary parental attachment was to his maternal grandparents, who were described by the patient as at best ambivalent about raising him and never interested or able to establish proper controls over him.

He was admitted to a unit that primarily treats cancer patients because the ward admits general medical patients on certain days of the week. This situation created the first difficulty, since the nursing and house staff working with cancer patients typically believe that each moment of life is precious and daily observe cancer patients making the best of very trying circumstances with few complaints and an abundance of gratitude to the staff members. M.W.'s sarcasm, antagonism, and constant challenges to authority stood out in bold relief and quickly established him as a "deviant" of an exotic variety. Initially, he was not given definite limits on his behavior or told what the expectations of him would be. He refused to adjust to the role of patient, rejecting hospital gowns in favor of flashy counterculture garments, such as a T-shirt emblazoned with a picture of a transvestite movie star. In the beginning the staff was fascinated and covertly entertained and amused by his antics. He would not remain resting on his bed, but would state, "I've got to take care of my business," and leave the hospital for several hours daily with a heparin lock protruding from his arm. The nursing staff reported that often M.W. returned with a severely ataxic gait and suspected that he was stoned (intoxicated via drugs), but they were afraid to confront him because they feared the usual string of hostile, sarcastic responses from him. Nor were the house staff or the attending physician able to deal directly with M.W., and thus his behavior went unmentioned and continued to escalate.

Mental health consultation was requested by the patient after he noticed the swimming pool in the psychiatric section of the hospital and asked the house staff about its use. The staff eagerly seized this opportunity for assistance and told M.W. he would have to talk to one of the mental health team. In addition, at this time M.W. had begun taking shots of gin from a bottle he kept at his bedside. This also distressed the staff, but again they made no comment. At the point of intervention by the psychological consultant, M.W.'s room was being bypassed on the morning rounds by the medical staff, who feared angry confrontations with him. M.W. was spending almost all of his waking hours away from the hospital, and the nursing staff felt completely helpless and were minimizing contact with him to avoid friction.

The request for consultation came one week before discharge and only after five weeks of quasi hospitalization, so M.W. was seen only twice by the consultant. M.W. wanted to discuss only use of the swimming pool, denied he had any personal difficulties that had led to drug use, insisted his drug usage was so slight it was unworthy of discussion, and claimed his SBE was only an "accident." He was offered a referral to an outpatient clinic, at which he sneered. He was seen again four months later when he was rehospitalized for SBE on a different service. When the liaison team member discussed his progress with the house staff and nurses on the new ward, it was apparent that the identical behavioral cycle, including patient and staff alike, was starting once again.

Case 2

C.H. was a 26-year-old, single, white female, admitted for SBE resulting from admitted use of intravenous heroin. She also reported a troubled life history. Her nuclear family unit was intact until she was 13, when her parents separated. She described her mother as "changing and becoming unbearable" from that time on; her mother shot herself in the head ten years later. C.H. had been self-sufficient, in a manner of speaking, from age 18 and had worked at a variety of jobs. Her addiction history revealed a series of bouts with heroin, never extending beyond several months in any one period and always in response to the loss of a crucial figure on whom she depended. Her present bout of drug use was in response to the death of her son, aged nine weeks, due to "crib death."

A series of stormy confrontations occurred immediately with the house staff over her stated needs for pain medications, as well as her accusations that her intern was sexually interested in her and would not care for her "as a person." She initiated the request for mental health consultation, the house staff quickly followed through, and she was seen in the second week of her six-week hospitalization. After several history-gathering sessions, the psychological consultant brought the director of the University Drug Program to see her, and the director presented his program simply to C.H. with the request that she "think about it" and let him know if she wanted to know more about it. At the same time, the consultant met with the intern and resident managing C.H. and stressed the importance of convincing her that an essential part of her treatment involved dealing with the problems that led her to use drugs. In addition, the female resident talked with C.H. about her complaints and accusations against the intern. This intervention led to a period of "splitting" the two, with the female seen as an idealized figure and the male viewed as ineffectual, nonunderstanding, and a bad doctor. During this period, the stormy outbursts subsided, as did the wrangling and demands for pain medications. C.H. did choose to ask for more information about the drug program and arranged for outpatient therapy after discharge. She has continued in psychotherapy, remains drug free, and has not been rehospitalized.

Case 3

B.W., a 26-year-old, married, white man, came to the Emergency Room febrile and complaining of a week-old abscess on his left forearm, which had been caused by a self-injection of drugs. A diagnosis of cellulitis was made and hospitalization recommended, but the patient refused admission. He returned to the Emergency Room the next day requesting a refill of Demerol, which had been prescribed some time ago by a private physician. He was advised to return to his physician for any refills and for treatment of his cellulitis.

One week later he again returned, stating that his private doctor had heard "something in my heart." The patient stated he had used heroin six years prior to admission, and in the previous year had intermittently injected Talwin, Demerol, morphine, and barbiturates. The hospital records revealed previous admissions for withdrawal seizures, as well as a brief admission to the Drug Detoxification Program.

A presumptive diagnosis of bacterial endocarditis was made, and he was per-suaded to accept hospitalization. Intramuscular antibiotics were instituted, and the patient was given methadone for pain relief. On the second hospital day, microscopic hematuria was noted. He was seen by a member of the Infectious Disease Service, who agreed with the diagnosis of SBE and recommended a full course of intravenous antibiotics. Since therapy via peripheral veins was not possible, the placement of a subclavian line was recommended. On the third hospital day, the intern noted that the patient "tends to be manipulative" and was demanding an increase in pain medication despite obvious improvement of the infection in his left arm. During the evening of the fourth hospital day, the patient was found asleep behind the elevators. When awakened, he claimed to be making a phone call, yet his pupils were dilated and the subclavian line was leaking and shortly thereafter clotted. A urinalysis revealed the presence of morphine and short-acting barbiturates. On the fifth hospital day, the patient was again noted to be lethargic, with dilated pupils. This observation was re-peated the following day when various nonprescribed drugs and a burnt spoon were found in his possession. In the evening, in an apparent confused and angry state, he broke his IV bottle on the floor. Later the same evening, the psychiatry resident on call was asked to see the patient. He advised the establishment of clear, firm rules and suggested that the Psychiatric Consultation–Liaison Service be called the following Monday.

On the seventh hospital day (Saturday), the patient was seen by the attend-ing faculty physician. He was informed of the risks of inadequate treatment and of tampering with central venous lines. It was the attending doctor's opinion that if his misbehavior continued, the risks to all concerned outweighed the benefits of further hospitalization. Continued hospitalization was made con-tingent on strict adherence to the rules. The patient, abusive and profane, an-nounced he wanted to leave.

B.W.'s comment to a nurse before leaving was: "They're just a big bunch of liars up there." He denied throwing his IV bottle, insisting that it fell off the pole. He denied pulling out his IV line, stating that someone else must have done it. He felt that he had wanted to cooperate, but no one had listened to him and that had he been given the medication he needed, he would not have taken it on the sly. He returned later the same day requesting readmission, stating he wanted to get well. B.W. was told that if he agreed not to take nonprescribed drugs and to obey the rules, he would be guaranteed sleeping medication, analgesia, and freedom of movement consistent with his condition and general hospital policy. He agreed and was readmitted. Later that day, however, security officers found him on another floor. When a search revealed multiple drugs and a hammer, the patient was again discharged.

Following his discharge, the medical resident for the first time called a faculty member of the Consultation-Liaison Service to voice his anger that Psychiatry had not either transferred the patient to its Service or effectively controlled him on the medical ward. After obtaining a description of the week's events, the psychiatrist pointed out how complex the management of such a patient can be and stressed that no one from Psychiatry had been called until the previous Friday night. He also indicated that since the presumptive diagnosis was bacterial endocarditis, transfer to a psychiatry ward would not have permitted optimal medical management. The medical resident was urged to readmit the patient if he requested it and assured that the Consultation-Liaison Service would work closely with the medical team. The medical resident was also advised to inform the patient that the hospital would provide him with the care he needed if he agreed to obey the following rules: (1) to remain on the ward at all times; (2) to make no phone calls and have no visitors; (3) to abide by all patient rules; (4) to agree to spot checks of his personal belongings at any time. If any of these conditions were violated, he would be discharged.

The same afternoon the patient did return, and the medical resident struck an agreement with him. No sooner was he admitted than he flagrantly broke his promise and was discharged.

CONCLUSION

In spite of the myriad complexities in treating the medically ill addict, there are few reports in the literature about comprehensive interdisciplinary treatment programs. A small number of reports[8-11] clearly refer to the tendency of addict patients to be hostile, uncooperative, disruptive, and defiant and document the angry helplessness engendered in the treatment personnel. All propose the establishment of a multidisciplinary intervention strategy specific to the addict patient. It is noted that these programs were initiated because appropriate mental health persons were not being consulted even in the face of outrageous patient behavior.

The three patients described in the case reports were all treated in a university or a university-affiliated teaching hospital with active, well-known, and highly regarded Psychiatric Consultation-Liaison Services, but no specific intervention programs for medically ill addicts. Yet, as is clear from the case reports (especially 1 and 3), appropriate mental health professionals were not called soon enough.

In Case 1, there was a significant breakdown in communication among members of the operational group. The nursing, house, and attending staffs were quite disrupted. Even in the face of a patient who was obviously abusing drugs on the ward and leaving the hospital at will, the advice of a mental health person was not sought until the patient himself presented the staff with an opportunity to call for help. In Case 3, similar behavior was tolerated for many days, and it was not until the patient had been discharged for the first time that the Consultation-Liaison Service was formally consulted. It is probable that if these behaviors had occurred in a patient who was "legitimately ill," a member of the treatment unit would have requested an early consultation from Psychiatry.

In Case 1, the nursing staff expressed their concern to the house staff, who in turn expressed their concern to the attending staff. It was at this point that the breakdown occurred. It was the attending physician's responsibility to provide guidance and modeling for the house staff and nurses, who had appropriately admitted their inability to deal with the situation. However, the attending physician, also unable to handle the disturbance, guaranteed that denial of the seriousness of the problem would become the method of dealing with it. In Case 3, the attending physician was also asked to act, and he did so forthrightly, but at a point where his confrontation almost insured the patient's unwisely leaving the hospital with an untreated, potentially fatal illness.

It is reasonable to assume that all professionals involved in these cases took their medical responsibility seriously, yet they were helpless to know how to discharge it. Thus, they did nothing, including not asking for effective help. We hypothesize that a considerable degree of anger and frustration toward the patient, fueled by anxiety stemming from helpless responsibility, led to collusion among all parties to ignore the entire situation. Further, it seems that the involvement of a mental health professional must have been perceived at some level as threatening. The threat may have stemmed from fear of acknowledging the pervasive denial—a denial caused in part by the reluctance of the ward staff to accept their intense anger and resentment as natural and understandable, although these negative feelings could have been used to appreciate the dynamics and coping styles of the addict patient. From this understanding, there could have emerged the capacity to establish appropriate limits for the addict patient in a straightforward manner, free from hostility, or at the very least, with recognition that consultation of other professionals is needed early in the hospital course.

Cases 1 and 3 also clearly exemplify the key role of the attending physician, even though he may be present on the ward only for limited periods each day. The importance of modeling in the learning of clinical skills is a well-accepted axiom of medical education.[12-15] There is no situation where it is more critical than in the treatment of the addict patient. When the attending teacher-physician acts decisively, either directly with the patient at the bedside or by emphasizing the importance of obtaining mental health consultation, the possibility of successful treatment is greatly enhanced. Failure to carry out these functions instead promotes an attitude and style that can only ensure escalating indecisiveness, tension, and conflict within the entire system.

Case 2 is an example of successful treatment when the interaction among various members in the operational group is defined early enough. By clarifying the meaning of the addict patient's behavior, the liaison person was able in this case to generate renewed positive interest in the patient as a person. It was then possible for the nurses and house staff to accept their own feelings and approach the patient with confidence. In addition, the liaison person provided the patient with much-needed direct support, mainly by actively involving a drug counselor familiar with the addict's subculture.

The potential of positive, comprehensive care, however, is by no means guaranteed even when the mental health professional is called in at the appropriate time. The mental health professional must also be careful not to be guilty of the same denial and withdrawal that affect the primary providers of care; limiting his own involvement while telling others to become involved is a short route to provoking the resentment of the medical and nursing staff.

The mental health consultant, then, has several do's and don'ts in dealing with hospitalized drug addicts and medical wards. The do's include: (1) priming the service to feel that consultation for hospitalized addicts does not represent a failure on the part of the service; (2) seeing the patient as early as possible in the hospitalization to avoid ritualization of severely negative patterns within the system; (3) ensuring psychological aftercare along with other medical follow-up; (4) being aware that the mental health consultant may not be the best person to treat the addict after the initial evaluation (this may necessitate introducing staff members of local drug treatment programs who can fluently speak the addict's language, spot addict manipulations, and confront the addict honestly); (5) working with the staff to see that the addict patient is prescribed the same medication (type and dosage) that a nonaddict patient with the same medical problem would receive; (6) helping devise a logical, comprehensive, and understandable expectational system for the staff and ultimately for the addict; and (7) carefully evaluating the addict's escalating noncooperativeness for a psychotic base, since it has been felt that a significant percentage of addicts have underlying psychoses often masked by heroin or other drug usage.[7,16] The covertly psychotic addict will obviously require different interpersonal and pharmacological management than will the nonpsychotic addict.

The list of don'ts is shorter than the do's, but certainly no less important. First, never be persuaded to take sides within the system. Both sides will usually be able to argue an earnest case with excellent evidence about the faults, prejudices, and inappropriateness of the other. Second, never lose respect for the addict patient's propensity to play two sides off against each other, a basic survival mechanism in a drug-using and dealing culture, which is predictably manifested in the hospital setting. This necessitates close and ongoing contact with the staff to insure clarity of communication. Third, do not trust the addict's visitors; they will often bring more than flowers, as reflected by one study, in which 66 percent of drug users were found to be on illicit drugs while hospitalized.[17] This finding has led us to conclude that it is essential that the addict patient have no visitors. This may seem a radical and authoritarian solution, but it is necessary to prevent the addict patient's social matrix from infiltrating the hospital system.

In consulting to any system, the mental health consultant always walks a thin line between patients and professional staff. Never is this line more tenuous and unstable than when the "patient" is the medical system that contains an addict.

REFERENCES

1. Kunstadter, R., Klein, R., Lundeen, R., Witz, W., and Morrison, M. Narcotic withdrawal symptoms in newborn infants. *JAMA*, 168:1008-1010, 1958.
2. Krause, S., Murray, P., Holmes, J., and Burch, R. Heroin addiction among pregnant women and their newborn babies. *Am. J. Obstetrics Gynecol.*, 75:754-758, 1958.
3. Strain, J., and Grosman, S. *Psychological Care of the Medically Ill: A Primer in Liaison Psychiatry*. NewYork:Appleton-Century-Crofts, 1975.
4. Meyer, E., and Mendelson, M. Psychiatric consultations with patients on medical and surgical wards: Patterns and processes. *Psychiatry*, 24:197-220, 1961.
5. Wurmser, L. Psychoanalytic considerations of the etiology of compulsive drug use. *J. Am. Psychoanal. Assn.*, 22:820-843, 1974.
6. Hoffman, M. Drug addiction and hypersexuality. *Compr. Psychiat.*, 5:262-270, 1964.
7. Wellisch, D., Gay, G., and McEntee, R. The easy rider syndrome: A pattern of hetero and homosexual relationships in a heroin addict population. *Family Process*, 9:425-430, 1970.
8. Lipner, J., Harris, P., Katz, S., Meltzer, J., and Shands, H. Hospital management of heroin addicts undergoing cardiac surgery: A team approach. *Br. J. Addic.*, 68(4): 341-344, 1973.
9. Schiller, C., and Rechter, R.W. The heroin addict on the rehabilitation ward. *Arch. Phys. Med. Rehab.*, 55(9):431-432, 1974.
10. Bergel, A., and Gross, I. Drug abuse patients in a general hospital. *Hospitals*, 48(10): 658-661, 1974.
11. Galanter, M., Karasic, T., and Wilder, J. Alcohol and drug abuse consultation in the general hospital: A systems approach. *Am. J. Psychiat.*, 133:930-934, 1976.
12. Auerbach, D.B. Liaison psychiatry and the education of the psychiatric resident. In: *Consultation-liaison Psychiatry*, ed R.O. Pasnau. New York:Grune & Stratton, 1975, pp. 277-284.
13. McKegney, P.F. Consultation-liaison teaching of psychosomatic medicine: Opportunities and obstacles. *J. Nerv. Ment. Dis.*, 154:198-205, 1972.
14. Kaufman, M.R. The teaching of psychiatry to the non-psychiatrist physician. *Am. J. Psychiat.*, 128:610-616, 1972.
15. Kardner, S.H., Fuller, M., Mensh, I.N., and Forgy, E.W. The trainee's viewpoint of

psychiatric residency. *Am. J. Psychiat.*, 126:1132-1138, 1970.

16. Gendreau, P., and Gendreau, L.P. The addiction-prone personality: A study of Canadian heroin addicts. *Canad. J. Behav. Sci. Rev.*, 2:18-23, 1970.

17. Razani, J., Farina, F.A., and Stern, R. Covert drug abuse among patients hospitalized in the psychiatric ward of a university hospital. *Int. J. Addictions*, 10(4):693-698, 1975.

CHAPTER 3

Will I Die?
The Child with
Life-Threatening Illness

SUSAN D. DISKIN

> They took the joy away and left the fears.
> Hurt is in blossom, no one to tie
> The broken string of lonely tears,
> Will I die?
>
> —BB, a twelve-year-old

The sick child evokes an immediate affective response. We naturally associate youth with seemingly invincible health, vibrancy, and idealism. To confront a youngster who is restricted to a hospital bed, away from home and the companionship of his friends, appears cruel and incomprehensible, and these sentiments are magnified in the case of a child battling a serious, possibly life-threatening illness.

The consultant to a pediatric service is faced with the task of coordinating communication between the child, his family, and the medical staff under these conditions of heightened emotions. This chapter will describe the case of a young adolescent with cancer and his struggle to maintain hope and courage in the face of grave fears. This child's position in his family system made illness and hospitalization especially threatening and gave rise to a complex pattern of resistances to treatment. The situation was further complicated by the investment of the medical staff in this experimental, poignant, and often exasperating case.

THE CHILD

The consultant was introduced to Johnny C. by his physician on the Oncology Service because the boy refused to receive injections. Johnny was a 12-year-old who was apparently well known throughout the hospital. The comments of one nurse seemed to typify reactions to both Johnny and his mother: "Johnny is a likeable, cheerful kid who helps around the ward. He promises to cooperate, but something comes over him at the sight of a needle. His mother only complicates the situation and seems to blame us for trying to force Johnny to follow his programs. We can't do a thing with either of them."

Two years ago Johnny had developed a swelling in his left knee. He was treated by a local physician for an assumed sprain, but his pain seemed persistent. Mrs. C. feared that Johnny was developing arthritis, from which her own father had suffered, and further evaluation was sought at the university hospital, revealing an osteogenic sarcoma of the distal femur. In this disease, occurring most frequently in young persons, tumor cells destroy bone, form osteoid tissue, and sometimes permeate the marrow cavity. These tumors are highly malignant, and traditional treatment involves surgical amputation of the affected area. Johnny's case, however, was considered for an experimental procedure involving removal of the tumor, replacement with a bone graft, and chemotherapy for cancer cells which might have migrated to other organ systems.

Johnny was the only child of Mrs. C. He had been adopted as an infant, his biological parentage was unknown, and Mrs. C. had raised the boy with the help of her mother after a divorce from Mr. C. soon after the child had entered the home. The family were practicing Episcopalians in a lower-middle-class community, and Mrs. C. was beginning a career as a legal secretary.

Mrs. C. was informed by the oncology team of the severity of her son's condition and the possible loss of the limb. She became visibly distraught at the news and implored the doctors to find a way to save Johnny's leg. Johnny was also apprised of his condition, and he reacted similarly to amputation as a devastating alternative. The bone-graft procedure was therefore agreed upon by the family, but Mrs. C. needed urging to consent to postsurgical chemotherapy, since she feared the lethal potential of high-dosage medications. Agreement, however, was obtained, and Johnny's prognosis was deemed favorable.

The bone-graft procedure was performed, and chemotherapy was begun on a regular basis. During this period, Johnny was wearing a supportive leg brace and moving about with crutches until his bone was sufficiently strengthened. He seemed to be adapting well, maintained regular school attendance and good grades, and continued his participation in social activities. Mrs. C. was hopeful, and even Johnny's dog, Wiggles, responded by protecting his master's leg from harm during play.

One day this pet was accidentally struck by a car. Johnny was quite shaken, and his mother tried to console him by emphasizing the dog's strength and courage. When the animal died the following morning, he was deeply mourned by the family. Soon afterward, Johnny entered the hospital for chemotherapy. During this visit, he expressed unwillingness to undergo necessary bloodwork or insertion of intravenous tubes. The nurses solicited his cooperation, and a consulting psychologist attempted to reduce anxiety through deep muscle relaxation and hypnosis. These efforts were initially successful, but Johnny soon began to jerk his arm away whenever a needle appeared. Once Mrs. C., encouraging her son's cooperation, was heard to say, "Be brave; be strong." To this Johnny replied, "Wiggles was brave, and look what happened to him." Eventually force was required to accomplish any needle procedures, amid Johnny's kicks and screams that the staff was "killing" him.

Johnny's refusals to receive injections increased over subsequent hospitalizations. Chemotherapy was temporarily interrupted since required monitoring of blood levels could not be carried out. At this time, Mrs. C. also began voicing doubts about the necessity for treatment. She referred to the experimental nature of the protocol and felt that Johnny's reactions should be attended to as signals from his body about what was required to counteract disease. The family was referred to a psychotherapist in their community to help with the stresses imposed by the illness. Johnny had by this time developed a full-blown phobia of needles and chemotherapy procedures.

PHOBIAS: THEORY AND TREATMENT

Phobic reactions have received extensive consideration from both psychoanalysts and behaviorists. The psychoanalytic position was explicated by Freud in 1909 in the classic case of Little Hans.[1] The analytic treatment of this five-year-old boy in the oedipal phase of development revealed how fear of a retaliatory father could be displaced to a formerly neutral object. Rather than confront his anxiety over harbored oedipal wishes and fantasied retribution, the boy began to fear horses in the street. The phobia thus served as a defense against anxiety, in which an internal threat was transformed into an apparently objective fear.

Freud[2] conceived of phobias as defensive-organization patterns occurring in individuals who have some developmental conflict in the area of sexual adjustment. He stressed an oedipal fixation with accompanying castration fears, the centrality of displacement and avoidance, and an actual traumatic encounter with the phobic object as the factors predisposing to the genesis of a phobia. This defensive style is seen as usually adaptive, at the expense of restricted ego functioning. When periodic eruptions of anxiety nonetheless occur, expansion of avoided areas or reliance on more extreme defenses is required. Borinstein[3] and

Schnurmann[4] have offered case studies demonstrating similar psychodynamic structures underlying phobias in young children.

Arieti[5] has proposed a view that does not require a sexualized aspect to underlying anxiety. Phobias are seen as cognitive restructurings in which abstract sources of stress are concretized. When the origin of the fear has been focused on an external object, the individual is much better able to adopt a successful defensive adaptation to it. When threat is localized in a circumscribed sphere, this area can be avoided, and reality testing in other situations can be maintained.

The psychoanalytic position has been criticized for both insubstantial research evidence and undue insistence on the sexual basis of all phobias.[6] The behaviorists have postulated an alternative model based on principles of Hullian learning theory. As outlined by Rachman and Costello,[7] phobias are viewed as conditioned anxiety reactions or behaviors acquired in a context of fear. Formerly neutral stimuli in an anxiety-producing situation become associated with fear, evoking an avoidance response in the organism. These behaviors then become conditioned to a range of environmental features through stimulus generalization. According to Eysenck,[8] escape from threat is reinforcing and will increase performance of phobic responses. These behavioral repertoires are maladaptive because they are impermeable to new learning even when actual danger is no longer present. Since the individual has experienced aversive consequences and wishes to avoid their repetition, he will continue the same behaviors without exposing himself to current reality.

Dollard and Miller[9] have offered some rapprochement between psychoanalytic and behavioristic views. These authors conceptualize the formation of the phobic response system according to a learning model. However, they attribute the original anxiety state in which a phobia develops to intraorganismic variables, quite often the results of childhood conflicts in the areas of sex and aggression, and believe that predisposition to anxiety fosters the growth of phobic patterns.

The behaviorist viewpoint is supported by case studies and experimental investigations with children and animals. Watson and Rayner's[10] famous case of Albert demonstrated acquisition of persistent fear responses when a child's play with a white rat became associated with aversive environmental stimuli. M.C. Jones,[11] in her case of Peter, reported successful elimination of a youngster's fear of furry animals and objects through the use of reconditioning and reinforcement techniques. Lazarus and Rachman[12] employed relaxation and systematic desensitization to reduce anxious reactions to hospitals in a fearful 14-year-old boy.

Insight-oriented treatment methods seek to explore the historical roots and unconscious conflicts that have given rise to phobic patterns of defense. It is likely, though, that unless the basic source of anxiety is discovered, the phobia will be replaced by other symptoms. In contrast, learning theorists focus on extinction of phobic responses and acquisition of alternative adaptive behaviors.

Using the concept of reciprocal inhibition, Wolpe[13] illustrated how the bond between phobic stimuli and anxiety can be diminished by a re-pairing of threatening cues with responses incompatible to fear. By gradually approaching the phobic area under conditions regulated by the therapist, the individual can learn to overcome previous anxieties.

Recent research on phobias has concentrated on comparisons of therapeutic efficacy of traditional psychotherapy and behavior modification.[14] The differential effectiveness of various techniques within learning-based therapies has also been the object of study.[15] Conclusions about the success of psychodynamically based interventions in the treatment of phobias is limited by a paucity of controlled evaluations of outcome; however, available data would suggest that monosymptomatic phobias are more amenable to change than complicated patterns of multiple fears.[16]

Research evidence has been more systematically accumulated by advocates of learning approaches who emphasize objective goal setting and quantification of outcomes. Like verbal psychotherapy, behavior modification has been more effective in cases in which the phobia is more circumscribed and of shorter duration.[17] Techniques of systematic desensitization appear especially promising. Wolpe[18] has reported that behavioral methods have successfully achieved symptom removal in close to 90 percent of adults who originally presented with various phobias or anxiety states. The adequacy of conditioning methods without adjunctive psychotherapy has also been defended by Lang and Lazovik,[19] who successfully treated 24 snake phobics without evidence of symptom substitution. Systematic desensitization has also been used effectively to eliminate phobias in children.[20,21] Short-term interventions seem capable of producing enduring behavior change when salient anxiety-producing stimulus properties are identified.

These data justify a good deal of optimism about learning techniques. However, more comprehensive controlled research is needed to specify the optimal match between presenting symptomatology, patient characteristics, and therapeutic mode (desensitization, modeling, implosion). As a tentative conclusion, it would appear that systematic desensitization is the treatment of choice for elimination of specific behavior patterns. Conditioning methods might also be usefully integrated with more traditional approaches to increase the individual's receptivity to personal change.[22]

CONSULTATION

The consultation occurred during Johnny's fourth hospitalization for attempted continuation of the chemotherapy protocol. He was a bright, healthy-looking child with freckles and brown hair falling over his eyes, and he usually wore a T-shirt with a motorcycle racer over his pajamas. Johnny appeared an affable fellow who responded receptively to the explanation of why the consultation had been requested and how it might be helpful. He was also supported by the reassurance that many children in the hospital found it beneficial to talk about their feelings with someone who was not part of the medical staff.

When we focused specifically on his illness, Johnny became less talkative. He demonstrated an accurate understanding of his condition and the purpose of chemotherapy and, with some urging, voiced some vague fears of the powerful dosage of chemicals he was to receive, which required an immediate "rescue" solution to prevent tissue damage. In the same context, Johnny spoke sorrowfully of the loss of his dog, Wiggles, who had been a beloved companion and protector. He also appeared uncomfortable at the thought of disappointing the doctors and nurses when he refused injections.

However, Johnny's distress at not receiving chemotherapy seemed equivocal. Worries over his present condition or future prognosis were also largely denied. Despite his evident desire to please others around him, Johnny was unable to explain why he jerked his arm away from needles, saying, "I don't know—I just don't like them."

Johnny's mother seemed initially reserved when the consultant introduced herself as someone interested in helping her son with his fear of procedures. Mrs. C. disclosed her own frustrations in this regard and described the burdens of providing consistent emotional and financial support, adding that she had left her studies to attend to her son. At the time of consultation referral, she was angry at the hospital staff, who, she felt, blamed her for Johnny's behavior. Though she herself had a distaste for injections and hospitals, she felt bewildered by the intensity of her son's reactions: "I really don't know. They say he needs these treatments, yet we really can't know for sure. Sometimes I think Johnny is the only one who knows what he needs."

Effective consultation begins by considering any single problem in its total context. This case involved a child, his family, the medical staff, and the manner in which these systems interfaced. A first step was to clarify the staff's expectations of the consultant and to define the services that could realistically be provided. Assessment was needed of the strengths and deficits in the environment that would support renewed functioning and resumption of chemotherapy.

The ward staff who had requested psychological consultation faced a management problem. Johnny's resistances were preventing the progress of medical procedures for which the nurses were responsible. In addition, the staff was sensitive to the boy's emotional predicament and realized that Johnny's behavior probably expressed certain resentments and fears.

Johnny had been admitted willingly to the hospital four times, but each time verbally and physically balked at needle procedures. He then became upset and angry at the staff members who tried to urge cooperation. Sensing their frustration, he shunned contact with doctors and nurses by whom he felt criticized. He thereby avoided chemotherapy and became less accessible to medical personnel who might have been able to enlist his compliance. In addition, Mrs. C. wavered in her conviction about the necessity for completion of the chemotherapy protocol, despite repeated assurances that these procedures were designed to prevent the growth of life-endangering cancer cells.

Although the hospital staff had initially taken a sympathetic and noncoercive stance toward Johnny, this attitude was not long tenable. Nurses became irritated by the boy's excessive time demands, which ultimately resulted in failure. Some of the staff expressed their puzzlement and anger over this patient's rejection of life-saving medications. These reactions were accompanied by guilt and hopelessness.

A central function of a phobic defensive organization is avoidance of that which would otherwise represent danger. Johnny was faced with serious hospitalization that would have evoked fear and anxiety in most patients; yet his disturbance about this matter was not directly apparent. Johnny's reaction to the sight of a needle, however, could not have escaped the notice of even the most casual observer. It appeared that the boy's fears of illness or death were being displaced to aspects of medical treatment and becoming manifest in the needle phobia. He also evidenced identification with the stricken dog Wiggles, whose bravery had been followed by death. Instead of confronting the ominous fear of dying, Johnny exhibited terror in response to injections, and to the degree that he was able to avoid procedures, he seemed to experience some relief and often was able to return home. Some mastery was thus possible over the underlying anxiety direct thoughts about illness would have elicited.

Johnny's unascertained prognosis compounded the more typical fears of a hospitalized young adolescent. The boy was confronted with pain, loss of control over body functions, and restricted mobility. His sensitivity to his mother's preoccupations further interfered with his candid voicing of concerns and arrival at a level of realistic hopefulness. Moreover, these stresses were occurring when Johnny would ordinarily have been facing the developmental tasks of separation from family and personal individuation.

Adolescence is also a time of increased sensitivity to one's own body image as an important component of self-esteem. This illness, which enforced medical dependency, seriously impeded Johnny's assertion of autonomy. From this perspective, his refusals to undergo procedures, however self-defeating, could be viewed as efforts to establish independence and personal control.

Mrs. C. had invested all her efforts for the past two years in care and concern for her only son; nevertheless, she felt the nursing staff blamed her for her inability to control Johnny's resistances. These tensions prevented more effective communication and collaboration with those figures who might have been able to provide Mrs. C. with emotional support during this stressful period; mutual anger served as a rationale for limited cooperation with the medical staff.

Johnny and his mother appeared to share a belief system with regard to the boy's disease. Weisman and Hackett[23] have lucidly outlined the interpersonal ramifications of denial in which active avoidance of certain real perceptions is collusively maintained to preserve relationships with significant others. It seemed that to acknowledge the gravity of Johnny's illness would have been intolerably distressing to mother and son and threatened both with separation and loss of their closest family member. Resistance to needle procedures offered the immediate gain of isolating the family from the staff members who were painful reminders of their fearful predicament; compliance with hospital regimens would have required recognition of the seriousness of Johnny's condition and acceptance of treatment risks.

This case brought both doctors and nurses in direct contact with their feelings of helplessness, consequent anger, and desires to be rid of this troublesome, sad situation. Provoking rejection from the hospital ideally suited the purposes of this frightened mother and son. The rage and impotence experienced by this family were mirrored by the intensity of feeling they evoked among staff members. It must have worried Johnny that no one seemed capable of controlling his behavior or, by extension, his disease. In a sense, his resistance could be viewed as a plea for effective limits.

Children are dependent on their elders for many needs. When they become ill, it may appear that adult caretakers have in some way failed to provide adequate safeguards. Exposure to sick youngsters may elicit guilt in healthy staff members entrusted with their care. If unrecognized, such reactions may unfortunately result in abandonment or rejection of child patients and their families when they require support, and a request for consultation in such a case may reflect a wishful transfer of responsibility and guilt to an external source.

When psychological complications arise, the consultant may find himself the unwitting recipient of expectations for an immediate "cure" so that medical intervention can progress without interruption. The rapid elimination of difficulties, however, may not always be realistic. It is the consultant's responsibility to articulate the limits of his capabilities and to provide some estimate of the time his program will require. Exaggerated expectations can thus be more nearly aligned with possibility. Where goals are not explicitly outlined, failure to effect quick resolution of difficulties may generate anger and cynicism in the referring party.

The presented case was atypical in that a patient of Johnny's age would usually have been assigned to a pediatric unit. Because of the complicated nature of the chemotherapy protocol, however, the boy was placed on the oncology ward. One can speculate whether the problem of his management would have become so extreme if it had been handled earlier by staff members more experienced with children. The specialized interests and training of many pediatric staffs can advantageously attune primary caregivers to a range of psychosocial and medical needs; however, the expectation should not be engendered that hospital personnel must or should handle those problems more typically assigned to mental health professionals. The consultant's service is to provide an objective, outside opinion on how role responsibilities can be most effectively carried out or, when appropriate, to suggest referrals for adjunctive care.

INTERVENTION

Intervention in this case consisted of three parts. A primary focus was the re-establishment of behavior control over Johnny's resistances so that chemotherapy could be continued. Toward this goal, a program of in vivo desensitization was initiated to weaken the association between anxiety and needles. Under relaxed conditions Johnny was exposed to the phobic stimuli for increasing periods of time. He rated aspects of the treatment environment according to their fear-inducing potential, and these stimuli were then presented in serial order until reported distress significantly diminished. Decreases in Johnny's anxiety were encouraged by social reinforcements from the clinician and medical staff who observed his behavior change. Desensitization sessions were held with the actual technicians to facilitate generalization of Johnny's cooperative responses to the hospital ward. Use of the same staff members not only solidified Johnny's association of these figures with low anxiety, but also bolstered these nurses' confidence and expectations of success.

Attention was next directed to the emotional needs of mother and son. Supportive psychotherapy provided Johnny and Mrs. C. with the opportunity to voice many feelings related to the illness, hospitalization, and medical staff. It was hoped that without being pressured to confront their denial, they could express their fear and hostility more constructively than in noncompliance with ward procedures.

Another goal was improvement of the C. family's communication with, and trust of, the medical staff. For this purpose, the consultant's presence as a figure not directly associated with the unit was critical. The consultant enjoys a unique position as a nonpartisan agent who can maintain objectivity and avoid over-involvement in any one aspect of a system. For many patients, the availability of a concerned and understanding outsider is of tremendous value, since some individuals are quite hesitant to express themselves openly to those responsible for their physical care.

The third phase of the intervention concentrated on the medical staff. At the outset the goal was portrayed as the restitution of a working equilibrium between the C. family and ward personnel that would permit Johnny's treatment to be carried out effectively. The psychological aspects of the boy's situation were discussed to increase the staff's empathy for their patient's experience, and their own feelings of helplessness and anger were directly addressed in group meetings where emotional ventilation and alleviation of guilt were possible.

A program was also devised for handling Johnny's resistances if they recurred on the ward. It was decided that a stepwise approach that permitted gradual extinction of anxiety offered the highest probability of success. A modified desensitization procedure was developed to facilitate abatement of fear before procedures were continued. The nursing staff was also instructed in principles of contingent reinforcement delivery, which aimed at achieving greater behavioral control through systematic praise for Johnny's gradual moves toward compliance. The consultant obtained periodic feedback about the program's efficacy, and modifications were implemented as needed. A general climate of cooperation evolved and replaced the contentiousness that had formerly characterized interactions between the C. family and the hospital staff.

Sensitivity to the psychosocial ramifications of illness and hospitalization is imperative in effective treatment of children and their families. Recent advances in therapeutic techniques offer an increasingly wide range of methods if difficulties do arise. Whether an intervention is ameliorative, however, will depend on definition of problems in a multidimensional framework and coordination of efforts among professionals. Emotional and physical stresses will exert complex pressures within any treatment milieu, and the consultant is challenged with the task of addressing the various needs of patients and staff. Only when a perspective is adopted that appreciates the functional relation between any problem and its environment can comprehensive health care be provided.

REFERENCES

1. Freud, S. Analysis of a phobia in a five-year-old boy (1909). In: *The Standard Edition of the Complete Psychological Works of Sigmund Freud,* 10:5-149, ed. J. Strachey. London:Hogarth Press, 1955.

2. Freud, S. Inhibitions, symptoms, and anxiety (1926). In: *The Standard Edition of the Complete Psychological Works of Sigmund Freud,* 20:87-172, ed. J. Strachey. London: Hogarth Press, 1959.

3. Borinstein, B. The analysis of a phobic child: Some problems in theory and technique in child analysis. *The Psychoanalytic Study of the Child,* 3:181-226. New York: International Universities Press, 1949.

4. Schnurmann, A. Observation of a phobia. *The Psychoanalytic Study of the Child,* 3:253-270. New York:International Universities Press, 1949.

5. Arieti, S. A re-examination of the phobic symptom and of symbolism in psychopathology. *Am. J. Psychiat.,* 118:106-110, 1961.

6. Wolpe, J., and Rachman, S. Psychoanalytic "evidence": A critique based on Freud's case of Little Hans. *J. Nerv. Ment. Dis.,* 130:135-148, 1960.

7. Rachman, S., and Costello, C.G. The aetiology and treatment of children's phobias: A review. *Am. J. Psychiat.,* 118:97-105, 1961.

8. Eysenck, H.J., ed. *Behavior Therapy and the Neuroses.* New York:Pergamon Press, 1960.

9. Dollard, J., and Miller, N.E. *Personality and Psychotherapy.* New York:McGraw-Hill, 1950.

10. Watson, J.B., and Rayner, R. Conditioned emotional reactions. *J. Exp. Psychol.,* 3: 1-14, 1920.

11. Jones, M.D. A laboratory study of fear: The case of Peter. *J. Genet. Psychol.,* 31:

308-315, 1924.

12. Lazarus, A.A., and Rachman, S. The use of systematic desensitization in psychotherapy. *S. Afr. Med. J.*, 31:934-937, 1957.

13. Wolpe, J. *Psychotherapy by Reciprocal Inhibition*. Stanford:Stanford University Press, 1958.

14. Gelder, M.G., Marks, I.M., and Wolff H.H. Desensitization and psychotherapy in the treatment of phobic states: A controlled inquiry. *Br. J. Psychiat.*, 113:53-73, 1967.

15. Rachman, S. Studies in desensitization. I. The separate effects of relaxation and desensitization. *Behav. Res. Ther.*, 3:245-252, 1965.

16. Yates, A.J. *Behavior Therapy*. New York:Wiley, 1970.

17. Snaith, R.P. A clinical investigation of phobias. *Br. J. Psychiat.*, 114:673-697, 1968.

18. Wolpe, J. The systematic desensitization treatment of neuroses. *J. Nerv. Ment. Dis.*, 132:189-203, 1961.

19. Lang, P.J., and Lazovik, A.D. Experimental desensitization of a phobia. *J. Abn. Soc. Psychol.*, 66:519-525, 1963.

20. Lazarus, A.A. The elimination of children's phobias by deconditioning. *Med. Proceed. S. Afr.*, 5:261-265, 1959.

21. Lazarus, A.A., and Abramovitz, A. The use of "emotive imagery" in the treatment of children's phobias. *J. Ment. Sci.*, 108:191-195, 1962.

22. Meyer, V., and Gelder, M.G. Behavior therapy and phobic disorders. *Br. J. Psychiat.*, 109:19-28, 1963.

23. Weisman, A.D., and Hackett, T.P. Denial as a social act. In: *Psychodynamic Studies on Aging: Creativity, Reminiscing, and Dying*, ed. S. Levin and R.J. Kahana. New York:International Universities Press, pp. 79-110, 1967.

CHAPTER 4

Life in a Venus' Flytrap: Psychiatric Liaison to Patients Undergoing Bone Marrow Transplantation

DAVID K. WELLISCH
FAWZY I. FAWZY
JOEL YAGER

> Hope is both the earliest and the most indispensable virtue. If life is to be sustained, hope must remain, even where confidence is wounded, trust impaired.
>
> —Erik Erikson

The UCLA Medical Center is one of several studying the effectiveness of bone marrow transplantation (BMT) in patients suffering from leukemia or aplastic anemia unresponsive to conventional therapy. We have noted that the BMT patient is at great risk; in addition to the stress of life-threatening illness, major procedures such as massive radiotherapy and chemotherapy and sustained reverse isolation threaten to overwhelm his psychological defenses. In response to the clearly perceived need for psychiatric consultation to this project, a multidisciplinary program for psychosocial care was instituted three years ago, offering routine comprehensive psychological attention to the patients, their families, and the medical team.

This chapter will describe in detail the management of two representative patients and discuss the special problems related to reverse isolation.

MR. A.

Mr. A. was a 26-year-old Filipino man, slight, intense, somewhat shy, with thinly disguised tension and desperation which he continually struggled to hide and control. He was admitted to the hospital for evaluation of the possibility of BMT ten months following the diagnosis of acute myelogenous leukemia. Multiple courses of chemotherapy had induced a remission after eight months, but that remission had lasted only one month.

Born in the Philippines, Mr. A. emigrated with his family at age seven to the United States. The family settled near Los Angeles, where his father worked as laborer and his mother as a secretary. He was the eldest of the siblings, with four younger brothers and two younger sisters. One younger sister had died in early childhood.

Mr. A. was a below-average student and dropped out of high school at age 17 to join the Marine Corps. He served in the infantry in Vietnam, much of the time in actual combat. He was twice wounded and hospitalized. On return to the United States he experienced three "nervous breakdowns;" their exact nature was unknown, but on each occasion he was briefly hospitalized and quickly returned to active duty. After discharge from the Marine Corps, Mr. A. was married for a short time to a Filipino girl. He was reluctant to discuss his marriage and provided scant detail. It was learned that the couple had been separated for seven months before he was hospitalized for bone marrow transplantation. Although Mr. A. felt he had failed in his marriage and did not want to talk about it, the marriage no longer appeared to be a major concern.

Hospital Course

This section chronicles Mr. A.'s hospital course and our intervention on a week-by-week basis. Psychiatry's involvement in Mr. A.'s treatment was not a series of discrete entrances and exits, but was constant and evolved over time.

Week One

After admission Mr. A. was found to be closely compatible with his 19-year-old brother on blood and tissue antigen typing and consequently could be offered BMT. Mr. A. readily accepted the idea of the procedure. Although the procedure was explained in detail to Mr. A., it later became clear that even though he may have heard what he was told at the time of consent, he simply could not appreciate the reality of the details until he was living in their midst a few weeks later.

The attending and house staff members felt from the very beginning that

Mr. A. was unusually anxious and nervous, and they requested a psychiatric consultation to evaluate the patient's mental condition and ability to withstand the rigors of BMT, including lengthy reverse isolation, extensive chemotherapy, and radiation.

The patient was first seen by the psychiatric consultant at the end of week one. He appeared frightened and tense and quickly mentioned his three "nervous breakdowns" in the Marine Corps, each of which required sedation and brief hospitalization. His two greatest fears were "isolation" and "being awake during surgery." Mr. A. did not appear to be psychotic during our first meeting, but he was clearly asking for help.

We recommended that 24-hour private-duty nursing be secured for him immediately so that he could form solid, dependable relationships on the ward *before* he became massively stressed. We also recommended that Mr. A. receive general rather than local anesthesia for all surgical procedures and that he be given adequate sleep medication to maintain proper sleep-wakefulness cycles.

Week Two

The second week was far more arduous. The patient was placed in reverse isolation, which protects susceptible, immunologically deficient patients, such as those with leukemia or aplastic anemia, from infection. Special environments are created in which staff and visitors who come into direct contact with patients are required to observe strict isolation precautions, which necessitate their donning masks, gowns, caps, and gloves. While reducing the likelihood of infection, this precaution also reduces interpersonal contact for the patient, specifically altering the extent and nature of the patient's touching and being touched.

Mr. A. was seen for several psychiatric interviews during this week. He said, "I'm not sick yet and can still handle things mentally, but when I get sick I get weak—and then I need mental help." He was concerned about keeping his brother, the donor, interested in the procedure because "he hates needles, especially big ones." This was the first time Mr. A. openly expressed fear of abandonment by his family. Later in the week, Mr. A. began to talk about Vietnam and related his fear of being confined to an experience of having been shelled in a bunker: "I finally ran out of there even though I knew I might be killed." At this point he first disclosed his fears of dying and said these fears were now constantly on his mind.

We continued to stress the importance of Mr. A's developing solid relationships with the nurses. There were now three regular nurses, and as soon as they were assigned to Mr. A., they were fully briefed and completely integrated into the team. They understood that Mr. A. felt he had little strength for coping with his situation and as the stress mounted he would probably regress and become quite dependent on them and his physicians.

By the end of the second week, Mr. A. had successfully endured the insertion of an arteriovenous (A-V) fistula in his left forearm under general anesthesia and seemed less anxious. We recommended that additional stimuli, such as television, radio, and a record player, be brought into his barren isolation room. The patient agreed to cooperate with our efforts to teach him relaxation exercises and self-hypnosis, which were intended to foster a sense of control. This instruction commenced during week three. Additionally, Haldol was substituted for the Valium and Dalmane he had been receiving, since these medications were overly sedating him.

Week Three

After taking Haldol for several days, the attending staff noted that Mr. A. was "well medicated," but nurses observed that his agitation was increasing. He began to resist taking oral antibiotics required for GI sterilization. A course of chemotherapy (cytosine arabinoside and 6-thioquanine) was begun in massive doses designed to destroy his own bone marrow entirely.

During the first relaxation training session, a hypnotic trance was induced. In the midst of this trance, Mr. A. bolted awake and began to sob about the death, years before, of his baby sister. He cried out, "Her death was my fault! She swallowed my marbles which had germs on them! I killed her!" It was decided to discontinue hypnosis since it was felt that Mr. A. could not tolerate such an assault on his already tenuous psychological defenses.

During the third week, psychological testing was completed and revealed a Verbal IQ of 89, a Performance (non-Verbal) IQ of 81, and a full-scale IQ of 85. Significant anxiety and depression were noted and intruded on and impaired his ability to coordinate cognitive with perceptual-motor and fine-motor functions. Short-term memory and ability to concentrate were seriously impaired and far below his other cognitive abilities. Personality testing with the Rorschach and Minnesota Multiphasic Personality Inventory (MMPI) revealed a borderline state with elements of depression, hysteria, and anxiety in the neurotic range, as well as impaired reality testing in the psychotic range. At that time the overall organization of his defenses was weak, but intact, and his predominant defenses were neurotic rather than psychotic. One noteworthy response to a Rorschach inkblot was: "some kind of flower that traps a little animal, and the animal gets eaten by the flower." This response was striking in its parallel to his situation, where Mr. A. was trapped in an isolated and containing environment in which he experienced repeated assaults on his body. It was noted that at about this time his awareness and appreciation that these "assaults" were for his own good began to fade.

We met Mr. A.'s parents for the first time during the third week. His mother cried freely, but his father was smiling, passive, and unemotional. Mr. A.'s mother visited more frequently and stayed at the hospital for several days at a time. When we asked his parents about the circumstances of their daughter's death in the Philippines, they said she died of a "convlusion" and mentioned that they had never discussed or openly mourned her death with the children. Thus, the father's seeming emotional detachment and unresponsiveness to Mr. A.'s condition appeared consistent with a past coping style.

During the third week, Mr. A.'s A-V shunt became clogged by an infiltration of leukemic cells, and irradiation of the area was required to reopen the line. The nurses noted that "he's worrying about everything" and "he's tolerating procedures really very poorly." He also began to spike fevers and experienced episodes of shaking chills requiring supplementary transfusions of white cells from relatives.

The medical intern who was assigned to Mr. A.'s direct care left the service at this time, which was a difficult loss for both Mr. A. and the nurses. The patient developed, in short order, a macro-papular rash covering his abdomen and began to express an aggressively demanding attitude toward his new intern. It was felt that he had become extremely irritable and childlike in his behavior. An open conflict also developed between the new intern and one of Mr. A.'s nurses, who felt she "was not being heard."

Week Four

Mr. A.'s psychological distress peaked during the fourth week. He pleaded with staff to "just let me walk in the hall [break isolation] for a minute or two" and begged, "Can't you take out my IV for one night to let me sleep well?" He frequently exhibited rage, tears, and sulking withdrawal and tested established rules, especially those regarding his personal hygiene and health maintenance. He refused oral medications and began to spit out his pills. He was beginning to push the nurses' tolerance to the limit.

The nurses, however, began to notice that Mr. A.'s misbehavior was related to their taking rest breaks or days off during the week. One recorded, "He seems to punish me for going off by not cooperating before I go on break and only cooperating after I return." We discussed in detail with the nurses how Mr. A. appeared to experience (in a hostile fashion) even brief separation as abandonment. We decided to institute "cathartic" sessions for him with the psychiatric team, but resolved that the staff would not step back from previously established limits.

Mr. A. was about to receive additional chemotherapy (Cytoxan), to be followed by total body irradiation and finally by actual BMT.

Week Five

The patient's acting out, agitation, and noncooperation were major problems. Because of his constant vomiting and refusal to take medication, Haldol was not effective. His tantrums and threats escalated, and he demanded intravenous

Valium. We recommended that Thorazine concentrate be substituted to make him more comfortable and tractable, and this recommendation was quickly accepted. The attending physician noted, "He must be heavily sedated due to uncontrollable behavior until he has completed transplant." Nursing notes began to report more cooperation and somewhat less agitation.

Mr. A.'s room was now decorated to provide more visual stimulation. An entire wall was covered with a paper mural depicting a pastoral scene. Unfortunately, all was not pastoral with those caring for him. The nurses felt isolated and estranged from the physicians, and conflicts developed over appropriate management. At this time, Mr. A.'s sleeping patterns began to deteriorate, and his demands for sleep medication increased.

At the end of the fifth week, he received a final course of irradiation as the last step in preparation for BMT.

Week Six

Mr. A. received BMT on the first day of the sixth week. The marrow was administered intravenously, and the procedure was filmed (as the signing of the consent forms for the BMT had been). Two days later the psychiatric consultant noted, "Patient feels movie cameras are controlling him, I am controlling him, and that the picture on his wall is moving." He was frankly psychotic, but was not grossly disoriented. Thorazine, it was felt, was at this time oversedating him and was discontinued. Haldol was reinstituted.

Mr. A. was severely pancytopenic and required matched platelet transfusions from his brother. He continued to have spiking fevers. At the end of the week Mr. A. said, "I'm physically ill, but I'm not going insane." He was correct. His psychosis cleared and in its place significant depression emerged. He looked exhausted and overwhelmed.

Week Seven

The intern who had been with Mr. A. through the worst period left the Oncology Service at the beginning of the seventh week. The patient was too ill from the effects of radiation and chemotherapy to notice. The departing intern in his off-service note wrote, "He is quite cooperative." The new intern who assumed Mr. A.'s care wrote, "He is presently zonked on neuroleptics."

Christmas was near. Although Mr. A. did not notice the passing of Thanksgiving, he was concerned about Christmas. His family continued to visit, his mother far more frequently than his father. The nurses noted little resistance from the patient during this week. Haldol was discontinued, but his dependence and physical discomfort were at their height.

Toward the end of the seventh week, Mr. A.'s depression increased. During interviews he pleaded more strongly, "I want to go home. I'm sick of this hospital although I know I'm not ready to leave." A compounding medical problem appeared—extensive candida esophagitis that resulted in severe soreness on swallowing.

Week Eight

Mr. A. was now 16 days post transplant, and early signs were encouraging. Small areas of myeloid and erythroid maturation were seen in his bone marrow; his white blood cell count was 400 and rising.

Early in the eighth week Mr. A.'s anger emerged again, and he refused IV's. Thorazine was resumed and shortly afterward the intern noted, "Much better, less tense." Mr. A.'s white blood count was 2,000. His most annoying problem now became skin rashes and insufferable itching, possibly secondary to "graft versus host disease" (GVH). The nurses struggled without success to prevent him from constantly scratching himself. Because of the possibility that Thorazine was contributing to the skin reaction, it was discontinued, and Valium was reintroduced for anxiety. The intern recorded, "Patient again becoming a management problem, demands morphine sulphate but settled for IV Valium."

Week Nine

Mr. A. began to move out of his bed and about the room. Although both house staff (especially Mr. A.'s intern) and nurses seemed more perceptive about his feelings and consequent behavior, the nurses were exhausted and demoralized by this time and were finding it difficult to be always empathic. The intern noted, "Patient pleaded with me not to restart his IV. I feel when it is restarted he will again regress, become uncooperative, and vomit." Mr. A.'s scratching was continuous and his cooperation with the nurses, minimal; he scratched and bled until the sheets were soaked with blood and skin, and bedding often had to be changed as much as six times daily.

Mr. A. stated, "I was lonely over Christmas." His usual nurses were off duty, and float nurses were assigned for the days before, during, and after Christmas. He was furious about this situation and channeled his rage into nonstop scratching. A medication change was ordered again, back to Haldol. It was difficult for the staff, especially the nurses, to be patient and supportive. Psychiatric involvement was now apportioned, with approximately 80 percent for nurses and 20 percent for Mr. A. The skin rash and persistent fevers were major concerns. However, both the platelet (now 12,000) and white counts (now 3,800) were encouraging.

Week Ten

Mr. A.'s BMT continued to do well. Engraftment had definitely occurred. In his off-service note the intern described Mr. A.'s skin rash as "horrendous and life-threatening," and he admonished the oncoming intern to "Be honest with patient and don't tell him things which aren't true as this clearly causes set-backs."

Mr. A. was seriously despondent: "I don't care if I die. I've been here in the hospital so long it doesn't matter anymore." At the same time he was ambivalent about death at this point; he alternated between "I want to die" and "I want to go home." An angry split now occurred for the first time between his day and evening nurses. It became apparent that each had hostile, vindictive feelings toward the other, based on Mr. A.'s playing one off against the other. (For example, he told the evening nurse, "But my day nurse said I didn't have to do that.") Mr. A. further aggravated the split by beginning to view the day nurse as "racist, vicious" and the evening nurse as "good, understanding." Unable ade-quately to express or resolve his distress and ambivalence, it appeared that he had begun to project his own ambivalence onto the nurses, making them feel split and ambivalent. A good deal of profitable time was spent with the nurses over this potentially explosive situation.

On the day the new intern arrived, Mr. A. was found lying on the floor of his room after having pushed the emergency button. He stated, "I'm afraid of having another nervous breakdown." The new intern recorded this as an "overtly psychotic episode." We discussed Mr. A.'s defensive and coping maneuvers with the staff, and this incident was conceptualized as the patient's induction ritual for the new intern. It was apparent that Mr. A. needed to demonstrate to the intern in a dramatic fashion just how pressured he felt, and he did not want the intern to underestimate or overlook his feelings.

Soon Mr. A. began to complain of "unbearable body pain" and demanded intravenous morphine. The potential for addiction was discussed, and the intern was advised to stand firm and not use morphine, but rather judiciously prescribe phenothiazines.

At the end of the tenth week, Mr. A. was told that he could soon be dis-charged. His BMT was stable; his platelet and white blood cell counts were consistently improving. Isolation precautions were discontinued, and for the first time in nine weeks the door to his room was opened. In spite of weeks of pro-testing that he wanted "only to be able to leave the room for a minute," his initial reaction was to stay anxiously in his bed for two days. The staff repeatedly discussed with him the safety of leaving his room and praised his decision finally to venture into the hall. Clearly, what had been a torture chamber and "Venus' flytrap" had at the same time become a womb and cocoon.

Mr. A. left after almost 80 days of hospitalization. For the first week, he stayed in a nearby hotel with his brother and mother and was seen as an out-patient. He eventually returned to a suboptimal home situation. Weeks earlier, because of his father's refusal to visit Mr. A. or to talk with him on the phone, Mr. A.'s mother withdrew from involvement with her husband and stopped speaking to him.

During the week of outpatient follow-up, Mr. A. completed a second MMPI. His previously borderline profile had changed and now appeared more psychotic, revealing fewer available adaptive defenses.

Mr. A. refused further psychiatric support and discontinued the prescribed Haldol. His family reported that he "stared at the walls most of the time." He lived for almost a year and finally succumbed to a recurrence of leukemia.

MR. B.

Mr. B., a 57-year-old married man, the eldest of eight children, was a recently retired mechanical engineer who had been a reliable, steady, devoted family man. He was in vigorous health until four months prior to admission, when he developed a flu-like syndrome, which was treated symptomatically with aspirin. This syndrome resolved, but one month later he began to experience shortness of breath and easy fatigability. Medical evaluation revealed aplastic anemia. Mr. B. was then confronted with the reality of a commonly fatal disease. He learned that while life could be sustained temporarily by repeated blood transfusions, he would always live with the threat of rapid death due to hemorrhage or fulminating infection. The possible benefits of BMT generated some hope for Mr. B., and he was quite interested in the experimental program.

Initial Interview

Mr. B. was hospitalized at UCLA for an evaluation of possible BMT. During the first routine interview with the psychiatric consultant, Mr. B. was superficially cheerful. Although he tried to present himself as optimistic, gentle probing uncovered considerable anxiety. He could not fathom what might have caused his illness. Mr. and Mrs. B. were encouraged to ask questions regarding medical treatment, review the pros and cons of the procedure, and discuss the matter together before deciding whether to participate in the BMT project.

That evening Mr. and Mrs. B. met with the Oncology Fellow from the BMT team, who again described the seriousness of Mr. B.'s illness, the experimental nature of the BMT procedure, its research aspects, and the risks involved. Although Mr. B. was especially concerned with the fact that he was going to be the oldest patient ever to have this procedure at UCLA, he was nevertheless hopeful. It was impossible for either Mr. or Mrs. B. to acknowledge openly the risks at this time; their faith in God and their hope for a miraculous cure precluded serious consideration of the dangers of the treatment.

Hospital Course

Week One

By the time the psychiatric consultant returned for the second visit, Mr. B. had been transferred to an isolation room in preparation for the transplant. Mr. B. was alone, and he took the opportunity to share with the consultant his concerns about his wife. He felt guilty that he was sick and bedridden and that he might die and leave her to face a difficult life without his support. "We worked hard all our lives and saved some money so we could retire and start enjoying ourselves. I retired last April and my wife was due to retire in September. Then this hits us like a ton of bricks." Mr. B. was tearful while talking about his wife; his main concerns centered about her well-being after his death. It was becoming clear that Mr. B.'s motives for risking the procedure were closely tied to his wishes to continue to care for his wife.

The consultant's visits with the patient continued on a regular basis. An initial issue for Mr. B. was his problem in establishing a trusting and appropriately dependent relationship with his nurses; since he had been self-reliant his whole life, at the beginning he was reluctant and unable to put himself in their hands. The consultant also saw Mrs. B. individually to provide her an opportunity to ventilate and discuss her own anxieties.

At the end of the first week Mr. B. had completed his chemotherapy and was prepared for total body irradiation. Mr. B.'s brother, the scheduled marrow donor, was expected to arrive in the city shortly. This was both exciting and anxiety-provoking for Mr. B.—exciting in that he was going to see his brother for the first time in ten years, gratifying in that his brother was willing to come to Los Angeles to help, yet troubling in that Mr. B. worried that something bad might befall his healthy brother as a result of the procedure.

The patient's brother arrived and was apprised of the physical and psychological ramifications of being a donor. He knew that he would have minor surgery under general anesthesia so that the marrow could be aspirated from his hip. He also knew that he might be called upon to provide his brother with additional transfusions daily or every other day, which would require his remaining in the city for a prolonged time. He stated that he was prepared to help his brother, but admitted that he was concerned about the possible psychological conflicts he might experience if the bone marrow graft did not take and his brother died.

Week Two

Mr. B. completed the second phase of the protocol. He received total body irradiation followed by intravenous transfusion of the marrow graft. He weathered these without difficulties, although he, his family, and the staff were constantly alert for complications that might arise. The deep religious faith of the family throughout this period was striking and provided continued spiritual strength. His brother's presence helped Mr. B. a great deal. He gave Mr. B. considerable support and encouragement and was available for Mrs. B. at all times.

Ten days post transplant, laboratory tests indicated the transplant had successfully taken. Mr. B. said, "I told you I would make it." The staff, Mr. B., and his family were all optimistic, and preparation for his discharge was discussed. Mrs. B. was occupied with plans for her husband's return home. Having become emotionally invested in this delightful couple, the staff shared in the pleasure of his apparent success.

Week Three

Success was, however, short-lived. One week later Mr. B. developed severe "graft versus host" disease (due to immunological reactions between the graft and the recipient's own tissues), with fevers, chills, and stomatitis. From that point, although they superficially retained hope, everyone expected Mr. B. to die shortly. Mr. B. was not sorry about having gambled, but was sad that things had not progressed as he had wished.

Week Four

The consultant continued to see the family together and Mrs. B. separately. She had made peace with herself: "He wanted it, I wanted it, we tried, I will never be sorry we did, I just had hoped he would make it."

The remaining few days were full of sadness. Mr. B. lapsed into semiconsciousness. Mrs. B. and her brother-in-law stayed in the room almost all the time. Mr. B. died peacefully. Mrs. B. cried, hugged the nurses, the oncologist, and the psychiatrist, all of whom were present.

Post-terminal Phase

The psychiatric consultant continued to see Mrs. B. for several weeks. She was able to grieve and talked about her revised plans for the future. After several weeks she announced, "I am not coming anymore. I think I am ready to face up to the future, but I'll call you if I need you." It was agreed upon, and they said goodbye.

COMMENT

These two cases illustrate the range of adaptive responses in patients who undergo BMT. The multiple stresses of potentially fatal disease, extraordinary doses of toxic chemotherapy and radiation, and life in reverse isolation present challenges to human coping systems comparable to those of few other illnesses. Mr. B.'s ability to deal psychologically with these events was considerable, and in spite of the fatal outcome, he and his family were able to share openly the periods of hope and despair. He departed from his wife with sadness, love, and dignity, in a manner that facilitated her appropriate grieving. Mr. B.'s good life adjustment, close family ties, open communication patterns, and strong religious beliefs, all contributed to his effective psychological coping.

In contrast, Mr. A. entered with far fewer resources. His previous history of psychiatric impairment and the disturbed patterns of family communication presaged the likelihood of an especially difficult course. Yet in spite of the marked psychological disturbances, Mr. A. survived the procedures and lived for more than a year. His case suggests that a history of psychiatric disturbance need not be a contraindication to BMT.

The "Venus' flytrap" metaphor for the reverse isolation environment deserves comment. Although this environment does not impose sensory isolation, there are a number of stressful conditions. The first aspect of the flytrap is its inescapability; not unlike solitary confinement, it imposes considerable sensory monotony and tedium and grants few behavioral options. Individuals differ in their needs for stimulus, novelty and change, and it can be expected that persons with strong needs for change will be greatly stressed in this situation and will be likely to feel as if they were going "stir crazy." The monotony can be reduced to some extent by providing television and radio and by frequently changing visually prominent objects in the room. Consultation with recreational therapists is helpful.

Another aspect of the flytrap is the absence of usual tactile comforts and their replacement by tactile assaults. For many persons, particularly the sick, being touched by caring, important persons provides a basic experience of closeness and reassurance. Balint[1] characterized the perceptual world of touch as friendlier than that of vision. Brown and Kelly,[2] in their description of bone marrow transplantation, also mention the stressful effect of patients' inability to be touched. The major touching experiences that patients have during the entire hospital course are intrusions, usually procedures that are uncomfortable and painful, such as aspirations or injections. Patients frequently attribute worsening of their condition to the procedures themselves rather than to the illness. In a closed environment, unable to leave the field, patients often feel picked at, probed, and slowly consumed.

Appropriate management requires a sensitive, flexible, and multifocal approach aimed at the patient, the family, and the patient's caretakers. For the patient, empathic availability and listening, clear and honest communication, the opportunity to ventilate and to be appropriately dependent, relaxation and meditation training in select cases, and judicious psychopharmacological management are essential. The family requires support, education, and encouragement to remain close to the patient throughout the procedure without being intimidated or turned away by the technical trappings. Staffs require education concerning psychological responses to illness and specific help to allow them to deal with patients in a compassionate and effective manner and to handle their own reactions to caring for terribly ill patients under particularly trying circumstances. Alertness to conflict between staff members is especially important, and problems need to be openly discussed and resolved as quickly as they are identified.

The image of the Venus' flytrap silently enfolding its helpless victim is a vivid and useful metaphor for the special psychological difficulties of the patient placed in the reverse isolation environment. By breaking the silence and allowing the patient as much control as possible, the psychiatric consultant may be able to persuade him that the outcome is sometimes worth the struggle.

REFERENCES

1. Balint, M. Friendly expanses—horrid empty spaces. *Int. J. Psycho-Anal.,* 36:225-241, 1955.
2. Brown, H.N., and Kelly, M.J. Stages of bone marrow transplantation: A psychiatric perspective. *Psychosom. Med.,* 38:439-446, 1976.

CHAPTER 5

Infertility and Habitual Abortion: The Search for a "Psychological Factor"

GORDON D. STRAUSS

Just one other mound
Of sand, whereon no green thing ever grew
Once more I clasp,—and there is nothing
there.

Edna St. Vincent Millay,
Collected Sonnets

In their outcome, at least, infertility and habitual abortion are equivalent for the woman who wishes to bear children: both frustrate that wish. Yet the literature in obstetrics and gynecology and in psychiatry has kept them separate. Occasionally, as in the case described in this chapter, the equivalence becomes evident when both processes occur in the same woman. However, whether separate or together, the presence of infertility or habitual abortion will often lead the treating physician to consider a psychological or emotional etiology. As the literature over the past 30 years reflects, the locus of attention in the search for the "psychological factor," especially in infertility, has shifted from the woman alone to the couple. We shall examine this shift and review a case in which the semantic differential was used as a tool for understanding dyadic marital conflict in the psychological assessment of infertility.

The author wishes to express his appreciation to Kay Jamison, Ph.D., Ransom Arthur, M.D., and Donald A. Schwartz, M.D., for their help in preparing this chapter.

53

INFERTILITY

Several concepts should be defined before proceeding. First, there are two ways to define psychological infertility. The narrower definition is a failure to conceive in the absence of any physiological or anatomical abnormalities; this definition excludes 90-95 percent of all infertile women.[1] An alternative, and less restricting, definition recognizes that finding an "organic" cause for infertility does not rule out psychological factors. Indeed, as Sandler[2] points out, it is well established that such conditions as amenorrhea, spasm of the fallopian tube, and dry or scanty cervical mucus can all be precipitated by "psychological stress." Twenty-five to 30 percent of patients with infertility can be considered within this broader definition of psychologically based infertility.[1,2]

Traditionally, the medical evaluation of infertility is directed toward determining the physical abnormality. There are a number of well-established causes of infertility in women. The obstetrics-gynecology literature speaks of five factors in sterility:[3] (1) The ovarian factor (failure to produce or release an egg which can be fertilized); (2) The tubal factor (failure of the egg to enter the outer end of the fallopian tube and/or failure of the egg to progress along the tube); (3) The cervical factor (inadequate cervical mucus, either in quantity or quality, to allow proper migration of sperm cells); (4) The male factor (failure to deliver an adequate volume of spermatozoa with normal morphology and motility); (5) The uterine factor (failure of the fertilized egg to implant securely in the uterus). Much of the study of the psychological aspects of infertility appears to be a search for a correspondingly specific "psychological factor."

Early Theories

In the second volume of her *Psychology of Women,* Helene Deutsch[4] not only formulates a psychoanalytic theory of psychologically based infertility, but also describes a series of personality types or character styles that she believes are representative of infertile women. She thinks that the important dynamics in infertility are unconscious fear and guilt, though she acknowledges that "psychologic treatment proves ineffective if it is opposed by incorrigible organic factors." More influential than her dynamic formulations is the typology of sterile women derived from observations in her analytic practice. Deutsch describes five types, but since the last of these is "emotionally disturbed," only the first four will concern us here.

The first type is a woman who is immature and dependent, a "physically and psychologically infantile woman." The second is a woman who is not immature, but whose "rich motherliness" is focused exclusively upon her husband. The third type is a woman whose infertility reflects a diversion of interest into areas other than motherhood; this type Deutsch subdivided into those whose interests are in the erotic aspects of their marriage and those whose interests are diverted by career or other ideology. Finally, there is the type that Deutsch describes as "masculine-aggressive," who "refuses to accept her femininity." Although Deutsch's typology has some interest in itself, its main importance lies in the fact that it has in large measure inspired much of the work done in this area.

Besides Helene Deutsch, the other significant original representative of the analytic tradition in the study of infertility is Therese Benedek. She views infertility as a psychodynamic defense[5] and postulates that the infertile woman is immature (compare Deutsch's first type), but equipped with a strong ego allowing effective repression of conflict about motherhood. Infertility is a result of this repressive process. She goes on to speculate that women who have similar conflicts about motherhood, but who have weak egos will fail to repress the conflict, become pregnant, and then develop mental illness. According to Benedek, treatment involves a process of maturation and emotional growth. This maturational model is important because it provides a plausible basis for the "cure" for infertility through the process of adoption and subsequent pregnancy; this will be discussed later in this chapter.

The Infertile Personality

One of the strongest traditions in the psychiatric study of physical illnesses, originating with the work of Franz Alexander, is the concept of a personality type or character style specific for each psychosomatic illness. Infertility has been the object of repeated studies to determine the psychological profile of women with this disorder. Kroger's work[6] is representative of many of the early studies. From his study of infertile women, he concludes that there are three types: women who are both physically and emotionally immature, women who are highly masculine and aggressive, and women who show a mixture of both patterns.

What is most striking about these findings is their similarity to the first and fourth of Deutsch's "types" of infertile women. Indeed, in a study by Rothman et al.[7] done ten years after the Kroger study, the words are a little different, but the conclusion is quite similar: infertile women can be characterized by their conflicts around dependency and hostility. Similarly, a recent article by Cox[8] cites a study by Mai, in which a group of 50 infertile women were compared to controls from a family planning clinic; a significantly greater number of hysterical and aggressive personality disorders were found among the infertile women.

In any critical assessment of these studies, the most important fact is that they are all retrospective. The infertile women are identified, they are studied, and then conclusions are drawn about their psychological makeup. While such conclusions may suggest areas for emphasis in treatment when such patients are identified, they offer no predictive value. Deutsch herself recognized this limitation: "this same type [her first type], with similar bodily and psychic character-istics, is found among women who conceive with particular facility."[4] An alternate approach has been taken by Hare et al.[9] They studied a group of pa-tients with a particular psychiatric disorder (obsessional neurosis) and looked at the incidence of childless marriages. They found a much higher rate of childless marriage in obsessional neurotics than in the general population in Great Britain (29 vs. 19 percent). The difficulty in interpreting these results is that it is not at all clear that childless marriages imply infertility.

Beyond the issue of methodology there is a more significant aspect to ex-amining infertility with respect to particular personality types or to psycho-analytic theories. In either case the assumption is made that the core of the problem is intrapsychic: in the manifest personality and/or in the underlying dy-namics. Generally de-emphasized or ignored altogether is the possibility that the key to understanding infertility lies in the interaction of the woman with her environment. Hence, the notion of infertility as a stress reaction is a useful one to consider.

In contrast to the traditional ideas about infertility as an "intrinsic" process, a stress-reaction model *does* focus on the interaction of the woman with her environment. At the same time, it is readily compatible with modern psycho-physiological concepts of target organ sensitivity to diverse or generalized stresses. Indeed, through the (presumed) relation of emotional states to the hy-pothalamus, there is a plausible basis for one or more of the accepted factors in infertility being mediated through psychological causes. A stress model of infertility is also useful because it facilitates thinking of infertility as a systems problem.

The system that has been the most fruitful for understanding infertility is that of the marital dyad. Although a systems approach is generally thought of as a comparatively recent development—and indeed in this area it *is* only in the more recent literature that such research is reported—the potential impor-tance of the woman's interaction with her husband was mentioned by Deutsch in 1945.[4] That this important area was being ignored was documented by Marcel Heiman[10] in the later 1950s. He reviewed the major studies on infer-tility during the preceding decade and found that only an occasional study mentions the role of the husband and in no study is that role examined. Heiman urged that subsequent work take into account the interaction of the infertile woman with her husband. Heiman's plea has been generally neglected, so much so that as recently as 1971 a paper appeared in the literature suggesting that psychiatrists not be called in to evaluate infertility because of the unlikelihood that a systems view would be taken; the article advocated the use of marriage counselors instead.[11]

Gradually the literature on infertility has begun to reflect awareness of the importance of the marital dyad. Increasingly, there are references to "the infertile *couple*" instead of the infertile *woman*.[12] Representative of this shift in emphasis is a recent study by Platt et al.[13] designed to examine the issues of "locus of control" and self-concept in infertile couples. It made use of the semantic differential as a measure of self-concept and the Rotter scale for internal-external control. Also assessed was the general level of emotional disturbance. They found that compared with controls, infertile couples were more likely to perceive the locus of control for events in their lives as external to themselves. In both males and females in infertile couples, there was a significant discrepancy between their concept of "present self" and "ideal self," as might well be expected; there was also a discrepancy between their views of themselves and their concept of "father" (for males) or "mother" (for females). Infertile females, but not their husbands, were found to have more emotional disturbance than controls.

The study by Platt et al. is representative of the newer work in this area for several important reasons. First, it places emphasis on the marriage system rather than the infertile woman alone. Second, the authors present their data as well as their conclusions, allowing meaningful replication. Third, it is considerably more sophisticated than most studies in this field in that a control group was used. As Noyes and Chapnick[14] point out in their critical analysis of the literature in this area during the 35 years between 1937 and 1962, most studies have used either case reports or cohorts of infertile women without control groups.

HABITUAL ABORTION

Perhaps because it is less common, habitual abortion—defined as three or more spontaneous abortions—has been the subject of fewer psychological investigations than infertility. Certainly one important difference between the two is that while physiological or anatomical abnormalities in the female do not automatically eliminate psychological contributions to the etiology of infertility, women who habitually abort are considered appropriate for psychological investigation *only* if the aborted fetus is without evidence of genetic aberration or congenital deformity.

As with infertility, attempts have been made to identify the personality type or character style of the woman who habitually aborts. The study by Grimm[15] is perhaps the best known and employs the best methodology. She studied 61 habitual aborters in comparison to a control group of 35 women, half of whom were pregnant and half of whom were nonpregnant women referred for a possibly psychosomatic obstetrical or gynecological problem. All subjects were given the Wechsler Adult Intelligence Scale, the Rorschach, and the Thematic Apperception Test. Performance criteria were established for aspects of each test, and then the habitual aborters and controls were compared using a chi square measure of statistical significance. Grimm's conclusions may be summarized briefly. She characterizes the habitual aborter as more likely to (1) have an impaired ability to plan and anticipate, (2) have poorer emotional control, (3) be more conventionally conforming and compliant, (4) experience greater "tension" about hostile affect, (5) have stronger feelings of dependency, and (6) have "greater proneness to guilt feelings." (All findings at least $p < .05$.)

Many of these findings by Grimm are replicated in a more recent study by Hertz.[16] Studying nine habitual aborters and an equal number of controls matched by age, culture, and socioeconomic status, in the context of "prolonged psychotherapy," Hertz found that these women had a "greater tendency to react with psychophysiological reactions under stress," showed "poorer emotional control," and had a diminished capacity for planning and "positive anticipation."

The functional similarity of infertility and habitual abortion was alluded to earlier. One of the striking aspects of the studies of the personalities and characters of habitual aborters is that the general conclusions sound rather like the descriptions of at least some of the infertile women. For example the immature-dependent type of infertile woman described by both Deutsch and Kroger appears similar in many ways to the habitual aborter described by Grimm, who shows marked dependency, poor emotional control, and inadequate ability to plan and anticipate. Just as no study has shown that infertile or habitually aborting women can be identified prospectively on the basis of personality characteristics, so too there has been no study to determine whether infertile women can be distinguished from habitual aborters by means of psychological evaluation. On the basis of the existing literature, it seems doubtful that such distinctions could be reliably made.

TREATMENT

If infertility and habitual abortion are hard to differentiate on the basis of personality factors, studies of treatment interventions do suggest some important areas of difference. Once again, the literature related to infertility is much larger. Perhaps the oldest and best-known "cure" for infertility is adoption. Nearly every clinician knows of at least one case where a woman, previously infertile, adopted a child and subsequently became pregnant. The prevalence of this phenomenon is sufficiently widespread that clinicians and the general public alike tend to believe there is a causal relation; indeed, even after going over the considerable evidence that adoption is *not* a cure for infertility, a colleague reacted by saying, "but it's such a *plausible* explanation! ... "

Plausible or not, the only support for the theory of an adoption cure for infertility comes from anecdotal reports or uncontrolled studies. Not even all of the uncontrolled studies, however, support the adoption theory. Banks[17] surveyed 100 infertile women who had adopted and received responses from 94;

TABLE 1

Six Studies of Childbirth After Adoption[a]

Author	N	Adopting Group Fertile couples	%	N	Control Group Fertile couples	%	Length of follow-up
Hanson & Rock[19]	202	15	7.5				2 to 12 years
Humphrey[20]	59	7	12				1 to 15 years
Weinstein[21]	256	35	14				9 to 12 years
Weir & Weir[22]	197	32	16	241	44	18	At least 5 years
Rock et al.[23]	249	57	23	113	40	35	5 to 15 years
Sandler[24]	25	18	72	25	11	44	At least 2 years

[a]From Humphrey.[18]

of those there were only four pregnancies, only one of which, he felt, could be related to adoption.

Perhaps the most graphically convincing article in the literature is that of Humphrey.[18] He summarizes the results of six studies between 1950 and 1969 (see Table 1). Three of the studies were without control groups and showed that the percentage of previously infertile women who became pregnant after adoption ranged from 7.5 to 14. The other three studies were controlled; in the two with the largest N's there was a greater percentage of nonadopters who became pregnant. Only in a single study did the percentage of adopting women who became pregnant exceed that of the nonadopters; this study used a relatively small N, and the differences that did emerge were not statistically significant.

Two points should be added. First, although the data show that adoption does not provide a cure for infertility, there is still the question of what is allowing these previously infertile women to conceive (this would apply to the non-adopters who subsequently become pregnant as well). Certainly, at the theoretical level, Benedek's[5] notion that infertility reflects immaturity and fears (of incompetence as a mother, among others) fits nicely with the formulation that through a process of maturation and growth, psychologically based infertility can be expected to improve. If adoption has a curative role, it may lie in speeding up the rate at which this maturation occurs by providing the woman with the experience of motherhood, though not of birth. None of the studies have looked at whether there are differential rates at which adopting and nonadopting infertile women subsequently become pregnant.

There is another point to be made from examining the literature on subsequent pregnancies in previously infertile women: given a "spontaneous" rate of anywhere from 7.5 to 44 percent, studies of various therapeutic interventions with infertile women are of little value if they do not include an adequate control group. Indeed, early claims for psychotherapy, both individual and group, in the treatment of infertility consistently ignored this issue.[25-27]

The literature on habitual abortion differs from that on the treatment of infertility in two respects. First, adoption, the focus of so much of the study on infertility, has not been examined in relation to habitual abortion. More striking is the fact that there *does* appear to be evidence that psychotherapy can play a meaningful role in the treatment of habitual abortion.

In 1957 Weil and Steward[28] published a case report of a 31-year-old woman with a history of seven spontaneous abortions. During her eighth pregnancy, she had weekly supportive psychotherapy and concurrent serial measurements of human chorionic gonadotrophin (HCG). There appeared to be a general correlation between the changes in HCG level and the patient's emotional status as manifested in therapy. The pregnancy went to term, and the woman delivered a normal infant.

This suggestive beginning was followed up by Tupper and Weil[29] in a systematic and controlled study of 38 women with a history of habitual abortion. All of the women had complete physical and gynecologic examinations, measurement of urinary 17-keto and 17-hydroxy corticosteroids, routine blood tests, psychological testing, and a psychiatric interview. Half of the population had weekly psychotherapy during their pregnancies. Therapy was divided into four phases. In the initial phase rapport and motivation were established, the husband was interviewed, the couple was instructed not to have sex for the first three to four months, and information about anatomy and physiology were provided. The second phase consisted in encouraging a certain amount of dependency on the psychiatrist (in part by permitting telephone calls to the therapist at times of major or minor stress), discussing past family relationships, and exploring present life situations. In the third phase, which corresponded to the beginning of fetal movements, there was greater emphasis on the patient's independence, a shortening of the length of interviews, and a "shift in interest from the therapeutic situation to the child-rearing process." The last phase included discussions of childbirth, relaxation exercises, and hypnosis. The results summarized in Table 2, indicate that the women who had psychotherapy had significantly ($p < 0.01$) more full-term live births than the women who had only an initial workup and then routine prenatal care.

While the study by Tupper and Weil can be criticized because the women were not assigned to therapy on a random basis (therapy was offered to all, but geography and other unspecified reasons kept half of the population from participating), they turned out to be well matched for such factors as the number of previous abortions, average age, educational level, years of marriage, and the number who had had previous live births. Methodological flaws notwithstanding, this study strongly suggests that supportive psychotherapy during pregnancy can play an important role in the treatment of habitual abortion.

TABLE 2

Results of Pregnancies in Experimental and Control Groups[a]

Description	Total cases	Full-term live births		Abortions	Premature deliveries
		No.	%		
Experimental group					
Habitual aborters given supportive therapy during pregnancy	19	16	84	2	1 (died)
Control group					
Habitual aborters interviewed on a maximum of two occasions	19	5	26	13	1

[a]From Tupper and Weil.[29] Chi square 8.74; $0.01 > p > 0.005$.

CASE REPORT

Many of the issues touched on in the review of the literature can be given greater focus and made less abstract through examination of clinical case material. The following case combines the problems of infertility and habitual abortion and demonstrates the utility of a systems approach. It also emphasizes the usefulness of the semantic differential in working with couples.

Mrs. A. was a 34-year-old, married white woman who was referred for psychiatric evaluation by her gynecologist. She had sought gynecologic consultation because she had been unable to become pregnant for six years; she also had a history of spontaneous abortions six, seven, and nine years prior to her current consultation. She had had no full-term pregnancies and had no children. Before her visit to the referring gynecologist, her diagnostic workup had included two hysterosalpingograms (both normal), analysis of her husband's semen (normal), and an unsuccessful one-year trial of Provera. She had a history of regular menses, preceded by mild bloating and depression; she and her husband had intercourse regularly. Except for a history of uterine fibroids and benign cysts of her breasts, the patient had an essentially negative medical history; there was a family history of diabetes, but the patient had a normal glucose-tolerance test.

Her recent gynecologic evaluation demonstrated a normal Basal Body Temperature curve, normal serum progesterone, poor preovulatory cervical mucus, and, on endometrial biopsy, retarded histological progression of her endometrial tissue. The gynecologist concluded that Mrs. A. had "luteal phase insufficiency, based upon poor estrogen stimulation of the endometrium in preparation for the effect of progesterone." The reason for the referral to a psychiatrist was that the gynecologist felt that she "had rather bizarre thought patterns . . . making it very difficult to follow her trend of thought. She also related . . . symptoms suggesting conversion reaction and had one episode of total body shaking following an examination during which she calmly described these episodes with classic 'la belle indifference.' " Therefore, the gynecologist wanted to know if there were serious psychiatric disease and, if so, whether solving her infertility problem would exacerbate her emotional problems.

Marital History

Mrs. A. and her husband had been married for 12 years. They met one summer at Yosemite Valley, where he was a clerk in a store. When they married, Mrs. A. was already a school teacher; Mr. A. got a job selling dry goods. Eventually, he was transferred to Southern California. Mrs. A. felt her husband was wasting his ability and convinced him to go back to college, where he got his B.A. degree and a teaching credential. For several years Mr. A. had been teaching history and geography in a junior high school. Two or three years ago Mrs. A. switched from full-time to substitute teaching because she felt it would be less stressful for her.

The A.'s lived in a tract home in Southern California. They had relatively few friends and rarely entertained. They used to go out to dinner and a movie or dancing periodically, but Mrs. A. had not had much interest in these activities in the last year and a half. When she was not working, Mrs. A. watched television—mainly afternoon soap operas. In the evening Mr. A. drank two or three martinis and one or two glasses of wine. He emphasized that his drinking never began more than one hour before dinner and that it did not interfere with his teaching because he did his lesson plans on the weekends. Mrs. A. did not drink.

They had intercourse two to three times a week; Mrs. A. hinted at one point that sex was more frequent before her husband drank quite so much. Neither of them expressed dissatisfaction with the quality of sex, but Mr. A. stated that he wished it could be more frequent and attributed the problem to his wife's "nerves" rather than to his drinking.

Family Backgrounds

Mrs. A.

Mrs. A. was born and grew up in central California. Her father was dead, but her mother was alive. She was an identical twin; there were no other siblings.

Mrs. A.'s father worked for the railroad; at age 40, when Mrs. A. was two, he suffered a skull fracture, and from that time until his death 27 years later, he had periodic episodes of abrupt change in personality, accompanied by heavy drinking. Mrs. A. described her father during those episodes as becoming "hyperactive, argumentative, and grandiose." He was hospitalized psychiatrically several times, but apparently no diagnosis was ever given to the family. He died of vascular complications of surgery for an abdominal aortic aneurysm.

Mrs. A.'s mother was an independent career woman of 64 and in good health. She was without psychiatric history; she was interviewed during the evaluation of the A.'s and appeared to be without manifest psychiatric disturbance.

Mrs. A.'s twin sister was married and the mother of two children. The first she conceived and bore without complications. Subsequently, she too had difficulty conceiving and carrying a pregnancy to term; she had three spontaneous abortions. Three years before Mrs. A.'s consultation she became pregnant again after using Provera; the pregnancy was very difficult and Mrs. A.'s sister was essentially invalided until she delivered. Mrs. A., her husband, and her mother all agreed that the sister's health did not return to its prepregnancy level.

Mr. A.

Mr. A.'s family was originally from the Northeast; his parents were retired and living in Arizona. Mr. A.'s grandfather was a physician, and two of his uncles were doctors, too. They were all alcoholics as well. His father was a successful businessman who was described as stable, well organized, and responsible. His mother was said to be somewhat eccentric. Mrs. A. once stated she felt her mother-in-law would like to be a gypsy and travel around the country.

Mental Status, Composite

Before turning to the content of the evaluation sessions, it may be useful for the reader to form a clearer picture of Mrs. A. and her husband. What follows are two composite mental status examinations, based on several interviews.

Mrs. A.

Mrs. A. always presented as a neatly dressed and groomed tall, dark-haired woman who sat quietly. She was without marked psychomotor activity, but did create an impression of being slightly tense. Her speech was usually rapid and difficult to interrupt. She was extraordinarily tangential—more so than any other nonpsychotic patient the author could recall. She also tended to be circumstantial with periodic lapses in logic, though without loss of coherence. Her thinking was well organized with a highly intellectualized flavor to it; there was no evidence of loose associations, hallucinations, or florid delusions. Nevertheless, she did have a variety of ideas that appeared peculiar or extreme. For example, her concerns about the risk to her physical health from becoming pregnant seemed out of reasonable proportion. While she did not manifest paranoid delusions, she occasionally showed a *style* of thought that *was* paranoid: for example, she suspected previous doctors of systematically withholding information from her. She never expressed suicidal or homicidal ideas.

Mrs. A.'s mood was regularly one of tense friendliness; she created the impression that she was making a significant effort to be cooperative. Affectively, she was somewhat constricted and shallow, but she was always socially appropriate. She tended to deny ever being angry in a session with the interviewer. She often seemed to be quite controlling.

There were never any doubts about the clarity of her sensorium, and she was always fully oriented. Similarly, memory function was intact. Her store of general information was adequate, and she appeared to be slightly above average in intelligence (she made repeated references to herself as an intelligent, educated woman). Her judgment was conventional in most respects; her assessment of her husband was realistic with regard to the existence of a drinking problem, but she had no sense of a need for her to help bring about a change. She had some insight into the role emotional conflict played in her symptoms, but consistently chose to focus on the possible causal effect of having been on exogenous estrogens in the past.

Mr. A.

Mr. A. was a tall man with close-cropped hair, always neatly dressed and groomed, always in a short-sleeved sport shirt that showed him to be rather muscular (it was summer). Quiet, almost shy, he would always sit outside on a brick planter reading a book as he waited for his wife. His speech was relatively slow, and he gave the impression of choosing his words with some care, although not always with precision. For example, he would frequently pause before answering a question and then give an answer which, while sounding adequate at first, was often really quite vague and general. His thoughts were organized, and he was without any evidence of psychotic processes. While openly guarded, he nonetheless gave the impression of ultimately being more direct and straightforwardly honest than his wife.

He usually tended to be in a rather serious mood, but was not without a sense of humor on occasion. A self-defined "loner," he did not usually show much variation in affect, but never seemed inappropriate. Only rarely would there be a brief flash of anger directed at his wife. Mr. A.'s sensorium was always clear, and he was fully oriented. He had good memory function, and in no way did his cognitive function appear to have deteriorated because of his drinking.

Initial Evaluation Sessions

During the first session, Mrs. A. and her husband were each seen separately, followed by a conjoint interview. Mrs. A. touched on a variety of issues; among them were her doubts about her husband's desire for children, her critical attitude toward doctors, her preoccupation with the risks of pregnancy, her willingness to consider adoption (and her husband's opposition to this), and her "ill-ness." The latter referred to various symptoms of anxiety—flushing, diaphoresis, palpitations, tremor, tachycardia, hyperventilation—which had become particularly troubling in the previous six months; this had led Mrs. A. to discontinue her substitute teaching, to seek repeated medical evaluations, and to remain at home. Mr. A. discussed his personal style as a loner, saying, "I don't like having friends." He also talked about his interest in having children of his own; he opposed adoption because "I don't want somebody else's reject." He expressed concern about whether his wife could handle the stress of being a parent.

In the second session Mrs. A. was seen alone. She again mentioned her fears about pregnancy, focusing on the possibility of another spontaneous abortion; she worried that she might "go to pieces" should this occur. She also spoke of her husband and his family, comparing herself to his father—"we both like stability." She spoke in condescending terms about Mr. A., saying that it seemed to her that he "keeps seeking father figures."

It was during the third session that Mrs. A.'s mother was interviewed. She described the relationship between Mrs. A. and her twin sister and mentioned that both sisters had married in the same summer and both had married men with the same first name. She compared Mr. A. to her own late husband in that both could be charming and both drank too much.

As the evaluation progressed, it became less and less clear just what Mr. and Mrs. A. saw as the central issue: whether it was her inablity to conceive, her fear of becoming pregnant, her husband's opposition to adoption, her doubts about *his* sincerity in wanting children, or his doubts about *her* ability to cope with the stresses of parenthood. Conventional psychological testing of Mrs. A. and her husband confirmed the clinical impression that these individuals did not have gross abnormality of intellect or psychiatric function, but did not throw any additional light on these issues. What was needed was a way to assess their attitudes, to find out what pregnancy and parenthood meant to them. The semantic differential provided just such information.

The Semantic Differential

In a 1952 paper entitled "The Nature and Measurement of Meaning," Charles Osgood[30] first introduced the semantic differential as a way of assessing what people mean when they use words referring to certain concepts. It is essentially a tool to examine attitudes. Osgood described it as "a combination of associational and scaling procedures. It is an indirect method in the same sense that an intelligence test, while providing objective and useful information, does not directly measure this capacity."

Figure 1 illustrates one of the sets of semantic differential scales devised for use with Mrs. A. and her husband. There are 22 pairs of words, each representing opposite ends of a seven-point scale (for example, good-bad, masculine-

1.	good	____:____:____:____:____:____:____:	bad
2.	masculine	____:____:____:____:____:____:____:	feminine
3.	active	____:____:____:____:____:____:____:	passive
4.	stable	____:____:____:____:____:____:____:	changeable
5.	optimistic	____:____:____:____:____:____:____:	pessimistic
6.	calm	____:____:____:____:____:____:____:	excitable
7.	positive	____:____:____:____:____:____:____:	negative
8.	warm	____:____:____:____:____:____:____:	cold
9.	strong	____:____:____:____:____:____:____:	weak
10.	cautious	____:____:____:____:____:____:____:	rash
11.	relaxed	____:____:____:____:____:____:____:	tense
12.	fair	____:____:____:____:____:____:____:	biased
13.	sensitive	____:____:____:____:____:____:____:	insensitive
14.	enthusiastic	____:____:____:____:____:____:____:	bored
15.	capable	____:____:____:____:____:____:____:	incompetent
16.	cooperative	____:____:____:____:____:____:____:	uncooperative
17.	gentle	____:____:____:____:____:____:____:	rough
18.	confident	____:____:____:____:____:____:____:	uncertain
19.	carefree	____:____:____:____:____:____:____:	troubled
20.	considerate	____:____:____:____:____:____:____:	selfish
21.	spring	____:____:____:____:____:____:____:	winter
22.	full	____:____:____:____:____:____:____:	empty

Figure 1. Semantic Differential Scales*

---

*Editors Note: Scales of Figures 1, 5, 6, 7, 8 differ from those of 2, 3, 4.

TABLE 3

Response Sets

	Mrs. A		Mr. A		Mr./Mrs.
Extremes	22		44		2.00
Nonextremes	80		85		1.06
Neutral	27		43		1.59
Generally positive	190	186	138	120	0.72 ... 0.64
Generally negative	26	13	40	39	1.53 ... 3.00

feminine, active-passive). At the bottom of the page, a concept is given against which each of these seven-point scales is applied. For the A.'s the following concepts were used: *Man, Woman, Husband, Wife, Mother, Father, Gynecologist, Psychiatrist, Pregnancy, Children, Parenthood,* and *Friendship.* The instructions specify that the center space is to be used only when the concept is neutral or irrelevant with respect to the scale and that otherwise each concept is rated as being slightly, moderately, or extremely related to one end of the scale or the other.

Several kinds of information can be obtained from the semantic differential. Most obviously it is useful in assessing attitudes about issues when an individual has many different and conflicting feelings. By having the subject rate a number of concepts, information can be gleaned about his or her cognitive response set—that is, does the person tend to be generally positive or negative; do responses tend to be extreme, or are the opinions expressed in a more modest or cautious fashion?

Table 3 illustrates these points with regard to Mr. and Mrs. A. The numbers in the columns labeled *Mrs. A.* and *Mr. A.* refer to the number of boxes checked using all 12 sets of 22 scales. For example, Mrs. A. marked either of the extreme boxes 22 times, while her husband did so 44 times; that he was twice as likely to make an extreme response is reflected in the third column, where his responses are expressed as a fraction of his wife's. The row labeled "Nonextremes" refers to responses made in the boxes nearest to neutrality. Most of the scales can be dichotomized so that one end represents a more positive response. For most of the scales used with the A.'s the positive end is toward the left side (for example, good, safe, happy). Therefore, the rows in Table 3 labeled "Generally positive" and "generally negative" refer to the number of boxes checked, excluding the most extreme boxes, in the specified direction. There are two numbers in each column in these categories because one scale, that for the concept *Father,* was markedly different in general pattern from the 11 others for both Mr. and Mrs.

A. The second number represents the totals less the boxes checked on the one aberrant concept.

While the information about response set is of interest and can be useful in assessing an individual's cognitive style, the more powerful use of the semantic differential is in working with couples or families. It is well established that problems in communication are frequently encountered in couples or families. One way to deal with this situation is to help a couple recognize where their attitudes are similar and where they are divergent. It seems reasonable to assume that for any issue a couple may have basically similar or dissimilar attitudes. Moreover, they may perceive the degree of congruity accurately or they may distort it: they may agree and think they agree, agree and think they disagree, disagree but think they agree, or disagree and think they disagree. When a third party becomes involved, either for an evaluation or for therapy, it may be quite difficult to know which of these situations prevails.

This was the case with the A.'s. After several interviews they had created the impression that their views about the desirability of children, pregnancy, and parenthood were quite divergent, and, indeed, *they* perceived substantial disagreement. However, as Figures 2-4 indicate, their views on children, pregnancy, and parenthood are more striking for their similarities than for their differences.

A different pattern emerged when the A.'s rated the concepts *Husband* and *Wife*. From the interviews one might have expected that each of the A.'s would have rated the same-sex concept more positively and the opposite-sex concept more negatively. However, they were divergent only in their views of *Wife*. There were no significant differences on any of the *Husband* scales, and the concept was basically positive for both. In contrast, there were impressive differences on nearly half of the scales for the concept *Wife*, which Mr. A. consistently rated more negatively (Figures 5 and 6).

Even more revealing were the scales rating the concepts *Mother* and *Father*. Here, Mr. and Mrs. A. were most divergent, and more striking yet, they diverged in exactly the opposite direction on *Father* and on *Mother*. *Mother* (Figure 7) was rated more highly by Mrs. A., with major differences from Mr. A. on about one-third of the scales. However, as mentioned earlier, for the concept *Father* (Figure 8) the discrepancy between Mrs. A. and her husband was greater than on any other. There are only two scales, masculinity and sensitivity, where they did not differ to a major degree. On this concept the A.'s completely reversed their usual response patterns: Mrs. A. was markedly negative, while her husband was almost totally positive.

The semantic differential clarified a number of issues, and it was possible to formulate several hypotheses, which were tested in the final sessions with the A.'s. First, it was possible to help them correct their misconceptions about each other's views on pregnancy, parenthood, and children. (One consequence of this was that Mr. A. began to take a less rigid position with regard to adoption.) More important, the attitudes reflected in the scales on the concepts *Mother* and

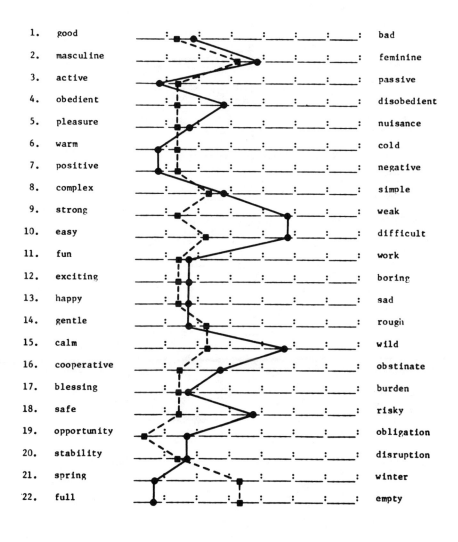

1.	good									bad
2.	masculine									feminine
3.	active									passive
4.	obedient									disobedient
5.	pleasure									nuisance
6.	warm									cold
7.	positive									negative
8.	complex									simple
9.	strong									weak
10.	easy									difficult
11.	fun									work
12.	exciting									boring
13.	happy									sad
14.	gentle									rough
15.	calm									wild
16.	cooperative									obstinate
17.	blessing									burden
18.	safe									risky
19.	opportunity									obligation
20.	stability									disruption
21.	spring									winter
22.	full									empty

Mr. A. ●————

Mrs. A. ■— — — — —

Figure 2. Children

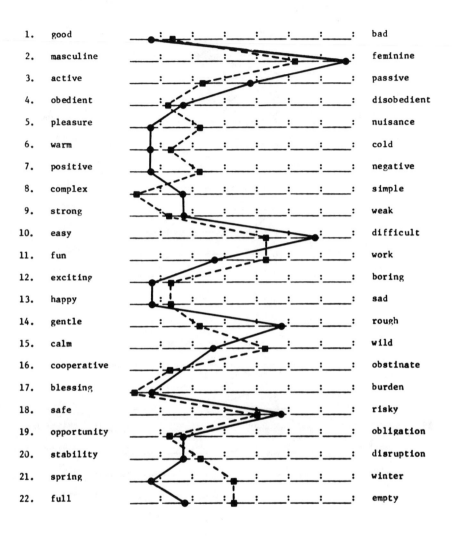

1.	good							bad
2.	masculine							feminine
3.	active							passive
4.	obedient							disobedient
5.	pleasure							nuisance
6.	warm							cold
7.	positive							negative
8.	complex							simple
9.	strong							weak
10.	easy							difficult
11.	fun							work
12.	exciting							boring
13.	happy							sad
14.	gentle							rough
15.	calm							wild
16.	cooperative							obstinate
17.	blessing							burden
18.	safe							risky
19.	opportunity							obligation
20.	stability							disruption
21.	spring							winter
22.	full							empty

Mr. A. ●———
Mrs. A. ■-----

Figure 3. Pregnancy

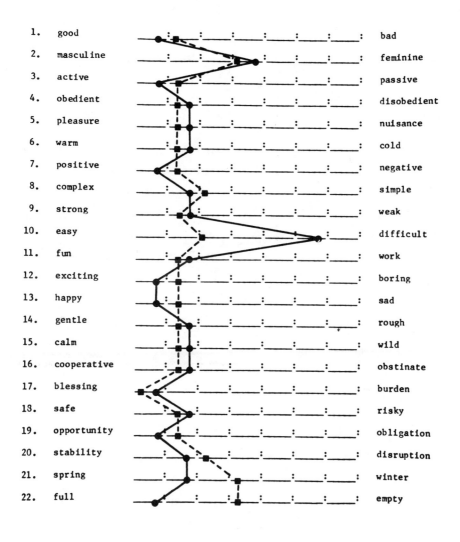

1.	good	bad
2.	masculine	feminine
3.	active	passive
4.	obedient	disobedient
5.	pleasure	nuisance
6.	warm	cold
7.	positive	negative
8.	complex	simple
9.	strong	weak
10.	easy	difficult
11.	fun	work
12.	exciting	boring
13.	happy	sad
14.	gentle	rough
15.	calm	wild
16.	cooperative	obstinate
17.	blessing	burden
18.	safe	risky
19.	opportunity	obligation
20.	stability	disruption
21.	spring	winter
22.	full	empty

Mr. A. ●——

Mrs. A. ■------

Figure 4. Parenthood

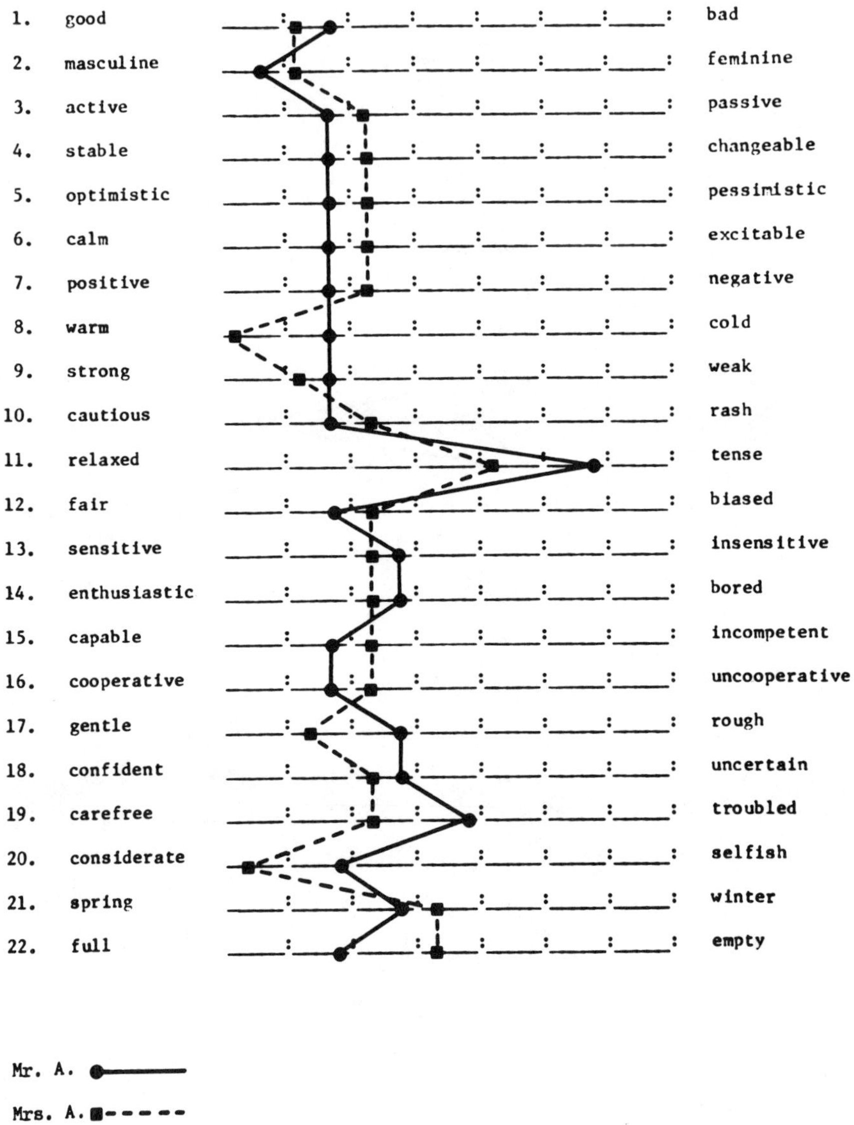

1.	good	bad
2.	masculine	feminine
3.	active	passive
4.	stable	changeable
5.	optimistic	pessimistic
6.	calm	excitable
7.	positive	negative
8.	warm	cold
9.	strong	weak
10.	cautious	rash
11.	relaxed	tense
12.	fair	biased
13.	sensitive	insensitive
14.	enthusiastic	bored
15.	capable	incompetent
16.	cooperative	uncooperative
17.	gentle	rough
18.	confident	uncertain
19.	carefree	troubled
20.	considerate	selfish
21.	spring	winter
22.	full	empty

Mr. A. ●———

Mrs. A. ■-----

Figure 5. Husband

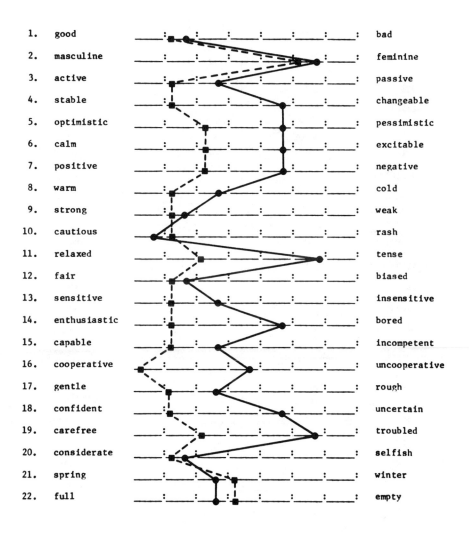

1. good — bad
2. masculine — feminine
3. active — passive
4. stable — changeable
5. optimistic — pessimistic
6. calm — excitable
7. positive — negative
8. warm — cold
9. strong — weak
10. cautious — rash
11. relaxed — tense
12. fair — biased
13. sensitive — insensitive
14. enthusiastic — bored
15. capable — incompetent
16. cooperative — uncooperative
17. gentle — rough
18. confident — uncertain
19. carefree — troubled
20. considerate — selfish
21. spring — winter
22. full — empty

Mr. A. ●———

Mrs. A. ■——————

Figure 6. Wife

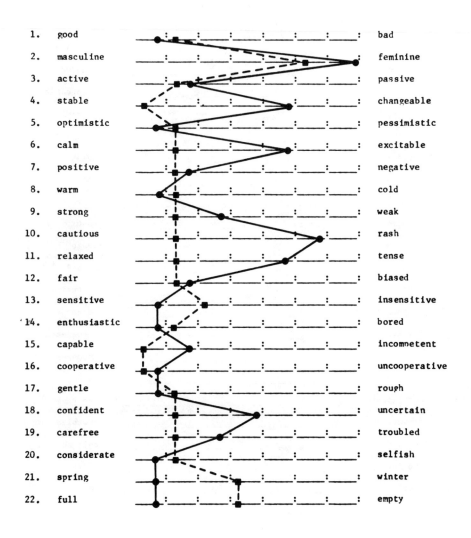

1.	good			bad
2.	masculine			feminine
3.	active			passive
4.	stable			changeable
5.	optimistic			pessimistic
6.	calm			excitable
7.	positive			negative
8.	warm			cold
9.	strong			weak
10.	cautious			rash
11.	relaxed			tense
12.	fair			biased
13.	sensitive			insensitive
14.	enthusiastic			bored
15.	capable			incompetent
16.	cooperative			uncooperative
17.	gentle			rough
18.	confident			uncertain
19.	carefree			troubled
20.	considerate			selfish
21.	spring			winter
22.	full			empty

Mr. A. ●————

Mrs. A. ■-----

Figure 7. Mother

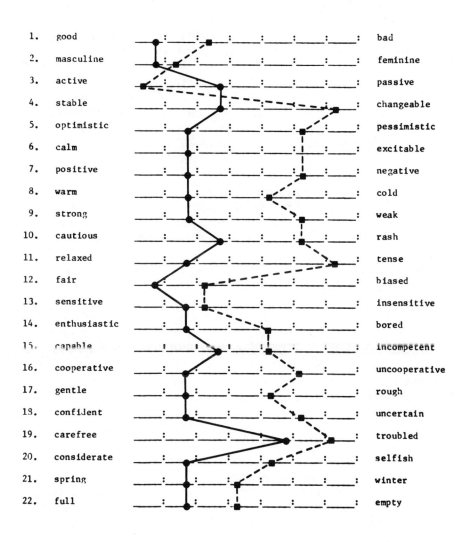

Figure 8. Father

Father were explored, and the following hypothesis was confirmed. The ambivalence each expressed in the interviews about the spouse's attitudes toward children and parenthood related to the oppositely diverging patterns on the semantic differential. Mr. A. desired children and felt reasonably competent to be a father; however, he had major misgivings about what would happen to his wife if she became a mother (recall that in his family his father was the stable one and his mother was more eccentric). In a complimentary fashion, Mrs. A. had few worries about herself as a mother, but harbored significant anxieties that her husband would recapitulate the pattern from her family when he became a father. The changes in her own father's personality occurred when she was quite young, and she carried the fantasy that they had been caused by her father's becoming a parent.

The evaluation of the A.'s was completed. The gynecologist was informed that neither Mrs. A. nor her husband had serious psychiatric illness and that the ambivalence about pregnancy and parenthood were, in part, reflections of marital conflict. They were referred for conjoint marital therapy, with the further recommendation that individual treatment be considered in the future. Worthy of note is the fact that on her first return visit to the gynecologist after the psychiatric evaluation, the quality of Mrs. A.'s cervical mucus was markedly improved.

This case epitomizes much, both reliable and questionable, in the literature on infertility and habitual abortion. Mrs. A. resembles both the dependent type described by Deutsch and Kroger and Grimm's habitual aborter who is conventional and compliant, with tension about the expression of hostility. Certainly when the initial referral was made, the presumption by Mrs. A.'s gynecologist was that *she* had a problem; serious consideration of her husband's role had ended with the examination of his semen. However, it is clear in retrospect that any attempt to understand Mrs. A.'s fertility problems without reference to her relationship with her husband was bound to fail.

In the evaluation of the A.'s, there at first appeared to be less rather than more clarity about the key issues. The semantic differential generated not only additional information about each individual (for example, cognitive response patterns), but also essential aspects about the dynamics of the marital system. Moreover, certain aspects of this case can be compared to findings in the more recent literature.[13,31] Like the couples studied by Platt et al.,[13] the A.'s clearly felt they had no control in the area of fertility. Unlike the couples in Platt's study, however, the A.'s did not show much discrepancy between their views of themselves and of the same-sex parent. Although it may be true in this case, as the literature in general indicates, that therapy may not ameliorate the A.'s infertility, the use of the semantic differential certainly was helpful in finding a point to begin treatment with this couple.

REFERENCES

1. Karahasanoglu, A., Barglow, P., and Growe, G. Psychological aspects of infertility. *J. Reprod. Med.,* 9:241-247, 1972.
2. Sandler, B. Emotional stress and infertility. *J. Psychosom. Res.,* 12:51-59, 1968.
3. Green, T.H. *Gynecology: Essentials of Clinical Practice.* Boston:Little, Brown, 1971.
4. Deutsch, H. *The Psychology of Women,* Vol. II. New York:Grune & Stratton, 1945.
5. Benedek, T. Infertility as a psychosomatic defense. *Fertil. Sterility,* 3:527-537, 1952.
6. Kroger, W.A. Evaluation of personality factors in treatment of infertility. *Fertil. Sterility,* 3:542-551, 1952.
7. Rothman, D., Kaplan, A., and Nettles, E. Psychosomatic infertility. *Am. J. Obstet. Gynecol.,* 83:373-381, 1962.
8. Cox, L.W. Infertility: A comprehensive programme. *Br. J. Obstet. Gynecol.,* 82:2-6, 1975.
9. Hare, E.H., Price, J.S., and Slater, E.T.O. Fertility in obsessional neurosis. *Br. J. Psychiat.,* 121:197-205, 1972.
10. Heiman, M. Toward a psychosomatic concept in infertility. *Int. J. Fertil.,* 4:247-252, 1959.
11. Farrer-Meschan, R. Importance of marriage counseling to infertility investigation. *Obstet. Gynecol.,* 38:316-325, 1971.
12. Shan, J.M., Schiff, I., and Wilson, E.A. The infertile couple. *Clin. Symposia,* 28(5), 1976.
13. Platt, J.J., Ficher, I., and Silver, M.J. Infertile couples: Personality traits and self-ideal concept discrepancies. *Fertil. Sterility,* 24:972-976, 1973.
14. Noyes, R.W., and Chapnick, E.M. Literature on psychology and infertility. *Fertil. Sterility,* 15:543-558, 1964.
15. Grimm, E. Psychological investigation of habitual abortion. *Psychosom. Med.,* 24:369-378, 1962.
16. Hertz, D.G. Rejection of motherhood: A psychosomatic appraisal of habitual abortion. *Psychosom.,* 14:241-244, 1973.
17. Banks, A.L. Does adoption affect infertility? *Int. J. Fertil.,* 7:23-28, 1962.
18. Humphrey, M.E. The adopted child as a fertility charm. *J. Reprod. Fertil.,* 20:354-356, 1969.
19. Hanson, F.J., and Rock, J. The effect of adoption on fertility and other reproductive functions. *Am. J. Obstet. Gynecol.,* 59:311-320, 1950.
20. Humphrey, M.E. *The Hostage Seekers—A Study of Childless and Adopting Couples.* London:Longmans Green, 1969.
21. Weinstein, E.A. Adoption and infertility. *Am. Sociol. Rev.,* 27:408-413, 1962.
22. Weir, W.C. and Weir, D.R. Adoption and subsequent conceptions. *Fertil. Sterility,* 17:283-288, 1966.
23. Rock, J., Tietze, C., and McLaughlin, H.B. Effect of adoption on fertility. *Fertil. Sterility,* 16:305-312, 1965.
24. Sandler, B. Conception after adoption: A comparison of conception rates. *Fertil. Sterility,* 16:313-333, 1965.
25. Abarbanel, A.R., and Bach, G. Group psychotherapy for the infertile couple. *Int. J. Fertil.,* 4:151-160, 1959.
26. Banks, A.L., Rutherford, R.N., and Coburn, W.A. Audiovisual group therapy for the

infertile couple. *Int. J. Fertil.,* 4:259-262, 1959.

27. Peberdy, G.R., and Snaith, L. Psychogenic infertility and functional reversion. *Int. J. Fertil.,* 5:111-119, 1960.

28. Weil, R.J., and Steward, L.C. The problem of spontaneous abortion: Psychosomatic and interpersonal aspects of habitual abortion. *Am. J. Obstet. Gynecol.,* 73:322-327, 1957.

29. Tupper, C., and Weil, R.J. The problem of spontaneous abortion: The treatment of habitual aborters by psychotherapy. *Am. J. Obstet. Gynecol.,* 83:421-424, 1962.

30. Osgood, C. The nature and measurement of meaning. In: *Semantic Differential Technique,* J.G. Snider and C. Osgood. Chicago:Aldine, 1969.

31. Wiehe, V.R. Psychological reaction to infertility. *Psychol. Rep.,* 38:863-866, 1976.

CHAPTER 6

Munchausen's Syndrome: The Consultant's Dilemma

CLAUDE T.H. FRIEDMANN

> Starting up in bed with a fitful, shuddering motion, I drew my basin toward me and bent over it with spasmodic twitchings and contortions of my whole body, such as no one could witness without profound emotion unless he had a heart of stone. "Nothing in me ..." I gasped between my writhings, lifting my wry and wasted face from the basin. "Threw it all up in the night . . . ." And then I launched upon my main effort, a prolonged attack of cramps and retching which made it seem that I would never breathe again. My mother held my head, repeatedly calling me by name in an effort to bring me to myself. By the time my limbs finally began to relax she was quite overcome and, exclaiming: "I'll send for Dusing!" she rushed out of the room. I sank back among the pillows exhausted but full of indescribable joy and satisfaction.
>
> —Thomas Mann,
> *Confessions of Felix Krull Confidence Man*

Munchausen's syndrome applies to an extremely intriguing, baffling, and difficult group of patients. Not only is their psychiatric diagnosis often elusive (we are never quite sure if a given patient is psychotic, sociopathic, or neurotic), but once made it is generally of little therapeutic benefit. Seldom are so many negative and angry feelings aroused in medical personnel as by these purveyors of factitious illness, and the psychiatric consultant is no exception. He must deal with his own negative feelings while soothing those of the medical staff, and finally, if he is fortunate to keep his patient beyond the point of diagnosis and the expulsion that usually follows, he will find himself facing frustration after frustration as he oscillates between rescue fantasies and rejective anger. And he will probably never really comprehend what makes such a patient "tick," though he may delve for hours into his patient's soul, the literature, and the collective wisdom of his colleagues.

Even the designation Munchausen's syndrome lends a bit of idiosyncrasy to this psychiatric problem. For Munchausen was not the person who discovered it, described it, had it, or cured it, nor is it the name of a town, hospital, saint, or individual in any way remotely connected with its medical or psychiatric presentations. Curiously, Munchausen was an eighteenth-century German baron who was given to tall tales.[1] In fact, R.E. Raspe, the baron's "biographer," a scholar and part-time geologist, may himself have been the perpetrator of the tales and the reputation.[2]

Richard Asher[3] explained the choice of eponym with his original description in *The Lancet:* "Here is described a common syndrome which most doctors have seen. Like the famous Baron Von Munchausen, the persons affected have always travelled widely; and their stories, like those attributed to him, are both dramatic and untruthful. Accordingly, the syndrome is respectfully dedicated to the baron, and named after him." Thus, the term is in many ways whimsical— perhaps in humor providing a defense against our almost utter helplessness in dealing with such patients. For these patients are indeed tellers of tall tales, extremely capable of triggering the best and most emergent medical and surgical services, but ultimately almost impossible to treat.

Asher reported three cases in his paper: (1) a 47-year-old seaman feigning intestinal obstruction and giving a history of capture by the Japanese with subsequent operations for fecal fistulae. He had a criminal history and multiple hospital admissions. After much quarreling with the staff, mixed with a willing recitation of his history, he left against medical advice. (2) A 29-year-old woman with clinical intestinal obstruction. She was subsequently found to have three aliases and several recent admissions to various hospitals with somewhat differing histories. (3) A 41-year-old woman who presented with an apparent bleeding ulcer. She too had had multiple hospital admissions (over a dozen!), which had generally terminated against medical advice. All three of Asher's patients had a large number of abdominal scars, had traveled widely, gave a dramatic but not quite convincing history of acute catastrophic illness, were evasive and truculent, and lied a great deal. They interspersed truth with a seemingly senseless web of falsehoods. They quarreled with the hospital staff and, when confronted with the nature of their illness, left against medical advice.

In 1957 John J. Chapman[4] presented the famous "Indiana Cyclone" to the

American medical community. The Cyclone was a 39-year-old wrestler and merchant seaman who presented to an emergency room with classic signs and history of thrombophlebitis and pulmonary embolism. He, too, had multiple surgical scars and was both ingratiating and obstreperous, believable and totally outlandish. His continual hemoptysis was suspected to be factitious, but this could not be proven. He caused so much trouble that the ward staff, hoping to send him away to Chicago, finally paid for his taxi ride to the bus depot. He returned to the hospital two days later, however, with fever, pallor, and evidence of thrombosis of the inferior vena cava. Then he went berserk and slashed his thigh, tearing up the ward in the process. He repeated the procedure a few days later and was sent to a state mental hospital—from which he escaped. He may be the only patient in history to have been described 16 separate times in the medical literature,[5] the last time in 1971.[6]

Eleven years after Chapman, Herzl R. Spiro[5] reviewed the literature. He found a total of 38 cases of Munchausen's syndrome. Men outnumbered women two to one in his series, and the presenting problems included nine instances of abdominal complaints, eight of dramatic bleeding or anemia, ten of neurological complaints, eight of fever, five of cardiac symptomotology, and five of skin lesions.

To the literature Spiro added his own case, that of a 30-year-old male who began to feign illness six years before, subsequent to the breakup of his first marriage. By age 30 the patient had had 39 hospitalizations (out of 53 tries) for factitious renal colic. This patient, like so many others, fulfilled the Munchausen legacy of tall-tale raconteur: he represented himself as a criminal lawyer, doctor, and private eye. He too had multiple surgeries and each time his fraudulence was exposed left the hospital against medical advice.

And so it goes. The number of case reports increases and the list of faked illnesses grows. Even new terms have been coined, such as "chronic factitious illness,"[5] hospital addiction,"[7] and "hospital hoboes."[8] These descriptions suggest the initial excitement, humor, verve, and seductiveness of these patients. Yet eventually a potentially dangerous, explosive, and entangling situation arises. For the patient, it can be lethal; for the physician, exasperating; and for the hospital and community, expensive. For the psychiatrist, it can be a dilemma of the first order.

THE PATIENT

The case of Mr. L., a 40-year-old, married, unemployed white male has been previously reported in the surgical literature.[9] As such, it was presented as a reminder to the surgical community of the existence of Munchausen's syndrome; no previous case of this malady had ever been described in their journals. The slant in this chapter will be somewhat different. An attempt will be made to relive the case through the eyes of the people involved at that time and to examine the role, feelings, and dilemma of the psychiatric consultant.

Mr. L. presented dramatically to the UCLA Emergency Room around midnight. He was agitated, in tears, and writhing in agony. He ingratiated himself 'quickly with the nurses and clerks by apologizing to them for "the bother" and appearing to be "brave" despite his desperate straits. The surgical resident was immediately summoned. He noted bilateral leg edema and severe calf tenderness and forthwith admitted the patient to the surgical service with a presumptive diagnosis of deep venous thrombosis. In the Emergency Room the patient stated that he had had a seminoma at age 13 with subsequent orchiectomy.

On the ward the patient gave a history of intermittent edema of six years' duration, including an admission for it to a local hospital in 1974. He claimed a 60-pound weight loss over the past year, the loss of his job because of the edema one month prior to admission, and severe sweating and fever to 102°F. during the three days before hospitalization. While talking, he pleaded for help, widening his eyes and motioning with his hands. Several times he grabbed the intern's arm. Then lying back in the bed, he assumed a posture of "courageous stoicism."

In his past history he again included the orchiectomy that he had described in the Emergency Room. This time, however, he ascribed the operation to a lymphosarcoma and added that he had also received bilateral inguinal irradiation for it. He admitted to at least seven surgical procedures: a colonic resection in 1969 for ulcerative colitis, a splenectomy in 1970 for splenomegaly, an open liver biopsy in 1971, a cholecystectomy in 1972, two incisional hernia repairs, and a laparotomy for gastrointestinal bleeding and abdominal pain three months prior to admission. He added that his brother had died of Hodgkin's disease at age 33. He gave this history freely, talking rapidly and in a serious tone of voice. He presented every indication of wanting to cooperate and get to the bottom of his problem. But his eye contact was very poor and his eyelids continually fluttered, leading the intern to speculate that there was something 'squirrely" about this fellow.

The admission physical examination revealed a pulse of 65, blood pressure of 130/90 mm. Hg, and temperature of 37°C. The left testicle was indeed absent, and there were multiple healed abdominal scars. Both legs were warm, edematous, and tender, but no erythema, induration, or palpable cords were noted. His lymph nodes were neither enlarged nor tender, his chest was clear, and there were no abdominal masses or organomegaly. The remainder of his physical examination was unremarkable. Admission laboratory values included a white blood count of 13,700 per mm.³ with 64 percent lymphocytes, many of which were said to be atypical. Since the diagnosis of deep venous thrombosis was still presumed, the patient was started on 6,000 units of intravenous heparin every four hours, bed rest, leg elevation, and local heat. He was also given 75 mg. of intramuscular Demerol every four hours for pain.

The next morning Mr. L. started along that familiar road which carries the Munchausen patient from "exciting emergency" to "difficult management problem." First, he began complaining of pain in his thighs and groin and pleading for more Demerol. A physical examination was immediately performed and found to be unchanged from the night before. Next, a hematology consultant, summoned regarding the abnormal blood smear and history of lymphosarcoma, repeated the blood count and found it within normal limits. Apparently a mistake had been made the night before—a curious coincidence indeed. The hematologist became skeptical after a talk with the patient, who began evidencing truculence and evasiveness when questioned about the supposed lymphosarcoma. The hematologist suggested that a psychiatrist be summoned. The question of fraudulence was in the air.

On the third day the patient became hostile and demanding. He openly quarreled with the nurses over medication. He complained of chills and fever, and an oral temperature was recorded at 39°C. But by this time the staff was suspicious. They suspected that the patient was a drug addict, and they felt increasingly manipulated over medication. Some began to doubt his pain, and others began to find inconsistencies in his stories. Not only did he alternate between lymphosarcoma and seminoma, he also threw in Hodgkin's disease. He threatened nurses with retaliation, implying Mafia connections. And, above all, he just "didn't look that sick" and "never looked anyone in the eye." As a result, the rounding surgeons ordered a rectal temperature taken; it was 37°C.

The nursing staff, feeling "snookered," began to demand the patient's immediate eviction from the ward. The clincher came when the surgeon who had operated on Mr. L. three months before was contacted. He reported that despite evidence of lower gastrointestinal bleeding and complaints of severe abdominal pain, laparotomy had revealed no abnormalities whatsoever. With this information, the heparin was stopped. The leg edema had completely resolved on bed rest. The surgeons, convinced that the patient was malingering, were prepared to discharge him. They requested an immediate psychiatric consultation.

After a brief interview with the patient, who was himself ready to leave the hospital, the psychiatric consultant contacted the local hospital that had admitted him in 1974. It was learned that the discharge diagnosis had been Munchausen's syndrome. Offered a transfer to a psychiatric ward for evaluation, Mr. L. balked. And while the surgical staff's anger was temporarily held in check by the suggestion that this man's behavior was disturbed rather than fraudulent, their message was nonetheless clear: "The patient will leave by tomorrow morning—either to a psychiatric unit or home, we don't care, but he will leave." The patient and staff had had enough of each other.

By never letting on what his decision would be, Mr. L. kept the staff guessing until the very last moment. He alternated between ingratiating statements and angry diatribes. When he agreed to the transfer, the consultant felt triumphant, only to have him balk again at the psychiatric ward door. Finally, he agreed to admission, or had he? For soon it turned out that he might have good reason for being on the ward—and for being in the hospital: he was about to be tried for manslaughter.

Mr. L.'s effect on the psychiatric staff paralleled his impact on the surgical unit. At first he was fascinating. Then he began to demand medication and to flaunt ward regulations. His history was given evasively and with limited credibility, yet much of it eventually proved factual. He seemed very happy when treated as an "interesting patient," enjoyed being videotaped and presented to rounds, and at times was very charming to his managing psychiatrist. But by the end of his stay he could not find a willing outpatient therapist, for he gave no indication of being able to set therapeutic goals, form a trusting relationship, or respond to any controls.

It came to light that Mr. L. had been indicted for the fatal shooting of his uncle, with whom he had had a "very close" relationship all his life. The shooting had occurred a month before admission, and shortly thereafter he had been hospitalized for leg edema in a nearby city. The date of his indictment coincided with his arrival at our Emergency Room. He described his uncle as his "only friend in the world," but also conceded negative feelings toward him. He maintained that the shooting was an accident. Further history from the patient, a review of an old record subsequently found at our hospital, and a review of the records of a 1974 admission documented 14 hospitalizations. The patient himself admitted to more than 40 hospitalizations since 1969, when he began having difficulties with his first wife. Currently he was having difficulty with the fifth. He admitted that the lymphosarcoma tale was a fabrication to obtain release from the Marine Corps in 1951. From time to time he also acted as though he were the son of a famous Mafia don and insisted the staff call him by that alias.

One month after his transfer to UCLA's Neuropsychiatric Institute, Mr. L. was discharged and agreed to outpatient treatment. At that time he indicated some capacity for introspection. He seemed upset that "People laugh at me and don't take me seriously" and seemed dimly aware that his maladies were factitious: "I never faked them, but sometimes I just knew my pains are not real." Although it was suspected that he had induced his edema by tying tourniquets around his legs, he still would not own up to it.

His parting shot, though, was yet to come. He never appeared for his outpatient appointment, but did manage to call the Chairman of the Department of Psychiatry to complain of poor treatment. He had finally succeeded. The consultant was furious.

DISCUSSION

This patient differs little from other Munchausen cases: presentation with factitious thrombophlebitis has been described no less than six times since

1970,[10-14] and one of these six patients,[13] plus at least two others,[15,16] also claimed to have lymphomatous disease. As Burnsten[17] has described, the presentations are always dramatic and difficult to diagnose, and the patients eagerly submit to painful procedures. The patients have pseudologia fantastica; they have traveled widely; their inconsistent stories and bizarre interactions with staff inevitably lead to discovery; they make their doctors and nurses angry; they disappear against medical advice.

Psychiatrists, as well as medical and surgical physicians, must continually remind themselves of the existence of these patients. Adherence to basic medical principles can save thousands of dollars and prevent needless procedures that waste time and risk patients' lives. Thus, physicians faced with a patient whose history is suspect should immediately contact the patient's previous physicians and obtain any available records. Once the diagnosis of factitious illness is confirmed, a psychiatrist should be consulted. He should immediately attend to the staff. Not only will the staff be angry at the patient for "conning" them and wasting their time, they will also be angry at themselves for being fooled. Fras and Coughlin[11] feel that if the anger is acted out against the patient, his likelihood of fleeing without further treatment will increase; as a result, the patient goes directly to another facility and begins the process anew.

Even if the psychiatric consultant can avoid the pitfalls of his own anger and convince the patient of the need for psychiatric treatment (here one can only suggest that each consultant use his own style), his problems have just begun. First, there is the question of life history and psychodynamics. Many of these patients report early experiences with doctors, hospitals, chronic illness, parental death, and sadistic parents.[18] Our patient was no exception. He recounted early childhood tortures by his father, who, he claimed, stuck toothpicks under his fingernails. Mr. L. described an orchiectomy at age 13 and also reported working as an x-ray technician from time to time. Several of his wives had been nurses. He also reported being placed in an orphanage at a young age after his mother's death; similar histories in Munchausen cases are quite common.

Several authors[5,18] have postulated that such experiences lead to low self-esteem, lack of basic trust, and a desire to re-create the early traumata in the adult situation. Menninger[19] postulated that polysurgical addiction is a method of avoiding anxiety, reproducing a sadomasochistic father transference, gaining love and sympathy, and sacrificing one part of the body in the unconscious hope of obtaining a prolongation of life or immortality. Ford[18] postulated that Munchausen's syndrome is a defense against psychotic decompensation.

Next, there is the question of diagnosis. Many of these patients are in fact diagnosed as psychotic, but many others are seen as sociopaths or hysterics, or even as having no psychiatric illness.[5] Ford demonstrated that many of these patients have markedly antisocial adult histories, and our patient was no exception. Indeed, psychological testing (consisting of a Minnesota Multiphasic Personality Inventory, Rorschach, and Thematic Apperception Test) administered to our patient tended to support the diagnosis of sociopathic character disorder.

Then the ultimate question: treatment. One consults. One deals with the staff's feeling, calms the patient, and perhaps effects a transfer to a psychiatric facility where a more complete appraisal of the situation is possible. The literature and the patient's life history may be reviewed and a psychiatric diagnosis established. Then one makes the discovery that there is only a single report in the literature of a "successfully" treated Munchausen syndrome,[11] and that with only a very brief follow-up. Therein lies the final dilemma. Quick diagnosis and judicious management can minimize cost, risk, and staff frustration, but as yet offer little chance of altering the unfortunate cycle of these patients' lives.

REFERENCES

1. Carswell, J. *The Romantic Rogue.* New York:Dutton, 1950.
2. Raspe, R.E. *Singular Travels, Campaigns and Adventures of Baron Munchausen.* London:Cresset Press, 1948.
3. Asher, R. Munchausen's syndrome. *Lancet,* 1:339-341, 1951.
4. Chapman, J.S. Peregrinating problem patients—Munchausen's syndrome. *JAMA,* 165: 927-933, 1957.
5. Spiro, H.R. Chronic factitious illness: Munchausen's syndrome. *Arch. Gen. Psychiat.,* 18:569-579, 1968.
6. Cramer, B., Gershberg, M.R., and Stern, M. Munchausen's syndrome: Its relationship to malingering, hysteria, and the physician-patient relationship. *Arch. Gen. Psychiat.,* 24:573-578, 1971.
7. Barker, J.C. The syndrome of hospital addiction (Munchausen's syndrome). *J. Ment. Sci.,* 108:167-182, 1962.
8. Clark, E., and Melnick, S.C. The Munchausen syndrome or the problem of hospital hoboes. *Am. J. Med.,* 25:6-12, 1958.
9. Friedmann, C.T.H., and Weinstein, M.H. Munchausen's syndrome: Report of a case. *Am. Surgeon,* 42:611-614, 1976.
10. Devereux, D.B., and Miller, T.R. More on Munchausen's syndrome. Letter to the editor. *Ann. Intern. Med.,* 80:283, 1974.
11. Fras, I., and Coughlin, B.E. Treatment of factitial disease. *Psychosom.,* 12:117-122, 1971.
12. Heym, H. The imposter patient: Munchausen's syndrome, with report of a case. *Del. J. Med.,* 45:155-160, 1973.
13. Lizzi, F., and White, R. Letter to the editor. *Ann. Intern. Med.,* 79:290, 1973.
14. Muller, J., and McDonnell, M.A. Case of Munchausen's syndrome: Philadelphia-Baltimore. Letter to the editor. *Ann. Intern. Med.,* 78:784, 1973.
15. Flynn, J.T. Munchausen patient. Letter to the editor. *Ann. Intern. Med.,* 78:315, 1973.
16. Mendel, J.G. Munchausen's syndrome: A syndrome of drug dependence. *Compr. Psychiat.,* 15:69-72, 1974.
17. Bursten, B. On Munchausen's syndrome. *Arch. Gen. Psychiat.,* 13:261-268, 1965.
18. Ford, C.V. The Munchausen syndrome: A report of four new cases and a review of psychodynamic considerations. *Psychiat. Med.,* 4:31-45, 1973.
19. Menninger, K. Polysurgery and polysurgical addiction. *Psychoanal. Quart.,* 3:173-199, 1934.

CHAPTER 7

Treating Violence Against Women: The Emergency Room Care of the Rape Victim

REGINA PALLY
SUSAN FUKUSHIMA

> Save me from such as me assaile,
> Let not my foes,
> O God, against my life prevaile:
> Save me from those
> Who make a trade of cursed wrong,
> And bred in bloud, for bloud doe long.
>
> Mary Sidney Herbert, Countess of
> Pembroke (1561-1621), *Psalm*

Forcible rape is the fastest rising crime of violence in the United States.[1] It has been estimated that a rape occurs every ten minutes, and approximately one woman in ten faces the prospect of a rape or an attempted rape in her lifetime.[2] These alarming data suggest that rape is emerging as a critical social and interpersonal problem and highlight the need for an organized treatment program for rape victims. This chapter will describe the steps in creating and implementing such a program.

According to popular belief, rape is an infrequent event, victimizing only women of questionable morals. The myth holds that no woman can be raped against her will, so that if a rape occurs, the woman must have been asking for it by provoking or misleading a man into overwhelming sexual passion. Contrary to this belief, the statistics indicate that rape is primarily an act of sexual violence to degrade and control the victim. It is a brief expression of physical power, a conscious process of intimidation, and a sexual invasion with long-term consequences for the victim.[3]

One of the most comprehensive statistical studies on the nature of rape and the rapist was conducted in 1971 by Amir[4] in Philadelphia. His data were drawn from police department files from 1958 through 1960, with a total of 646 cases and approximately 1,300 offenders. Although his study was limited by its reliance on police reports and reflected patterns of a city with an extensive ghetto population, it revealed facts that support the view that rape is a crime of violence. Here are some of his findings:

1. Rape can occur to anyone. Although most rapists attack women between the ages of ten and 29, the victim's age can range from 14 months to 90 years. Age and sexual attractiveness appear to be irrelevant to the rapist.

2. The rapist is characterized as a man with a median age of 23, although men from the age group 15-19 are most likely to commit rape. The offender is most often unmarried. Half of the offenders have a prior arrest record, although more recent estimates from the Federal Bureau of Investigation crime files report a previous arrest rate of 70 percent. More than 85 percent will go on to commit other crimes, including burglary, assault, robbery, and homicide, as well as other rapes. Most offenders live in the same neighborhood as their victims, and the victim and offender, in more than a third of the cases, knew each other as close neighbors or acquaintances.

3. Contrary to popular notion, the rapist is not a secretive, solitary offender. In 43 percent of the cases, rapists operated in pairs or groups. Far from being a spontaneous event, the act is usually well planned. In some instances the lone rapist or gang has a particular victim in mind. In others, the decision to rape is made in advance, but the selection of the woman is left to chance.

4. In 85 percent of the cases, some form of physical force, such as the display of a weapon, is required by the rapist to achieve his goal. In the remaining 15 percent, verbal intimidation or the sheer physical presence of the offender is sufficient. It is also noted that in group rapes there is an increased probability of violence and humiliation in the form of sexual deviation.

THE RAPE VICTIM

Before the late 1960s, most research focused on the sexual offender and the needs of sexually abused children, and there was relatively little written about adult rape victims. Several authors acknowledged the existence of a psychological crisis precipitated by the assault; Halleck[5] reported: "A wide variety of pathological reactions may be seen to follow sexual assault. . . . It is indeed difficult to conceive of any woman going through this experience without developing some symptoms." However, until 1970, only anecdotal accounts of the adult victim's response to rape had been reported.[6]

In 1960, the American College of Obstetricians and Gynecologists published a technical bulletin[7] on the emergency care of rape victims to establish standards for gathering medical and legal information. Although standards for the treatment and the collection of evidence were outlined and well defined, the psychological needs of the rape victim were not systematically studied until 1970, when Sutherland and Scherl[8] focused on the crisis specific to the rape victim. Since their study, other authors[9-11] have reported similar findings. Rape has been described as a critical situation comparable to severe stress reactions in which the victim experiences a sudden and unexpected loss—of trust in society and others, of self-respect, and of value as a person.

Symonds[12] has reported that in the moments just before a rape, the immediate response to the sudden, unexpected violence is one of shock and disbelief. When the realization of what is happening sets in, most victims experience fright that borders on panic. This fear is deliberately induced by the rapist, who may show the victim a weapon or threaten her life if she does not comply. This fear produces regressive and clinging behavior in the victim and heightens distortion in thinking and judgment. Symonds has termed this reaction "frozen fright" or "pathological psychological infantilism." All behavior is directed toward self-preservation with little or no energy left for overt resistance. In this atmosphere of terror, not only does the woman submit, but she may be cooperative and ingratiating to ward off further attacks. To the outsider, the behavior may seem friendly and may lead the rapist, the victim's family, the police, and even the victim herself to the false conclusion that she elicited or participated in the act.

There are individuals whose response to sudden, unexpected violence is not "frozen fright," but anger. They scream, hit, or yell. Although some rapists back down from such attacks, more often the criminal is antagonized and attacks the victim to beat her into compliance.

Following the rape, most women experience a stress reaction that consists of an acute initial phase of disorganization and a variable, prolonged period of gradual readjustment, beginning within two to three weeks. This reaction was first delineated by Burgess and Holstrum,[10] who call it the "rape trauma syndrome." These authors describe two modes of expressing the fear, anxiety, and anger during the acute phase following the rape. In the woman using the "expressed" style, reactions are manifested as crying, smiling, and restlessness; the woman using the second or "controlled" style, appears calm and composed. It is important to remember that the victim who maintains the "controlled" style may not be credible to the police, health professionals, or even her own family, and consequently may be unable to elicit the support she needs in the situation.

Fear of physical violence and death during the rape, followed by guilt and shame during the acute phase, are virtually universal.[11] It is common for the victim to feel she should have handled the situation differently. This is increased by society's tendency to blame the victim and focus on the sexual, rather than the violent nature of the crime. Symonds[13] remarks that there seems to be a marked reluctance to accept the innocence or accidental nature of the victim's behavior by others, and even by the victim herself. He believes that this stems from a basic need of all individuals to find a reasonable explanation for violent crimes; exposure to senseless, irrational, brutal behavior makes one feel vulnerable and helpless. According to Symonds, to attack the rape victim for some mistake or neglect that plausibly contributes to the crime protects both the victim and the community against pervasive feelings of helplessness and vulnerability.

It has also been suggested that guilt may be exacerbated by some of the victim's pre-existing unconscious wishes or fantasies of being raped or overpowered by men. However, like any wish or fantasy, these do not make the woman a willing victim, although they may add to the shame and confusion she experiences.[14]

Interestingly, the victim usually expresses little direct anger. Anger appears only circuitously in recurrent nightmares, explosive outbursts, or the displacement of hostility onto others. One explanation for this apparent apathy suggests that rape evokes childhood memories of the threat of punishment for misdeeds. The victim may feel that "If you act good, nothing bad will happen to you. Therefore, if something bad does happen to you, you weren't acting good."[13]

Somatic reactions in the acute phase include symptoms related to the physical trauma sustained, tension headaches, sleep and eating disturbances, and gynecological symptoms.

The second phase or long-term process of reorganization is variable and depends on the ego strength of the victim, the specific experiences related to the rape, and the victim's social network. Changes of residence and phone number, and turning to family members for support have been observed to be common responses. Recurrent nightmares of violence or dreams relating to the rape occur, as well as phobic reactions relating to situations reminiscent of the circumstances of the attack. Many women report sexual fears and have considerable difficulty assuming normal relationships with men. This is especially true for women with no prior sexual experience.

Burgess and Holstrum[10] also note a "compounded" reaction, which occurs in victims with a history of physical, psychiatric, or social difficulties. These victims develop additional symptoms, including depression, psychotic behavior, psychosomatic disorders, suicidal behavior, alcoholism, drug abuse, and promiscuity. In victims who do not report the rape and have not resolved their feelings about it, they note a "silent reaction," which is characterized by sudden marked changes in mood, avoidance of relationships with men or marked changes in sexual behavior, sudden onset of phobic reactions, a persistent loss of self-confidence, and dreams of violence and/or nightmares.

Life-cycle considerations are found to determine specific areas of vulnerability for the woman.[11] In the case of the young single woman, the rape may be her first experience with sex and possibly impair her future ability to function sexually and trust men, as well as her confidence in independence and separation from her family. The married woman may fear the loss of her husband's love and respect and, if she has children, may struggle with the question of whether to tell them. The divorced or separated woman has an additional problem in that her apparent sexual availability makes it more likely that her credibility will be questioned. Since she has already experienced failure in her marriage, the rape may confirm feelings of being a failure as a person and raise questions regarding her ability to function independently. The middle-aged rape victim, in a period of critical reassessment of her life, may be especially liable to depression and feelings of failure.

IMPLEMENTATION OF A RAPE TREATMENT PROGRAM

Until 1976, the rape victim entering the busy UCLA Emergency Room was treated like any other patient. She waited (often an hour or two) before being seen by a physician. She came in contact with clerical personnel who were often cold and impersonal or perhaps even judgmental and unsympathetic toward her. Despite the fact that Los Angeles is "the rape capital of the United States," with the highest rate of rape of any city, the Emergency Room was not adequately equipped to treat rape victims, While enduring the delays and red tape of the Emergency Room, the woman experienced further "trauma," which compounded the trauma of the rape.

As psychiatric consultants to the Emergency Room, we felt the situation could be improved. Since the Emergency Room social worker had independently arrived at the same conclusion and had already discussed the idea of a rape treatment program with the staff, we worked together to investigate how rape victims were treated in other hospitals. We found that several medical centers had programs which had generally been motivated and created by nonphysicians (nurses and social workers). These programs were based on criteria established by the American College of Obstetrics and Gynecology[7] and the Southern California Hospital Association,[15] and our program was modeled after their guidelines. We sought to (1) make the Emergency Room staff more sensitive to the emotional needs of the victim; (2) provide the victim with more supportive, nonjudgmental, direct personal attention; (3) improve the collection of evidence by setting up a uniform procedure outlined in a detailed protocol; (4) design a medical chart to be used specifically for cases of suspected rape; (5) arrange for follow-up short-term counseling.

Because rape involves legal and law enforcement issues, the Deputy District Attorney assigned to a special county task force on rape and the UCLA Campus Police were contacted. The District Attorney informed us that California law requires that hospitals report all cases of suspected rape. If the woman has not come to the Emergency Room with the police, the police must be notified, even though the woman may choose not to talk to them. If she does choose to talk to the police, they will obtain a detailed account of the rape event, provide special slides and test tubes for the collection of evidence, analyze the evidence, and contact the Office of the District Attorney.

The police feel there are several reasons why a woman should cooperate with them. Even if she is not interested in prosecuting, her report may be helpful in apprehending a suspect who has raped other women, since by piecing together several women's reports, a modus operandi can be formulated which may aid police in arresting a suspect. In addition, if she has insufficient funds to cover her hospital expenses, a police report will facilitate her application for state aid.

If the woman agrees, the police will take her report in the Emergency Room, after informing her that she may terminate the interview at any point. The police have attempted to make the interview easier for the victim by training their officers in sensitive interview techniques and supplying women officers for this purpose. It should be noted that there are legal limitations on the confidentiality of information imparted by the victim. Information exchanged between the rape counselor and victim is protected only if the psychotherapist is a psychiatrist or licensed psychologist; the right of privilege does not extend to social workers, nurses, lay counselors, or nonlicensed psychologists.

If the woman decides to cooperate with the police, the District Attorney makes the final determination of which cases will go to court for prosecution. This decision is based on the likelihood of a successful conviction and is influenced by the following factors: (1) evidence of adequately documented sperm in the vagina; (2) signs of coercion; (3) the prior relationship of the felon to the victim; (4) the coherence of the woman's description of the rape event.

The role of the physician in the collection of evidence is of paramount importance, and if the task is accomplished properly and the chart is succinct and readable, there is little likelihood that he will be subpoenaed for testimony in court. Specifically, law enforcement officials stress that the physician should be sure that (1) the chart is clear and legible; (2) slides to document the presence of sperm are collected and handed over to the police; (3) any proof of trauma, such as torn clothing and wounds, is adequately noted on the chart; and (4) a police officer can attest to the fact that he has observed the physician collect the evidence and that it has been given directly to him.

With the help of an interested obstetrics-gynecology faculty member who designed appropriate examination, treatment, and follow-up procedures, a chart was assembled based on the Hospital Association guidelines. The chart was created to accommodate the Emergency Room situation, in which the gynecologist is usually a busy resident who may work only on a relatively short rotation basis. Much of it simply called for checking the appropriate answer. It included (1) questions about the rape and the woman's past medical and gynecological history, (2) a section for the physical examination with outlines of human figures so that signs of trauma could be indicated in detail, (3) a description of the types of evidence to be collected, and (4) a section describing the type of treatment given and the follow-up arranged.

Step One

Using the information we had obtained from various sources, the following protocol was written incorporating the medical, legal, and psychological aspects of treating the rape victim. It is now in use in the UCLA Emergency Room.

PROTOCOL

The success with which a victim copes and resolves the crisis of rape is significantly improved when proper medical, nursing, and psychological care is provided by supportive, nonjudgmental hospital personnel.

SECTION 1

I. *Pre-examination*

  A. Sexual assault patients are given priority status.
    1. They should either be taken directly to the examining room and the doctor notified of the patient's presence; or
    2. If the examining room is unavailable, the patient should be taken to a private waiting area.
  B. The triage nurse will notify the charge nurse and the charge nurse will act as a nurse coordinator or assign an appropriately trained nurse to act in this capacity.
  C. The patient should not be left alone at any time. She may be with a physician, police officer, nurse, family member, counselor, volunteer, or friend.
  D. The hospital staff should be supportive. This will be described under Specific Goals of Treatment.
  E. The nurse coordinator should explain all procedures and obtain all the necessary identifying information and special consents, using the Emergency Medical Center Sexual Assault Form. She should describe police policy, consent form policy, the physical examination, and the availability of counseling.
  F. If the patient has not reported the assault, the nurse coordinator will request a clerk to notify the campus police.

II. *Examination.* The Emergency Medical Center Sexual Assault Form is to be used as part of the legal medical chart.

    A. The nurse coordinator obtains the history using the history portion of the form. The history should include:

        1. A description of the event in the patient's own words.

        2. A checklist of the following specific details (obtained after description of the event).

          a. Exact time, date, and place.

          b. Exact type of sexual contact—oral, anal, or vaginal; number of assailants; and number of actual forced sexual encounters.

          c. Identifying data about the assailant(s)—appearance, mode of operation, words, threats or weapons that were used.

          d. Whether the assailant(s) used a condom or any other contraceptive protection.

          e. The type of force used—verbal threats, weapons, beatings, or other physical assault.

          f. The dates of the patient's last normal menstrual period and the last time she had coitus, with or without contraception.

          g. What, if any, actions she took subsequent to the assault—including douching, bathing, other medical attention or treatment prior to coming to the Emergency Room.

          h. Whether the victim had been under the influence of medications, drugs, or alcohol, at the time of the assault. Had she taken these on her own or had these been forced on her by the assailant(s)? What had the assailant(s) done, if anything, to prevent the victim either from reporting or identifying him (them)?

        3. A brief medical history including allergies.

        4. A thorough gynecological history including pregnancies, contraception, and gynecological problems.

    Note: It is important to remember that the history is taken for medical reasons and *not* to make a legal judgment as to whether the victim has been raped.

    B. The nurse coordinator should be present during the entire medical examination. If the patient consents in writing and if the doctor and nurse concur, a relative, friend, or counselor may be permitted to remain with the patient during the examination.

    C. The nurse coordinator should be present while the patient is undressing in order to note the condition of clothing, for example, rips, missing buttons, stains, etc.

    D. The physician should perform the examination in a manner that maximizes the patient's sense of comfort and security, safety and control. He should inform the patient of procedures as they are performed.

    The physical examination includes:

Part I: The general medical examination on all victims.

1. Look for evidence of trauma, obtain x-rays and other laboratory work as indicated, and give appropriate treatment.
2. The gynecological examination. Perform a thorough pelvic examination, looking particularly for trauma. Obtain cultures for gonorrhea, draw a baseline VDRL, and perform a rectal examination as indicated.

Part II: The examination done for collection of evidence, in addition to the general medical examination done on all victims.

1. Note the condition of the patient's clothing.
2. Check for trauma as before and record very precise detail. Photograph all visible trauma, if possible.
3. Note secretions. Look for dry blood and other secretions, collecting samples when possible, and obtain a sample of the patient's own blood and/or secretions for comparison studies.
4. Take samples for slides from areas that may possibly contain sperm. Depending on the history, these areas may include the mouth, vagina, and rectum. The specifics for exactly how to collect evidence are given in the appendix.
5. Advise all victims about the necessity for protection against possible venereal disease as well as pregnancy prevention.

III. *Counseling*

A. There is a psychiatric resident on call who is available to talk with the woman if she so desires.
B. If the psychiatric resident on call is a male and if the woman desires to talk with another woman, the rape hot line should be contacted.
C. The charge nurse will notify the social worker that a rape victim has come in and the social worker will arrange to have a counselor call the woman, if the woman agrees.
D. The nurse coordinator will explain to the woman that rape can have long-term effects and that short-term counseling will help her deal with the rape and ameliorate some of the psychological sequelae.

A patient information packet is given to the woman to take home with her. This packet contains information about rape, common reactions of the victim and significant others to rape, and phone numbers for legal, medical, or psychological follow-up.

SECTION II

The following information is important in the psychological management of the rape victim.

A. The psychological treatment of the rape victim is a direct response to the emotional state and needs of the victim. The aim of the treatment is to begin the process of re-establishing the victim's equilibrium.

B. Understanding one's own attitudes and prejudices is essential before working with rape victims. Rape evokes powerful emotions that may make others feel vulnerable and may be defended against by their becoming critical of the woman's behavior. For example, if the woman has taken some risk, such as hitchhiking, she may be blamed for using poor judgment. The sexual aspect of the rape can often arouse feelings that the woman was somehow responsible, since it has been the woman's traditional role to define how far a sexual encounter should go. To be effective, the person working with the victim must be sensitive to his or her own feelings about rape and, regardless of personal attitudes, avoid moralistic judgments.

C. Specific Goals of Treatment

1. Attempt to decrease the woman's sense of insecurity by providing her with a quiet, private room in which she is never left alone.

2. Allay her sense of anxiety and generalized mistrust by explaining all procedures carefully.

3. Attempt to diminish her sense of helplessness and increase her sense of control over the event.

   a. Allow her to talk freely. This will enable her to ventilate her feelings and help her reorganize her perceptions of the rape. Point out any distortions in her thinking. For example, the woman may feel responsible for what has happened despite evidence to the contrary, or she may interpret submissive behavior designed to protect herself as cooperation with the assailant.

   b. Predict possible postrape reactions such as anxiety, insomnia, physical complaints, and nightmares. The explanation may have value in making the disorganization of the next days more understandable.

4. Point out and reinforce the woman's adaptive behavior to increase self-esteem and decrease feelings of having been demeaned and degraded. If she has contacted the police, family, or friends, it may be indicated to her that she has made the first step in dealing with the rape. If she is interested in prosecution, demonstrate to her that she has dealt with her anger in a constructive way and that she may be helping other women who could be raped by the same man.

5. Attempt to lessen guilt and shame that result from the woman's feeling of responsibility for the event. The woman may have had no choice but to cooperate in the face of violence or threats of violence.

6. Alleviate her sense of isolation by telling her that this has happened to other women and that they have dealt successfully with their feelings about having been raped. She can be encouraged to contact significant

others to gain their support, or if she feels that no one will understand, the counselor can facilitate this communication or give her the option of professional counseling.

7. Deal with her sense of disorganization. Help her structure the immediate future. This might entail helping her plan where she will go, with whom, and how she will get there.

8. Encourage the woman to express her anger or, if she is already angry, acknowledge her anger and its validity.

9. Assess psychiatric disturbances such as suicidality, homicidality, or psychotic symptoms which may occur in addition to other stress symptoms.

10. If for personal reasons you are unable to deal with a particular victim, ask someone else to consult with you about the difficulties you are having or ask another counselor to see the woman instead.

Step Two

After writing the protocol, our next step was to train personnel to implement it. We focused first on the nursing staff, since they had initial contact with the victim. We prepared three training sessions. The first session was didactic, with basic background material about rape, an outline of the mechanics of the protocol, and a presentation of the psychological aspects of rape and its management. The second and third sessions involved role playing. The Emergency Room situation was simulated and nurses took turns at being the counselor or the victim. The rest of the group watched and gave their reactions. Our aim was to refine sensitive history-taking skills and to demonstrate how these skills could be used with the rape victim. A second aim was to make the nurses aware of their attitudes in dealing with rape victims. Most commonly, we encountered anxiety at the thought of being a potential rape victim; feelings of discomfort about the more intimate parts of the history, such as sodomy, oral, or gang sex; and difficulties in dealing with certain types of victims who aroused negative feelings, such as intoxicated or silent patients. These sessions were followed by a review and trouble-shooting session three months later, when actual problems the nurses had encountered were discussed.

We next trained a group of counselors who could provide 24-hour coverage. We asked for volunteers from all women social workers, psychologists and psychology interns, and psychiatric residents. The training sessions were similar to the ones offered the nurses and also included an orientation to the Emergency Room. With the counselors, we emphasized the similarity between rape counseling and crisis counseling. Since many in this group were used to a more traditional form of nondirective psychotherapy, we encouraged them to be active and open about their feelings with the rape victim, since the therapist needs to provide a good deal of structure and direction. We also encouraged them to communicate with, and enlist the aid of, the victim's significant others. Again, besides the didactic training, one of our aims was to help the counselors learn about their own attitudes so that these feelings would not interfere with their effectiveness.

Difficulties arose in organizing a 24-hour on-call schedule each month, since many of the women had other commitments. Rather than lose counselors, we switched our focus: psychiatric residents would take calls on a 24-hour basis, and the counselors would serve as backup for crisis counseling under our supervision. In training the psychiatric residents, we used the same format described above and incorporated it into an ongoing Psychiatric Emergency Care course. As the residents covering the Emergency Room rotate, we continue to train new groups. We realize that while the availability of the residents is an advantage, in some cases the woman may prefer not to talk with a male resident. Although this has not proved to be a major obstacle, arrangements can be made for the woman to speak to an Emergency Room nurse or to contact the Los Angeles Rape Hot Line, which has 24-hour phone coverage and is run by women volunteers.

The final group to whom we offered instruction were the nurses in the Gynecology Clinic, where the rape victims were being referred for follow-up. The clinic nurses wanted information on dealing with rape victims presenting with gynecological complaints, and we emphasized detection of victims with the "silent rape" reaction, who often present with nonspecific gynecological complaints.

Our final training will include the gynecology residents who cover the Emergency Room and a group of nurses who will teach other Emergency Room personnel how to work with rape victims. We plan to keep the Rape Treatment Program viable by encouraging ongoing programs offered by our graduates.

CASE HISTORIES

The following cases illustrate the program in progress. The first case demonstrates some of the difficulties the staff had in managing a victim before the Rape Treatment Program was instituted, and the second describes how the Emergency Room staff has responded to victims after institution of the program.

Case 1

The patient was a 29-year-old, single white woman visiting Los Angeles to attend a business conference. One evening she went to a discotheque for a drink. She left the discotheque alone and while walking down the street was harrassed by a young man. Another man drove up in a car and offered to help her. She accepted his offer and got into the car, whereupon the driver circled the block, picked up his accomplice, and drove to a secluded spot. She was raped and forced to perform fellatio on both of them. She was brought into the Emergency Room by the police and questioned by a female police officer. After her gynecological examination, psychiatric consultation was requested because of her distressed condition. The patient reported feelings of shame and guilt, felt degraded by the experience, and was ashamed to face her friends. She was allowed to ventilate her feelings, and some of her distortions about the rape were explored. Valium was prescribed, and a recommendation for psychiatric follow-up was made. This she refused, saying she would be out of town. She was escorted home by the police, but reappeared in the Emergency Room several days later and requested medication. Another psychiatric resident was immediately called, and she was given a refill of her medication. About 12 hours later, she returned to the Emergency Room, saying that she had lost the prescription. The psychiatric resident had not been trained in the area of rape and therefore did not know at that time that specific symptoms in the postrape period include anxiety, insomnia, and disorganization which may last for several weeks. Despite the fact that he refilled the prescription again, he recalled suspecting that perhaps the woman was abusing drugs, and after this incident, she was lost to follow-up.

Certain facts in this case are noteworthy. Before the program was established, it was uncharacteristic for a psychiatrist to be contacted. However, it was through the psychiatrist's report that we discovered the specifics of this case and realized the need for clear guidelines in the treatment of rape victims. The psychiatrist's help was sought in this instance because of the staff's reaction to the dramatic distress of this woman. In many ways this woman presented with common characteristics of a rape victim—disorganization and need for sedatives. And the staff's responses were also characteristic—inability to cope with her reactions, suspiciousness about her symptoms, and uncertainty about her basic needs.

Case 2

A 32-year-old, recently divorced white woman with three children had been raped while returning from the supermarket late in the evening. A man had approached her in the parking lot, put a knife against her back, and pushed her into his car. He drove to a secluded spot, where he forced her to undress and raped her in the back seat of the car. He then drove to a residential neighborhood and left her without her clothes. She was able to summon the police by enlisting the aid of the people in a nearby house, who also provided her with a bathrobe. When she arrived at the Emergency Room, she was calm and controlled. The nurse coordinator called a close friend of the victim, who arrived with clothing. The nurse talked with the friend while a police woman took the victim's report. The nurse coordinator then called the gynecologist and explained the history to him, as well as the procedures for collecting evidence. The nurse obtained the woman's written consent to have evidence collected and, after the examination, helped the woman make concrete plans for the future, obtaining her consent to have a social worker call her the next day.

In the postrape period, this woman's major symptoms emerged as distrust of men, loss of self-esteem, and increased difficulties in coping with daily events. She had gynecological problems, including pelvic pain and vaginal discharge. The rape exacerbated already existing conflicts about her competence as a woman, wife, and mother.

In contrast to the first woman, this patient presented a "controlled" style. The nurse coordinator was able to recognize this as a common way in which victims present and was able to deal appropriately with the emotional needs the woman was unable to express. Like the first victim, this case illustrates the degree of disorganization these women experience. In this case the rape compounded difficulties the woman was currently experiencing around her divorce. Following crisis counseling, she continued in long-term therapy.

Our program, however much it represents improvement over previous methods of providing sensitive medical care for rape victims, is only a first step. The psychiatric consultant, after all, can only attempt to facilitate treatment of the patient and guide the staff to a deeper awareness of the complex emotional sequelae of rape.

The psychiatric community must devote its skills and knowledge to the larger task of understanding and eliminating the sources of violence against women. As Susan Brownmiller[3] concludes her study: "My purpose in this book has been to give rape its history. Now we must deny it a future."

REFERENCES

1. *Federal Bureau of Investigation Uniform Crime Reports for the United States.* (Washington, D.C.: U.S. Department of Justice, 1970). Quoted in Rada, R.T. Commonly asked questions about the rapist. *Med. Aspects Human Sex.,* 11:47, 1977.
2. Selkin, J. Rape. *Psychology Today,* 71-76, January, 1975.
3. Brownmiller, S. *Against Our Will.* New York:Bantam Books, 1975.
4. Amir, M. *Patterns in Forcible Rape.* Chicago:University of Chicago Press, 1971.
5. Halleck, S. The physician's role in the management of victims of sex offenders. *JAMA,* 180:273-278, 1962.
6. Factor, M. A woman's psychological reaction to attempted rape. *Psychoanal. Quart.,* 23:243-244, 1954.
7. American College of Obstetrics and Gynecology. *Technical Bulletin,* 14, 1960.
8. Sutherland, S., and Scherl, D. Patterns of response among victims of rape. *Am. J. Orthopsychiat.,* 40:503-511, 1970.
9. Werner, A. Rape: Interruption of the therapeutic process by external stress. *Psychother.: Theory, Res., Pract.,* 349-351, Winter, 1972.

10. Burgess, A., and Holstrum, L. Rape trauma syndrome. *Am. J. Psychiat.*, 131:981-1085, 1974.
11. Notman, M., and Nadelson, C. The rape victim's psychodynamic considerations. *Am. J. Psychiat.*, 133:408-413, 1976.
12. Symonds, M. The rape victim: Psychological patterns of response. *Am J. Psychoanal.*, 36:27-34, 1976.
13. Symonds, M. Victims of violence: Psychological effects and after effects. *Am. J. Psychoanal.*, 35:19-26, 1975.
14. Kirkpatrick, M. Rape: Who cares? Medical resistance to treating rape victims. Los Angeles:UCLA-Neuropsychiatric Institute, 1975 (Unpublished).
15. Hospital Council of Southern California and L.A. County Department of Health Services, Preventative Health Services. *Guidelines for the Hospital Emergency Department in Treating the Alleged Sexual Assault Patient.* 1976.

CHAPTER 8

"Change Me": The Request for Rhinoplasty

RICHARD G. NESS

> "But Amaril is going abroad to England," said Mountolive. "He has asked us for a visa. Am I to assume that his heart is broken? And who is Semira? Please tell me."
>
> "The virtuous Semira!" Clea smiled again tenderly, and pausing in her work, put a portfolio into his hands. He turned the pages. "All noses," he said with surprise, and she nodded. "Yes, noses. Amaril has kept me busy for nearly three months, travelling about and collecting noses for her to choose from; noses of the living and the dead. Noses from the Yacht Club, the Étoile, from frescoes in the Museum, from coins . . . It has been hard work assembling them all for comparative study. Finally, they have chosen the nose of a soldier in a Theban fresco."
>
> Mountolive was puzzled. "Please, Clea, tell me the story."
>
> "Will you promise to sit still, not to move?"
>
> "I promise."
>
> —Lawrence Durrell,
> *Mountolive*

The traditional tasks of the psychiatrist consulting to the plastic surgeon have been fourfold:[1] to identify severe personality problems and thereby screen out the small number of patients for whom cosmetic procedures are contraindicated; to clarify the patient's expectations and motivation; to provide definitive psychotherapeutic intervention when indicated; and to facilitate healthy psychological attitudes as an adjunct to surgery. Unfortunately, there have been no particular guidelines on exactly *how, when, why,* or even *if* such activity might prove useful to the plastic surgery patient. Examination of these expected roles of the psychiatrist indicates that there is little generally applicable knowledge in any of these areas; each patient must be studied as an individual whose request for corrective nasal surgery must be understood as a unique event in that patient's life.

Most commonly, the unsuspecting psychiatric consultant is called upon to demonstrate his ability to predict the future: whether a given patient is a good candidate for surgery. Implicitly, the question is, will the patient both immediately and ultimately be happy with the surgery (and surgeon) following his nasal reconstruction?

The earmarks of the bad rhinoplasty patient are perpetuated in cosmetic surgery lore:[2,3] beware of those with "unclear" motivation (the irrational patient or those directed by others to seek cosmetic surgery); the supersecretive, urgent, or demanding patient; those with purses full of pictures (or worse, the "you do what you think is best" victims); those with minor or subjective defects; the obvious psychotic; the polysurgical addict; and those expecting personality improvement as a side effect. A common conclusion of the writers describing such patients is: "The less prominent the defect, and the more subjective the need, the less likely it is that the patient will be satisfied."[3]

But there is little evidence that any single factor provides a sound reason for exclusion based on the "poor response" criterion, at least for the initial rhinoplasty request. We are better at predicting that those who have already been dissatisfied with previous nasal surgery are likely to be unhappy with future alterations.

Several examples of the lack of validity of textbook caveats are in order. Hay uses the only controlled patient samples found in this body of literature to show that neither the degree of psychological disturbance[4] nor the improvements in psychological functioning following rhinoplasty[5] are related to the initial degree of disfigurement. He also notes[5] that rhinoplasty is a procedure of little danger to the psychological health of unselected samples of patients. Although somewhat more psychiatrically disturbed than the general population, his patients are in frequency and degree less disturbed than selected samples of plastic surgery candidates reported in previous studies.

Various profiles of poor responders have been presented over the years. Together they include almost all the psychiatric diagnostic categories, but no one group of patients is singled out for whom surgery is contraindicated. For example, Knorr et al.[6] describe the "insatiable" cosmetic surgery patient, typically an unmarried male, aged 20-35, with low self-esteem, hyposexuality, grandiose ambitions, vague expectations regarding surgery, and no meaningful long-term relationships. Knorr[7] also describes a small group of female patients whose sense of loss of feminine identity following rhinoplasty leads them to seek further reconstructive surgery to undo what their soon-to-be exhausted surgeon has "done" to them. Book[2] describes "paranoid" personalities and depressed menopausal women as other patients requiring special examination prior to surgery. Over 25 years ago, Linn and Goldman[8] described "the psychiatric syndrome of the rhinoplasty patient," a subcategory of schizoid personalities with obvious ego deficits. These patients, however, weathered nasal surgery so well that the authors (anticipating Hay's controlled research by a generation) were forced to conclude: "Rhinoplasty is not a hazardous procedure from the psychiatric point of view." Linn and Goldman also anticipated the association of sexuality and nasal concerns, as Book[9] was later to review.

In summary, patients requesting rhinoplasty run a gamut of psychiatric disorders that would individually require consultation, but give no predictive clues based on diagnostic classification. A possible exception might be the group of patients with dysmorphophobia described in a fascinating study by Hay.[10] But even this nonspecific syndrome of gross psychopathology indicates a need for consultation based on the quantity of patient distress, not on the foreboding sound of the patient's psychiatric label. Perhaps the limited predictive value of psychiatric assessment is best expressed by Clarkson and Stafford-Clark:[11] "The essential criteria for endorsing surgery in cases where there is an established structural indication for it, are the degree to which the patient's overall appreciation of the possiblities and limitations of the procedure are consonant with reality, no matter how disturbed he or she might otherwise be."

The following detailed case presentation illustrates the need for individual assessment rather than reliance on a diagnostic cookbook in providing good psychiatric consultation for the rhinoplasty patient. Instead of classifying the patient described, the consultant attempts to understand his request for surgery and to recognize and answer questions more crucial than his surgical suitability. Any medical decisions will then be made in consideration of his person, and not just his nose.

A 45-year-old man, Mr. R., was referred for his first psychiatric consultation from the UCLA Plastic Surgery Clinic. The referring physician was aware that his patient's request for additional corrective surgery to his nose was clouded by some "apparent emotional factor" and that the patient was overconcerned with the physical appearance of his nose. Mr. R.'s medical history revealed that in July 1970, his first cosmetic surgery had been performed, consisting of rhinoplasty with submucus resection. During the following months, he had several courses of cortisone injections to reduce swelling secondary to surgery and in December 1970, had a second operation to remove nasal cartilage. In July 1971, he had another two-week course of cortisone injections. In January, April, and December 1972, he had internal resections of scar tissue. In January 1973, and again in November of that year, surgical excision of external nasal scar tissue was performed. Periodic cortisone injections were too numerous to count, but he did count them, claiming a grand total of 84 injections. In July 1974, during his last visit to the private plastic surgeon who had performed all the above procedures, the patient concluded that the physician "was tired of looking at my face," since he refused to perform any more surgery. The request for psychiatric consultation came in March 1975, after Mr. R. presented himself to the Plastic Surgery Clinic for removal of additional scar tissue and because of seasonal nasal stuffiness.

Mr. R. described his early years as vague, but pleasant ones. He was born when his father was 37, an age which was later to have significance in his own life. He remembered his father as a quiet, hard-working Russian immigrant who had settled in the Midwest and spent his adult life tending his own farm and working in a meat market. The patient stated explicitly that he had nothing in common with his father because "he was from another generation." More generally, the patient had "nothing in common with his family," especially the males. But it was his father whom he described as "never having expanded himself as an individual" and with whom it was impossible to form any sense of "identification." There were no strongly pictured male figures in the patient's background, and he reminisced wistfully, "If I would have had a brother, things would have been very different."

With more animation and detail than observed in any other part of his history, Mr. R. vividly described his father's physical appearance, specifically his nose, with near reverence for its physical beauty. The impression that the patient was describing a treasured and long admired work of art was unavoidable. When asked if he himself resembled anyone in the family, Mr. R. emphatically responded, "Not my father." The patient's early physical memories, then, were ones not only of looking very different from other members of the family, but also of being disappointingly ugly, "apelike," an almost alien strain in the family pedigree.

His mother was also described as a hard worker, a person who "watched over me." His two sisters, eight and ten years his senior, were present in memory only as shadows.

The patient remembered few significant life events during his growing-up years. He recalled taking up golf and pole vaulting in high school and being a fairly good student who liked gym and dancing. He was quite proud of his "nimble feet and excellent coordination" as an adolescent and was definitely "not a slob" during those critical years.

In college he studied psychology and architecture as well as fine arts. Unable to obtain satisfying work after graduation, he moved to California at age 28, held a number of different jobs, yet was most interested in finding employment as a cameraman or film developer in the movie industry. This he was to attempt unsuccessfully for the next 14 years.

Mr. R. met his wife, a successful film animator, one year before they were married in 1961. The patient described his 14-year marriage as "static," symbolized by the fact that he and his wife currently lived in the same apartment they occupied as newlyweds. He pictured himself emphatically as "heterosexual and potent," but admitted infrequent sexual contact with his wife. They had no children because he felt that he could not afford to raise any. He made a rather defensive distinction between his ability to have children, which of course was not questioned, and the lack of proper circumstances for their upbringing. As a pathetic rationalization that offspring were not missed in this relationship, he stated that his wife at 47 had no desire for children since she had already had a baby in a first marriage, who had died of complications three days after delivery.

The patient did describe one continuous creative interest, photography. He surprised himself with the vividness of some early memories of building his own darkroom at age 13 in the basement of the family house, but then remembered with regret that he had been too poor to afford anything but very rudimentary and primitive equipment. In 1967, he was finally able "to buy a good camera" and to realize some of his earlier dreams of becoming a prominent photographer. At one point it appeared that with his wife's help, he might be able to join a cameramen's union. Unfortunately, he was to "get screwed out of it overnight." Frustrated, depressed, and angry, he began eating and drinking heavily and gained ten pounds in weight. He became very aware of his altered body image and bought a set of barbells to work his body back into shape. Suddenly, almost overnight, he noticed that his nose began to grow because of "fat cell deposits," assuming a monstrously distorted size, which he described as a "banana bulb," a "big hump." Something, he felt, should be done about it. He was 37 years old at the time.

Mr. R., however, did manage to find a job as a nonunion worker in a film laboratory, where he was employed for the next two years. In 1970, at age 40, he lost this job to a younger man he was training for the same work. Within six weeks, Mr. R. was scheduled for his first cosmetic surgery. And this was the last time that he was to work steadily.

Mr. R. presented as a casually dressed man in dark clothing with tinted glasses. He had long, thinning hair, a rigidly held body, and a nasal voice. He was cautious and guarded, never quite sure of the appropriate response in such an interview situation. At critical times during the interview, he alluded to his diseased nose, pleading that the only way to understand him was through medical definition. It was as if there would be some miraculous cure for his problems if only, for the nth time, he could yet more clearly express to a physician the subjective experience of his own nose, now an ugly hump that needed to be "whacked off." His nose was a "swollen, turgid, organ" that woke him up in the early morning and also "disturbed his wife's sleep." "The weakest part of me is my nose," he said, a liability that he dated to a hay fever experience as a 12-year-old. "I'm not a big guy," he further related, "I have a small frame and everything seems to go to my face and hips." "I have lost my youthful face and the elasticity in my skin." "I'll probably even need a face lifting in five years." Interspersed with these descriptions of his failing physical appearance were clues to a more general existential position: "I'm caught up in the jungle;" "I'm on a treadmill to oblivion;" "No one would give me a job;" "I'm a professional job seeker;" "I haven't made it; I'm not involved with people; of course it's distressing and depressing not to have status when you know your own potential." What he could do without his infirmity was manifold: "I could get on with photography, stop wasting money and consuming time, sleep well, get out in the cool air again, stop staying away from people, and I'd be less irritable." In all, he was an innocent bystander as life's opportunities escaped.*

Rather than dwell on the issue of psychiatric diagnosis, the psychiatric consultant may make sense out of Mr. R's request for continued "search and destroy" missions on his nose by clarifying those inapparent, yet understandable, links between his thoughts, feelings, behavior, and life events. Since his presentation had a strong flavor of unresolved adolescent dilemmas, one should begin at that developmental era to understand his insatiable demands.

The primary task of the adolescent is to solve the complex problem characterized by Erikson[13] as identity formation. To become comfortable with a stable sense of "Who am I?," the adolescent ego has to rely on its "ability to integrate all previous identifications" into an "accrued experience" of self-sameness. We can immediately see how this developmental hurdle may have caused our patient to stumble, for his history shows an obvious lack of solid identification with significant others; he even used the phrase "identification with my father" to describe an experience noticeably missing from his earlier life and now providing only a sense of his incompleteness. Those building blocks of personality given to the child as welcome pieces of important "other selves" were not incorporated, and our patient was left with a perception of himself as empty or made of foreign materials.

A sense of not belonging to one's family is not far from a feeling of illegitimacy. If Mr. R. was unable to understand correctly who he was within his own family, how much harder was it as a teenager to answer, "Who will I become?" Such confusion, as Erikson describes, is the reflection into the future of whatever lack of inner sameness the adolescent continues to experience from childhood. The patient had done many things since his youth, but he had never *been* any of them. The dream of being a photographer was still a dream, 30

---

*It is interesting to compare Mr. R.'s self-portrait with Ruth Mack Brunswick's[12] description of the Wolf Man: "He neglected his daily life and work because he was engrossed, to the exclusion of all else, in the state of his nose. On the street he looked at himself in every shop-window; he carried a pocket mirror which he took out to look at every few minutes. First he would powder his nose; a moment later he would inspect it and remove the powder. He would then examine the pores, to see if they were enlarging, to catch the hole, as it were, in its growth and development. Then he would again powder his nose, put away the mirror, and a moment later begin the process anew. His life was centred on the little mirror in his pocket, and his fate depended on what it revealed or was about to reveal" (p. 265).

years after it became his first possible solution to the dilemma, "Who am I?"

Erikson's theory suggests a corollary that applied to Mr. R.'s developmental failure: an inability to come to grips with a developmental choice at the appropriate point leads to difficulty in solving succeeding life-stage tasks. The young adult, with his identity more or less established, has to tolerate and master the formation of intimate relationships. If he does not, a posture of interpersonal isolation, self-absorption, and withdrawal is established. In addition to his stagnation and infertility, Mr. R. described a lack of ability to relate to others; he spent even his leisure time watching television or at the movies, taking pictures, tending to plants, or riding around alone in his car.

According to Erikson's model, then, role confusion is compounded by the inability to establish both occupational and sexual identity. If Mr. R. failed to have the experience "I am a man like my father," it is no wonder he failed to somehow fully experience both "I am a man" and "I am a father." That these two were also confused with each other, the development of his symptoms tells us clearly. At age 37, unsuccessful once more in his attempt to define his competency by joining (that is by becoming *identified* with) a cameramen's union, he replaced an uncomfortable surge of emotion by an acutely formed (and deformed) nasal growth. Analgous to the growth spurt of pubescent genitalia as well as the pubertal nose,[9] a mysteriously expanding midline organ appeared. To this the patient hung on bravely until he lost what occupational identity he did have. He then abruptly had this incomprehensible and offending organ "whacked off."

But there is also significance to the coincidence of Mr. R.'s age at the time—37. The fact that he himself was born in his father's thirty-seventh year suggests that his final attempt to crystallize his own masculine identity was not only frustrated by role failure (a job lost to a younger man), but also produced his own congenitally ugly, sexually ambiguous offspring, a new and second nose. It is intriguing to speculate: if Mr. R. realized that at age 37 an ugly growth, his nose, suddenly interfered with his own life, how much blame did he take upon himself for the fact that a similar interference (his birth) victimized his father's thirty-seventh year? Nasal surgery would then assume the added component of undoing not only his primary failures in life, but also himself, the blot on his father's countenance. Saving face for Mr. R. thus entailed saving two faces, a not-so-impossible job for a man with "two noses." A failure at his own rebirth as a man, as a person with professional identity, and as a father, he began his quest for an ultimate surgical self-definition.

Mr. R.'s relentless search for someone, somehow to make his nose all right then becomes more understandable. As his image of being a competent and successful male faded with age, his attempt to redefine that man surgically showed its driving force: he needed to excise the symbol of isolation, stagnation, and aborted adult fruition; undo the shame of being a blot on others; and postpone a sense of ultimate despair. Unfortunately, he could not know where to stop, since he had never understood what he was supposed to be or even what he was supposed to look like.

This presentation makes clear that an in-depth assessment of Mr. R.'s needs in relation to the timing of the surgical request led to an easy recommendation: not only was further surgical intervention to be avoided, it was not even what he was searching for in the first place. The psychiatric consultant was then free to make himself available for the more urgent business of providing Mr. R. with the supportive framework in which his needs, mistranslated into a surgical request, could more properly and happily be met.

A patient like Mr. R. also invites an examination of issues central to the consultive process in psychiatry. For example, how do extremely different medical specialists "share" physician responsibility for the same patient?

The first trap to be avoided is collusion with an assumption of "mind-body duality." The separation of medical and psychiatric components is a paradigm of speciality task differentiation and has nothing to do with the packaged whole, the patient. In fact, patients themselves seem more aware of the indivisible components of physical and mental functions and find it more natural than their doctors to experience emotional and physical well-being as inseparable.

Another liaison effort is to set the priorities of speciality interventions. For example (as in our case), how does one choose between either reconstructive surgery or psychotherapy? When does one decide to do *both?* or *neither?* The only well-defined step in this process is to avoid the common antagonisms that may sabotage the consultive relationship. The plastic surgeon and psychiatrist cannot "save face" or evade responsibility at each other's expense. "We'd like to operate, but the psychiatrist says no" has the same destructiveness as the naive psychiatrist's "You can't cure your depression with cosmetic surgery, so forget it." Only when both plastic surgeon and psychiatrist begin to hear and feel "our patient" as a joint responsibility have they reached the point where whatever is decided will be the result of the best medicine has to offer.

This "best," a combined effort of responsibility toward the patient, still leaves room for the patient's remarkably different appreciations of his physician-surgeon and physician-psychiatrist. In fact, these relationships can become an active area of interdisciplinary learning, at the frontier of our understanding the necessarily varied care-taking roles possible to us. In the final outcome of the patient's request to "change me," the harmony of these roles may be just as critical as what either surgeon or psychiatrist can do alone.

REFERENCES

1. Jacobsen, W.E., Meyer, E., and Edgerton, M.T. Psychiatric contributions to the clinical management of plastic surgery patients. *Postgrad. Med.,* 25(5):513-521, 1961.
2. Book, H.E. Psychiatric assessment for rhinoplasty. *Arch. Otolaryng.,* 94:51-55, July, 1971.

3. Taylor, B.W., et al. Psychiatric considerations in cosmetic surgery. *Mayo Clinic Proc.,* 41(9):608-623, 1966.
4. Hay, G.G. Psychiatric aspects of cosmetic nasal operations. *Br. J. Psychiat.,* 116: 85-97, 1970.
5. Hay, G.G., and Heather, B.B. Changes in psychometric test results following cosmetic nasal operations. *Br. J. Psychiat.,* 122:89-90, 1973.
6. Knorr, N.J., Edgerton, M.R., and Hoopes, J.R. The "insatiable" cosmetic surgery patient. *Plast. Reconst. Surg.,* 40:285-289, 1967.
7. Knorr, N.J. Femine loss of identity in rhinoplasty. *Arch. Otolaryng.,* 96(1):11-15, 1972.
8. Linn, L., and Goldman, L. Psychiatric observations concerning rhinoplasty. *Psychosom. Med.,* 11:307-314, 1949.
9. Book, H.E. Sexual implications of the nose. *Compr. Psychiat.,* 12(5):450-455, 1971.
10. Hay, G.G. Dysmorphophobia. *Br. J. Psychiat.,* 116:399-406, 1970.
11. Clarkson, P., and Stafford-Clark, D. Role of plastic surgeon and psychiatrist in the surgery of appearance. *Br. Med. J.,* 11:1770, 1960.
12. Brunswick, R.M. Supplement to "History of an Infantile Neurosis." In: *The Wolf Man by the Wolf Man,* ed. M. Gardiner. New York:Basic Books, 1971.
13. Erikson, E. *Childhood and Society,* 2nd ed. New York:Norton, 1963.

CHAPTER 9

After Being Turned Inside Out: The Team Approach to the Ostomy Patient

GREGORY J. FIRMAN
ELLEN E. LINN

> Yet in the actual practice of his art, where he has to do with man as he is, should the physician devote all of his efforts to the body alone, and take no account of the mind, his curative endeavors will pretty often be less than happy and his purpose either wholly missed or part of what pertains to it neglected.
>
> —Jerome Gaub,
> *De regimine mentis, 1747*

Some 90,000 new ostomy surgeries, either temporary or permanent, are performed annually in the United States[1] for a number of disease processes: obstruction, tumor, inflammatory bowel disease, or congenital abnormalities. The liaison psychiatrist is often called to see these patients for problems specific to the ostomy as well as for those psychiatric problems encountered in any medical or surgical patient. The recent emergence of the specialized enterostomal therapist, who is usually a registered nurse with training in ostomy care, has focused attention on the unique problems, both medical and psychological, of the ostomy patient.

This chapter will describe the importance of the team approach in the management of adults who have had ostomy surgery, with special attention to cancer and inflammatory disease of the bowel.

OSTOMY CLUBS AND THE ENTEROSTOMAL THERAPIST

Colectomy with ileostomy for inflammatory bowel disease and ileal conduit procedures for urinary diversion became surgically feasible about 30 years ago. Although these procedures were successful in resolving the underlying physiological problem, physicians and nurses were unable to provide adequate postoperative education and care for their ostomy patients. The patients were hampered in their psychosocial and occupational adaptation by leaking appliances, excoriated skin, and feelings of social isolation. Out of several informal support and self-help groups, the United Ostomy Association was developed. The UOA, formed in the early 1950s, is a worldwide network of rehabilitative clubs that offers continuing education and social activities for its 20,000 members, as well as visitation services for new ostomates.[2,3]

In 1964, the first Enterostomal Therapy Training School was opened at the Cleveland Clinic by Dr. Rupert Turnball. Currently there are ten accredited programs in the United States and approximately 500 active enterostomal therapists.

Enterostomal therapy is a relatively new nursing specialization, which is gaining increasing recognition. The role of the enterostomal therapist has developed in response to the highly specialized technical and psychological needs of the ostomy patient. These nurses provide direct patient care during the pre- and postoperative periods, with emphasis on rehabilitation. They assist in patient and family teaching and consult with physicians, nurses, and professionals in allied disciplines regarding the care of stoma patients. Because many enterostomal therapists are themselves ostomates, they are also excellent role models for the patient. By their choice of nursing speciality, they demonstrate to the patient that they do not share the distaste or disgust for ostomy care frequently shown nonverbally by other staff members.

REVIEW OF THE LITERATURE

The literature on ostomy patients may be divided into three categories. The first group includes large-scale surveys of the problems of ostomy patients; the second consists of in-depth explorations of the psychodynamics of patients; the third examines therapeutic considerations and modes of adaptation.

Surveys

One of the largest studies of the first type is that of Roy et al.,[4] who surveyed 497 cases of permanent ileostomies at the Mayo Clinic. Of the 75 percent of patients that responded to their questionnaire, almost 89 percent considered their subsequent health good to excellent. Management of the ileostomy and appliance was not considered a major problem by 84 percent, but the remainder experienced significant problems with soreness and excoriation of the skin around the stoma. Nearly all (95.6 percent) returned to their previous occupations, and sexual habits were unchanged in 87.2 percent. The authors emphasize the desirability of early surgery for patients with inflammatory bowel disease (ulcerative colitis or Crohn's disease), since total rehabilitation and improvement in level of function were so good and the operative mortality was minimal (3.3 percent) in elective cases. This was opposed to a mortality approaching 19 percent for surgery performed on an emergency basis for acute toxic megacolon, hemorrhage, or intestinal perforation.

Baird et al.[5] surveyed 92 patients with colostomies, 80 percent of whom were over 50 years of age at surgery and most of whom had undergone surgery for cancer. In this group, 14 percent were not informed or did not understand that the surgery would "put their bowels on the outside." Twenty percent felt the physician had only partially explained the surgery, and 66 percent felt they should have been told more. It is also of interest that 38 percent felt that they left the hospital without full knowledge of self-care of their colostomies. Seventy percent relied only on the physician for advice on management of the colostomies, apparently because the hospitals involved had no trained enterostomal therapists on the staff. These authors emphasize the importance of ostomy groups for both psychological support and education of the patient.

Based on an English survey of 61 patients with permanent colostomies, George et al.[6] report a much poorer outcome in these patients compared to those with ileostomies. Besides the usual run of physical and dietary problems, more than one-third of the patients had curtailed their social life postoperatively, and more than half had given up some type of leisure activity. Most felt depressed following the operation, and approximately 40 percent continued to have periods of depression. It should be emphasized, of course, that typically, colostomy patients are much older than those patients with ileostomies, and the underlying disease process, although not specifically mentioned in the study, is usually colon cancer. The possible relation between the personality types of ulcerative colitis or cancer patients and the outcome of their surgery has been alluded to in the literature,[7,8] and further exploration should be of great value in the psychological care of ostomy patients.

In articles published in 1968 and 1969, Druss et al. focus on the psychological response to colectomy with ileostomy and to partial colectomy with colostomy. In the first of these studies,[9] a questionnaire was sent to 41 patients who had had ileostomies secondary to chronic ulcerative colitis. The mean age at onset of disease was 28 and at surgery, 35 years. Surgery had been performed from two to nine years prior to the survey. In 95 percent of these patients, general physical health was improved, and most preferred the surgical procedures to continuing to function with the disease. Even in this group, however, most felt unprepared for the surgery psychologically and considered that postoperative care of the ostomy and instruction in handling it were inadequate. It is important to note that the psychological adjustment of these patients was invariably related to key figures in their lives. If that "significant other" supported the patient, then the patient himself tended to do well; conversely, the patient's readiness to adapt to the procedure influenced those close to him. The authors found no evidence of "symptom substitution" following ileostomy, but rather a sense of freedom, with ego expansion indicated by cultivation of new interests and new confidence. The good functional outcome, however, did not correspond directly with the reported intrapsychic sense of well-being. Sexually, 20 percent of male patients had potency problems, some of which were felt to be related to autonomic trauma from resection of the rectum. Female patients did not have as high a percentage of sexual problems. In all cases, however, acceptance by the spouse or other sexual partner was an important factor in sexual adjustment, since self-esteem was usually mirrored through the other person's eyes. As other studies had found, ostomy clubs were felt to be helpful in adjustment; work performance generally improved; and the previously described range of physical problems (odor, gas, skin problems) were encountered. The patients felt that about a year was needed to adjust to life with an ileostomy. Most patients required two to three additional hospitalizations for stoma revision, obstruction, or prolapse.

The second study by Druss et al.[10] surveyed 36 patients with abdominal-perineal resections for colon cancer. Their average age was 56 years at surgery and 61 years at follow-up. These patients, regardless of their preparation, described shock at the first sight of the colostomy. Two-thirds reported symptoms of postoperative depression, and most of the depressed patients were those who claimed to be inadequately prepared. Younger patients tended to be the most depressed in this group. First attempts at irrigation were almost always anxiety-provoking, and the patients felt that the initial reaction of the hospital staff to the irrigation procedure was important in determining their own attitudes. Similarly, a majority felt instruction and a good relationship with a physician or nurse were decisive in carrying them through the postoperative phase and to eventual adjustment. In this group, only 45 percent were still having sexual relations at follow-up. Thirty-five percent of the patient group had no change in sexual activity pre- and postoperatively, and 41 percent were less active. Consistent with the findings of George et al., 72 percent had a deterioration in their social relationships, usually related to the fear of producing odor or the anxiety of leaving the security of their home.

As noted above, there were many differences between the ulcerative colitis-ileostomy group and the carcinoma-colostomy group with regard to age, underlying disease, and extent of surgical procedure. However, they were similar in that (1) each lost an organ, (2) there was no anal sphincter control, (3) defecation was now from the surface of the body and from the front, and (4) a new organ (stoma) was created, with concomitant changes in body image.

In any case, the carcinoma-colostomy patients tended to have worse reactions than the ulcerative colitis-ileostomy patients because (1) they felt well before surgery and therefore could not conceptualize a "trade-off" of stoma for symptoms, and (2) the illness and surgery occurred at a time of general decline in most of their lives. The authors felt that the universally experienced initial depression was largely related to several factors: loss of an organ, mutilation and perceived castration (especially in males, with the creation of a hole, often bleeding, in the front of their bodies), physical unattractiveness, inability to vent their anger at a powerful authority figure (the surgeon) who in fact had mutilated them, and inability to avoid violating the socially introjected "code of cleanliness," which dated from the toilet-training period. The depression was usually worked out within about a year, with each patient using previously established defensive styles.

Two main patterns of defense were observed. The first were obsessional, which the authors believe to be the higher level. These involved bowel-retraining efforts and cleanliness rituals. The rituals helped the patient attain a sense of mastery analogous to gaining anal sphincter control in early childhood. Phobic defenses, on the other hand, were less successful and involved a restriction of activities, a sense of hurt and wounding, and an idea of premature old age. Ninety percent of these patients were in good physical health one year after the operation, but were nevertheless incapacitated by psychological factors. Based on these findings, the authors make recommendations for postoperative management: encouraging full information and support from the hospital personnel; ensuring that the patient has mastery of the colostomy before leaving the hospital; including family members in discharge planning to secure their crucial acceptance of the patient and the colostomy; and mobilizing ostomy groups for support, role modeling, and problem sharing. It is interesting in this regard that colostomy clubs are fewer and less active than ileostomy clubs, most likely because of the character of their membership.

Psychodynamic Studies

Although psychoanalytic studies do not have direct relevance to immediate clinical care, they are useful in pointing out various unconscious fantasies experienced by ostomy patients. An in-depth paper by Orbach et al.,[11] reporting on a study of 48 patients who had had colostomies, focuses on their body concepts five to ten years following the colostomy. The underlying disease is not mentioned, but it probably was carcinoma of the rectum. The method of inquiry was a structured interview, supplemented by blindly scored Rorschachs.

Orbach and his colleagues found that the body concepts of patients after a colostomy were greatly influenced by a conviction of having been seriously injured, with the belief that their body intactness and integrity had been violated. On a fantasy level, the operation was perceived as a physical or sexual assault. Those who fantasied the surgery as a sexual assault were supported in this belief by the colostomy stoma, a new opening in the front of the body. Most men regarded this opening as evidence of having been feminized, while women often interpreted it as the addition of a second vagina. The bleeding from the stoma reinforced the fantasy of a second vagina because it was interpreted as menstruation. The Rorschach findings also emphasized patients' confusion about the body, anxiety about sexual adequacy and functional integrity in male patients, and concerns about body image, mutilation, and violation. Independent of the Rorschach, patients reported a sense of bodily fragility and weakness, which had a very important effect on their lives, as well as a reduction—sometimes drastic—of activities requiring mobility and the expenditure of energy. Finally, both the interviews and the Rorschach test findings were in agreement with respect to preoccupation about the bodily processes concerned with food intake and elimination.

During the interviews, the patients were asked for a detailed description of the interior of their bodies as they conceived them before and after an abdominal-perineal resection. Although most patients correctly located the position of the rectum, many held a similar misconception about its function: they believed that the intact rectum served as a storage depot in which the total amount of feces in the body collected in readiness for evacuation. On the basis of this belief, these patients assumed that "normal" evacuation completely emptied the body of its daily production of feces. Once the storage depot was removed and its accompanying function of collection was disrupted, however, they believed that the interior of the body had to be flushed entirely clean to avoid serious consequences. The relation of the colon and the intestines to the stomach was the source of some profound misconceptions regarding both position and function. Many patients conceived of the colon and small intestine as strikingly shorter than they actually are and as positioned in practically a straight line from the rectum to the stomach. In addition, they believed that the direction of the digestive process was reversible under certain conditions. The combination of these factors—short length, a straight line of descent from stomach to rectum, and the concept of reversibility—led them to believe that a "backwash" could occur. This imagined phenomenon was an upward movement of feces, which at its arrival in the stomach would then mix with undigested food. The outcome of this reversal of direction and of the mixture was believed to be deleterious to health or even possibly a danger to life, without the informant being able to specify how or why.

A relatively small number of patients held another misconception that involved a "replacement notion." This was a belief that the intake of food and the output of feces had to be approximately equal to avoid overloading the capacity of the interior of the body. That these replacement concepts were accompanied by an intense hypochondriacal concern is not surprising, since these patients must of necessity focus on bodily sensation and away from action and relatedness to others. The preoccupation with gas and odors, as well as fears of leaving their own bathrooms, added to the social withdrawal and fostered the development of hypochondriacal symptomatology.

The findings of this study must be understood in relation to the subjects, who were primarily elderly cancer patients of a low educational level. Moreover, nearly half of them were foreign-born. Even so, this work emphasizes the undesirability of medical personnel's assuming a knowledge of basic anatomy and physiology on the part of the patient. Indirectly, it underscores the need for more effective preoperative orientation and education, preferably from a physician or nurse with specialized training. We stress the word "effective" because Epstein and Lasagna[12] have shown that a lengthly factual presentation alone is, in fact, not assimilated by most patients. Careful presentations, with repetition, feedback, and "mini-tests," are probably of more value for both information and consent.

A second paper by Orbach,[13] drawing on the same population as in his previous paper, focuses on ideas of contamination in postoperative colostomy patients. Structured interviews were again used, this time emphasizing the practices, feelings and beliefs of patients before, during, and after irrigations and during the interval between the irrigations.

Repetitive, ritualized practices (called "controls") by colostomy patients were a major finding. The primary objectives of patients relying on controls were to facilitate evacuation during irrigation and to prevent spillage (spontaneous evacuation) while in the community. Women who were greatly concerned with personal hygiene and the cleanliness of their homes prior to surgery spent a long time in irrigation and introduced large amounts of water and disinfectants into their colon following colostomy. Many of these women expressed ideas of contamination following the loss of anal sphincter control, and they acknowledged, moreover, that these ideas had existed before surgery in a less extreme form—for example, in the belief that the body should be purged of poisonous wastes each spring by purgatives, such as sulphur and molasses.

Loss of control over the evacuation of substances assumed to be poisonous was basic to the formation of severe ideas of contamination. With the removal of the rectum, many patients believed that the necessary storage place, which shielded the environment from uncontrolled toxicity, was also lost. As a consequence, many women and a few men assumed that feces no longer stored in the rectum would increase the probability of contaminating the environment during irrigation. Their explanations as to how the contamination occurred were similar to early medical conceptions that infections were carried by odors or vapors. It is interesting that nearly twice as many of these rituals were practiced by women as by men. These rituals had as their primary objectives the detoxification of feces still in the colon and the decontamination of the body surface.

Decontamination, as opposed to detoxification, did not have the interior of the body as a reference, but was rather concerned with the exterior of the body and the immediate environment of the bathroom. It seemed that more women than men were intensely anxious about the potential contamination of the self or others, at least in the population studied.

Therapeutic Considerations

Of the articles dealing primarily with therapy, one by Jackson[14] focuses on the stages by which a patient adapts to his colostomy. She points out that the initial defense mechanism of denial can be quite effective in slowing down the internalization of the situation to a pace compatible with emotional stability. After this, either on the patient's own initiative or on that of the staff, the denial gives way to a more realistic confrontation and accompanying depression, to reluctant resignation, and then—ideally—to a determination to succeed.

Dlin and Fischer[15] emphasize the need to tailor educational and psycho-therapeutic interventions to the individual patient. Specific areas for preoperative exploration should include general evaluation of personality and maturity, indications for surgery, previous surgical experiences of the patient or his family members, the meaning of the surgery to the patient as revealed by his fantasies, and whether the patient's unconscious wish is to live or die.

McCawley et al.[16] postulate some degree of sexual and body image concern, as well as depression (related to loss of anal control, of the resected organ, and of sexual appeal or potency) in every ostomy patient. They recommend attending to these areas even in the absence of expressed concerns.

CASE EXAMPLES

Case 1

Mrs. C. was a 72-year-old widow with a six-year history of low-grade bladder carcinoma. She was born in Europe and had spent time in a concentration camp during World War II. She came to the United States with her husband, who became involved in banking, had a substantial income, and left her well provided for after his death some 20 years earlier. She had a history of recurrent depressions from age 28 and twice required electroconvulsive therapy. In the fall of 1975, her psychiatrist gave her a "medication" for her depression, which she discontinued on her own after a month "because it wasn't working."

Mrs. C. was a well-dressed woman who took great pride in her appearance. She currently lived with a housekeeper in a comfortable apartment. Her interests were music, languages, and current events. Socially, she had a small group of friends who seemed very supportive of her needs. She had no children.

Her bladder carcinoma was treated initially by cobalt therapy and later by partial cystectomy. Following the latter procedure, she began to have bouts of severe lower abdominal pain, aggravated by voiding. In December 1975, instillation chemotherapy into the bladder was begun. These treatments were too painful to her, however, and she pleaded with the urologist to perform a radical cystectomy and ileal conduit (Bricker procedure). The pros and cons of this procedure were discussed in a conference involving the urologist, the patient, and the enterostomal therapist. The urologist was reluctant to perform the surgery, both because of Mrs. C.'s past psychiatric illness and because of the low grade of the tumor. The patient, however, insisted that she could not live with the bladder pain, and the surgeon agreed to perform the procedure. The enterostomal therapist made several preoperative visits during December 1975, to reinforce the preoperative teaching and to answer the patient's questions concerning the impending surgery and the stoma. She was also seen by the psychiatric service to evaluate her for surgery in light of her history of depressions and dependent life style. The health care team was able to explore Mrs. C.'s anxiety about the surgery, her anger and resentment about the disease, and her depression related to her altered body image and anticipated invalid life style.

Her postoperative course was complicated by lack of cooperation in self-care and some degree of depression and withdrawal. She required great encouragement to eat or perform any of her self-care, although she did not require further ECT or antidepressant medication. On discharge, her stoma and appliance were functioning well, and she was independent in her stoma care.

A visiting nurse referral was made to help with the adjustment from the hospital setting to the home. Initially, Mrs. C. regressed in her self-care, but over the next four months she became partially independent. She would change her own appliance with the nurse watching, but again became agitated and depressed when the visiting nurse attempted to terminate her visits.

In April 1976, the nursing visits were terminated because of a lapse in Medicare coverage. Although she was made to assume the responsibility of her stoma care, Mrs. C. tried without success to find somone whom she could pay to do this service for her. She even tried to impose the responsibility of her stoma care on her ostomy visitor.

By the fall of 1976, Mrs. C. was performing her own ostomy care, but she had not integrated it successfully into her pattern of daily living. She had curtailed some of her social activities, and she remained mildly depressed.

Comment: The postoperative regression and depression seen in this woman were predicted on the basis of her history of recurrent depressions, her dependence, and her advanced age. Education, frequent supportive visits by the psychiatrist, enterostomal therapist, ostomy visitor, and the necessity of self-care imposed by the termination of Medicare were all helpful in an adaptation which, given her circumstances, may be considered optimal.

Case 2

Mr. H., a 52-year-old, divorced custodian living alone, was admitted for symptoms of ulcerative colitis of one month's duration. At the time of the surgical consultation, he was not responding to medical treatment consisting of hyperalimentation and steroids, and colectomy and ileostomy on a semi-emergency basis were recommended. No history of psychiatric problems was elicited.

Mr. H. was at first totally opposed to the proposed surgical procedure and stated he would rather die than have an ostomy. The psychiatric consultant found that his primary concerns involved his altered body image, care of the stoma, and feelings of isolation from his family and friends, who lived in an adjoining city from which he had been transferred to UCLA for tertiary care.

In view of these expressed concerns, the psychiatrist recommended continued education and support by the nursing staff and enterostomal therapist. The enterstomal therapist was able to help the patient deal realistically with his altered body image, worries over resuming social and sexual activities, and doubts about how much physical activity he could tolerate. He responded well to the enterostomal therapist's interventions and expressed particular surprise on learning that infants, children, and young adults also needed ostomy surgery for various medical reasons and that their adaptation was usually good. He was also visited by an ostomy patient of the same age and sex, who was doing well emotionally and physically.

After about a week of preoperative preparation, Mr. H. underwent a total colectomy and ileostomy. For the first five or six postoperative days, he became markedly depressed, wishing to die and refusing to view or care for the stoma. As his physical condition improved, with much encouragement from the nursing staff, he gradually became independent in his self-care.

Since Mr. H. lived alone some two hours' drive from the medical center, he was referred to the local Visiting Nurse Association, enterostomal therapist, and community mental health center. One month after his discharge, he was no longer having extensive periods of depression. He had been fitted with a reusable ostomy appliance by his local enterostomal therapist and had become active in an ileostomy club.

Comment: Preoperative education, gentle probing for areas of major concern, and role modeling were all of great help in this man's adaptation to his stoma. Also important were his stoical, practical-minded personality, the symptomatic relief gained by the surgery, his prompt return to work, and his involvement in the local ileostomy club. His pattern of adaptation, though much different from that of Mrs. C., was fairly predictable if the same factors were considered: personality pattern, psychiatric history, underlying disease process, age, and social supports.

Case 3

Ms. M., an attractive, 19-year-old, single college student who lived with her brother and widowed father, had been diagnosed as having ulcerative colitis three years prior to surgery. She had had two major exacerbations requiring hospitalization, and she had been treated medically with Azulfidine, cortisone enemas, bulk agents, and Donnatal during the year preceding surgery. Response to medical therapy was poor, however, and she developed a toxic megacolon four days before surgery.

Ms. M. had no history of psychiatric illness, and she was doing well in school. Her mother had died when the patient was 13 years old, and she had assumed the role of homemaker, caring for her father and brother. She had a steady boyfriend, with whom she was sexually active.

Two preoperative visits were made by the enterostomal therapist, with the aim of education and exploration of concerns. Ms. M. was anxious about the impending surgery, and most of her questions centered around body image and sexuality. Ileostomy with total proctocolectomy was performed. After surgery, she was anxious to learn ileostomy care, and her father and boyfriend were both supportive in this. She was able to discuss the ileostomy openly with her boyfriend, and he viewed her stoma and appliance before hospital discharge.

After discharge, the patient was followed in the Surgery Clinic. She experienced postoperative anxiety and depression, manifested by erratic mood swings, shaking, nightmares, and insomnia. She was treated with Valium and frequent supportive visits by the surgeon and enterostomal therapist.

Two months postoperatively, Ms. M. had resumed sexual relations and was orgasmic. Her mood pattern had returned to normal, and she was having no difficulty sleeping. She chose to drop out of college temporarily and seek a job until she decided on her educational goals, and she was making plans to move to her own apartment.

Comment: This young woman's rapid psychosocial adaptation was aided by support from significant others in her life and by the symptom relief afforded by surgery. Frequent brief supportive visits and minor tranquilizers were helpful during the immediate postoperative period and were soon tapered.

DISCUSSION

Several important points can be gathered from the review of literature and case studies. First, ostomy patients may react to the surgery in a wide variety of styles. The most important variables are the underlying disease process, the age and life situation of the patient, life-long psychological and adaptational styles, the symbolism of the ostomy to the individual, basic instruction and education, and the attitudes of significant others and supporting groups.

Second, every effort should be made to measure the patient's understanding of the disease process and the proposed surgery. Any knowledge lacking must be painstakingly and repeatedly presented and questions frequently asked to gauge the patient's comprehension.

Third, brief supportive therapy and empathic exploration of the meaning of the disease and surgery to the individual patient is important in carrying him through the successive stages of adaptation to the ostomy and the inevitable accompanying depression. Past adaptational styles, social resources, and the reaction of significant others are important predictors of adaptation to the ostomy.

Fourth, the patient should have mastered self-care skills before discharge from the hospital.

The enterostomal therapist is becoming increasingly important, not only as a technical expert, but also as a role model. Ostomy visitors are similarly important supportive figures and role models to the extent that the patient can identify with them.

As Jackson[17] states, "Independence in their care alone does not in any way support the possibility that they have accepted the ostomy." Rehabilitation in its fullest sense is a long-range program—beginning in the preoperative period—to help the ostomate achieve maximum autonomy and a high quality of life.

REFERENCES

1. Lenneberg, E. Role of enterostomal therapists and stoma rehabilitation clinics. *Cancer,* 28:226-229, 1971.
2. Rowbotham, J. Advances in rehabilitation of stoma patients. *Cancer,* 36:702-704, 1975.
3. Mizrachi, N. Ostomates help each other deal with sexuality. *Hosp. Trib.,* August 16, 1976, pp. 13-15.
4. Roy, P. et al. Experience with ileostomies: Evaluation of long-term rehabilitation in 497 patients. *Am. J. Surg.,* 119:77-86, 1970.
5. Baird, N. et al. Colostomy problems—the patient's viewpoint. *J. Kans. Med. Soc.,* 68:1-4, 1967.
6. George, W. et al. Problems of a permanent colostomy. *Gut,* 16(5):408-409, 1975.
7. Fox, B. Issues in research on premorbid psychological factors and cancer incidence. *Cancer Prevention and Detection,* 1977 (In press).
8. Engel, G.L. Studies of ulcerative colitis. II. The nature of the somatic processes and the adequacy of psychosomatic hypotheses. *Am. J. Med.,* 16:416-433, 1954.
9. Druss, R., et al. Psychologic response to colectomy. *Arch. Gen. Psychiat.,* 18:53-59, 1968.
10. Druss, R. et al. Psychologic response to colectomy—II. Adjustment to a permanent colostomy. *Arch. Gen. Psychiat.,* 20:419-427, 1969.
11. Orbach, C. et al. Modification of perceived body and of body concept following the construction of a colostomy. *Arch. Gen. Psychiat.* 12:126-135, 1965.

12. Epstein, L., and Lasagna, L. Obtaining informed consent: Form or substance. *Arch. Intern. Med.*, 123:682-688, 1969.
13. Orbach, C. Ideas of contamination in postoperative colostomy patients. *Psychoanal. Rev.*, 61(2):269-282, 1974.
14. Jackson, B. Colostomates: The mosaic of stress and implied care. *Aust. Nurses J.* 4(10):24-27, 1975.
15. Dlin, B., and Fischer, H. Psychiatric aspects of colostomy and ileostomy. In: *Modern Perspectives in the Psychiatric Aspects of Surgery,* ed. J. Howells, New York:Brunner/Mazel, 1976, pp. 321-342.
16. McCawley, A. et al. The psychological problems of ostomates. *Connecticut Medicine,* 39(3):151-155, 1975.
17. Jackson, B. Colostomates' reactions to hospitalization and colostomy surgery. *Nurs. Clin. N. Am.*, 11(3):417-425, 1976.

CHAPTER 10

The Child with Ulcerative Colitis: Play Therapy as a Rehearsal for Surgery

BETTY PFEFFERBAUM
CHARLES HOLLINGSWORTH

> Space is not the measure of distance. A garden wall at home may enclose more secrets than the great Wall of China, and the soul of a little girl is better guarded by silence than the Sahara's oases by the surrounding sands. I dropped down to earth once somewhere in the world. It was near Concordia, in the Argentine, but it might have been anywhere at all, for mystery is everywhere.
>
> Antoine de Saint Exupéry,
> *Wind, Sand and Stars*

Ulcerative colitis in children is an extremely difficult management problem for the pediatrician and surgeon—and for the psychiatrist who is inevitably asked to take part. The course of the disease is marked by frequent exacerbations and remissions that are thought to be affected by both emotional and biological factors. Many studies have shown significant correlation between important (real or symbolic) loss of interpersonal relationships and the exacerbation or precipitation of symptoms in predisposed individuals;[1] other studies have placed less emphasis on emotional factors and more on biological or genetic determinants.[2] This continuing dispute has often hindered effective liaison between pediatrician, surgeon, and psychiatrist. Current thinking, however, is best summarized by Engel,[3] who while pointing to the lack of definite evidence of psychological causative factors, nevertheless considers the disease neither exclusively functional nor organic, but rather one that demonstrates the interlocking nature of biological and psychological mechanisms.

Ulcerative colitis is characterized by inflammation and ulceration of the colon. It tends toward chronicity, although there are some fulminating cases with rapid deterioration. It is usually accompanied by anorexia, weight loss, and anemia; occasionally it may be accompanied by arthritis, skin lesions, and stomach ulcers in children. However, the more common complications associated with the pediatric age group are growth retardation and delay in the onset of puberty.[4]

The disease is especially severe in the pediatric age group; over 90 percent of involved children have moderate to severe activity of the colitis, while less than 50 percent of adults have this degree of activity. The severity and debilitating nature of the disease often necessitate surgical intervention, and in many pediatric patients colectomy may be indicated within two years of onset.[4] There are no absolutes for recommending surgery, but in the patient with involvement of the entire colon and continuous symptoms, it seems unrealistic to persist in medical treatment, particularly when physical, social, and intellectual development is impeded.[5]

Though the chronic continuous type of colitis may present a less debilitating course, it is the more dangerous clinical pattern in children, since the major catastrophic complications such as perforation, fistula formation, and cancer are more frequent in this form of the disease.

Despite the fact that the mortality rate in children with ulcerative colitis has been greatly reduced in the last decade and drug-related improvement can now be obtained in many cases with Azulfidine and corticosteroids, a significant and ever-increasing number (over 40 percent) of patients ultimately require surgery because of the serious threat of cancer.[6] Devroede[7] found that cancer develops in three percent of children with ulcerative colitis within the first ten years after onset and then increases by 20 percent per decade for those at risk after the first ten years. According to Devroede, the estimated probability of developing cancer is 43 percent within 35 years of the onset of ulcerative colitis. Four high-risk factors are associated with the development of cancer in children with ulcerative colitis: extreme severity of the first attacks; involvement of the entire colon; continuous, rather than intermittent, symptoms; and onset of the disease early in childhood. The child that we shall describe presented with all of these factors.

O'Conner et al.[8] in a controlled study have reported that psychotherapy is related to improvement in the physiological status of the disease. In contrast, McDermott and Finch[2] found no specific correlation between the degree of psychological involvement and the course of the disease. Nor could a favorable physiological response be correlated with the intensity, duration, or type of psychotherapy. These authors, however, do describe significant improvement in the emotional states of the majority of children with ulcerative colitis who were treated psychiatrically as part of a combined medical, psychiatric, and surgical program. This improvement was not, though, associated with reversal or improvement in the bowel disease, as O'Conner had reported, confirming impressions that other etiological factors play a role in maintaining the progression of the disease.

Engel[1] has stressed that the fact that surgery is indicated does not represent a failure of psychotherapy. Indeed, psychiatric attention to a child facing surgery may be the crucial determinant of the success of the procedure and the child's eventual healthy adjustment.

The following case history describes the child psychiatrist's participation as a team member in the preparation of the child, family, and staff for surgery and its sequelae.

CASE PRESENTATION

Michele was first seen in the Pediatric Clinic when the staff requested assistance in preparation for her surgery. She was a beautiful child, quiet and courteously cooperative, whose eyes seemed to ask the questions she could not verbalize: "Why are you here to see me?" "Why are you asking me so many questions?" "What have I done wrong?"

Although there was a strong history of bowel disease in Michele's family, no one had been afflicted at such an early age. Michele was only eight years old when she became ill with abdominal pain, diarrhea, and rectal bleeding while away at summer camp. This necessitated hospitalization, where a diagnosis of ulcerative colitis was made. For two years Michele was followed closely and treated conservatively with Azulfidine and steroids. Yet rehospitalization was required on three separate occasions. In the meantime, Michele suffered a succession of painful and demeaning experiences: having to leave her classroom suddenly because of urgent diarrhea, needing to wear sanitary napkins to prevent soiling her clothing, and concealing soiled undergarments from her parents.

The primary problem itself would have been more than enough to tax the limits of a little girl, but Michele was beset with difficulties that antedated her physical illness. Her family situation was complex and chaotic. Michele lived with her father, an unemployed construction worker, her paternal grandmother, and her older sister and brother. For reasons that are unclear, Michele's mother had given up custody of her children and maintained only visitation rights. Michele, who was accustomed to seeing her mother once or twice a week, was acutely aware of the hostility and bitterness between her parents.

Psychological factors and family dynamics, once held to be causative and now felt to be at least provocative in patients with ulcerative colitis, were clear in this family. The patient has typically been described as dependent on the mother or mother figure, with fantasies of mother's omnipotence and with repressed rage toward the disappointing mother.

Engel[1] feels that ulcerative colitis develops in a child who has evolved an ego that is functionally and permanently dependent on the mother. He stresses the difficulties these children have in object relatedness. He also believes that these patients tend to be less adaptive and that care must be taken to protect them from new and unnecessary tensions. He states that the colitic process begins or reappears in a setting in which the patient feels, consciously or unconsciously, that he has suffered or will suffer the loss of an important object relation. Using clinical observations for his data, Engel concludes that this real or imagined traumatic separation may be accompanied by biochemical or physiological alterations which permit initiation of a variety of pathologic processes in tissues, including those characteristic of ulcerative colitis. The child may experience exacerbations even in the hospital setting. Pasnau[9] has correlated some exacerbations with loss of medical caretakers with whom the child had established a significant relationship.

While Michele herself would rarely speak of her mother, there was evidence that she had placed her in an exalted position: the grandmother described Michele's desires to please the mother to the point that Michele waited on the mother and served her meals when they were together. Indeed, Michele's refusal to give the therapist more than occasional glimpses of her feelings toward her mother verified the importance she attached to keeping that relationship in a special, preserved position unreachable for mutual examination. We shall see later how Michele's anger at her absent mother encroached on every aspect of her life and was expressed in the therapeutic relationship.

The therapist's task would have been simpler if Michele's problems had been discrete and easily isolated. Yet Michele presented with difficulties in a number of other life spheres. Frustrations at home led to poor academic and social adjustment. Michele was early identified by teachers and classmates as a child with considerable behavioral problems: rule breaking, lying, stealing, low academic achievement, and identification with other girls who had singled themselves out as "problem children."

Michele was referred for psychiatric consultation five months before the anticipated date of surgery, which was to include total colectomy and permanent ileostomy. By that time she had experienced a two-year unremitting course of ulcerative colitis, and her physicians' explicit request was that the psychiatrist help prepare Michele and the family for surgery. Initially, a psychiatric nurse was employed to counsel the parents and grandmother so that the psychiatrist could focus attention on the child.

While adults are able to be verbal, children tend to express themselves through action. This was clearly true for Michele, who at times of stress found expression through disruptive behavior. For this reason, the therapist encouraged the use of play in therapy to give the child a vehicle for exploring her feelings and facing at her own pace her anxieties, fears, and expectations.

How, then, did Michele use play in therapy to reveal her concerns and, in sharing them, allow them to be mastered? One of the handiest tools of the child psychiatrist is simply paper and pencil. What better way to learn about a child's own body image than to ask him or her to reproduce in drawing a boy or a girl? In this activity Michele allowed a glimpse of herself when she invariably depicted a crippled person with an arm or a leg in a cast, an amputated limb, or a patch over a blind eye. She saw herself as this crippled person afflicted with a disease that identified her as different and deformed.

Other play therapy tools included dolls and puppets which became important participants in her life. In the earlier sessions Michele concentrated on that aspect of her life in which she perhaps felt least vulnerable: she talked about and played out her misbehavior. She used dolls and puppets to enact the theme of a child's disobeying and suffering the consequences of severe punishment. The therapist was quick to note that the punishment seldom fit the crime: for a simple lie, the child doll would be imprisoned! The therapist soon was able to understand some associations to the child's illness, though these were not interpreted to the child until much later. In fact, by the end of the first month Michele made her own connection. She found a doctor and nurse puppet and with them revealed her concept of the illness. The child puppet committed an offense (anything from telling a lie to bank robbery) and then suffered the consequences of a dramatic illness for which he was taken to the hospital, where he died and then miraculously returned to life. It was becoming clear how much Michele considered her illness and impending surgery to be punishment for her "misdeeds."

In later sessions, when Michele became more verbal, there was much talk of surgery and fear of dying. Anger, alternating with dependence, became common themes. In terms of dependence, Michele invested omnipotent powers in the therapist, hoping beyond hope to be spared the surgical procedure. With the anger, she expelled her rage in the awareness that once again she was left abandoned, frustrated, and frightened. And once again the mother she held in such high esteem could not rescue her.

Four months after the first session, Michele, her pediatrician, and her therapist met together so that the psychiatrist might know at first hand the information Michele received and help Michele learn how to tell her pediatrician what kinds of things bothered her. The brief appointment in the busy Pediatric Clinic, together with Michele's more defended posture, made her act differently in the presence of the pediatrician: she denied any concerns or fears about her illness or surgery. The pediatrician at first colluded in the silence by assuming that his kind, but matter-of-fact explanation of what would happen, his "don't worry," and Michele's nod of the head indicated she was reassured. The therapist was able to facilitate more open and honest communication between the child and her physician by interpreting Michele's need to please and placate him and by helping Michele give voice to some of her fears about anesthesia and dying.

Michele's disease did not abate, and preparation for surgery began soon after the conjoint meeting. An enterostomal nurse was introduced to Michele and became an integral member of the team, with the task of preparing Michele for colectomy and ileostomy. It was felt that Michele's reaction would depend heavily on her family's, and they were offered instruction on the procedure and its implications. It was agreed that Michele's independence regarding stoma care was to be encouraged.

Supportive therapy involving play continued to be a pivotal aspect of the preparation for surgery. An ileostomy doll was fashioned for Michele so that she could practice stoma care. Indeed, Michele became fond of the doll, took it home, and practiced cutting and applying the stoma bags to it. In her sessions she continued to use other dolls and the puppets to voice her apprehension about the surgery, and as the date of her surgery approached, she introduced new games into the therapy, such as "hangman." The psychiatrist was engaged in this game, in which Michele frequently spelled out words associated with her fears about surgery and her illness. Michele would often allow words such as "surgery" to be spelled, but not spoken, acknowledging how much terror she felt.

The surgical procedure itself was smooth and uneventful, and in the post-operative phase, Michele has begun to re-create in play what has been done to her. Identifying with the aggressor, Michele has expressed hostility via physical contact by introducing games such as tag, shoot-outs with toy guns, and boxing with batacas. Her need to manipulate and control the sessions dramatically increased after surgery, and these needs continue to be interpreted to her even now as she develops new capacities to manage her own bodily functions.

Michele's relationship with her mother continues to be emotionally charged. In one session after a week-long vacation, the therapist suggested to the child that this absence might have been reminiscent of other absences. With both anger and sadness, Michele responded, "You're not supposed to talk about my mother," and tearfully ran out of the room.

RECOMMENDATIONS

Ulcerative colitis in childhood is often a devastating disease. Frequent diarrhea, cramping pain, embarrassing episodes of soiling, and loss of one's sense of control over bodily functions prevent normal individuation and healthy growth and development. Although these considerations make surgery seem less mutilating, the stress of surgical intervention threatens even the most psychologically healthy children and families and makes psychiatric consultation imperative in some cases.

What general principles of management can then be offered? The consultant must realize that his duties are severalfold. He must take an active part in the health care team, consisting of pediatric and surgical physicians, nurses, specially trained enterostomal nurses, and stoma volunteers. The staff must be reminded about the sensitivity of these children to stress, especially loss, and taught how to discuss the innumerable details of the illness, surgery, and rehabilitation in age-appropriate ways. It is especially important to communicate to the team members how such a child may translate his or her anxieties into behaviors that may, unless their meaning is understood, adversely affect the working relationship with the staff and delay recovery.

While the classic description of the parent-child dyad may not hold for every case, the family dynamics must be considered, especially when family interaction becomes a source of stress and conflict for the child. In addition, the consultant may explore with the family ways to be supportive and accepting of the child without fostering undue dependence. The family needs sufficient information and support to ensure the child a safe haven for rehabilitation.

Psychotherapeutic interpretations with children suffering from ulcerative colitis must be cautious and supportive. The child must be allowed to take the lead so that fears, fantasies, and expectations before and after surgery may be taken up in his or her own way and pace. Play therapy may be particularly revealing and helpful in younger children, who must be given the opportunity to safely explore their anxiety, helplessness, anger, and loss and slowly confront the painful reality of a mutilated body image. Future difficulties must be kept in mind; with Michele, the important issue of sexual performance and adequacy have only begun to surface.

Novalis wrote: "It is certain my Conviction gains infinitely, the moment another soul will believe in it." Michele was a child who from very early in life visualized herself as crippled, abandoned, and unworthy. The consultant's job was clear: to promote an atmosphere of understanding and reliability, in which Michele's sense of frustration and defeat could be examined and in which she might feel less alone. Only then could this little girl re-enter the world with confidence and self-esteem.

REFERENCES

1. Engel, G.L. Studies of ulcerative colitis: V. Psychological aspects and their implications for treatment. *Am. J. Diag. Dis.* (New Series), 3:315-337, 1958.
2. McDermott, J.J., and Finch, S.M. Ulcerative colitis in children: Reassessment of a dilemma. *J. Am. Acad. Child Psychiat.*, 6:512-525, 1967.
3. Engel, G.L. Biologic and psychologic features of the ulcerative colitis patient. *Gastroenterology*, 40(2):313-322, 1961.
4. Ament, M.E. Inflammatory disease of the colon: Ulcerative colitis and Crohn's colitis: A Review. *J. Peds.*, 86(3):322-334, 1975.

5. Patterson, M., Castiglioni, L., and Sampson, L. Chronic ulcerative colitis beginning in children and teenagers: A review of 43 patients. *Am. J. Digest. Dis.*, 16(4):289-297, 1971.
6. Werry, J.S. Psychosomatic disorders. In: *Psychopathological Disorders of Childhood*, ed. H.C. Quay and J.S. Werry. New York:Wiley & Sons, pp. 155-159, 1972.
7. Devroede, G.J. Cancer risk and life expectancy of children with ulcerative colitis. *New Eng. J. Med.*, 285:17-21, 1971.
8. O'Conner, J.F., Daniels, G., Karush, A., Moses, L., Flood, C., and Stern, L. The effects of psychotherapy on the course of ulcerative colitis: A preliminary report. *Am. J. Psychiat.*, 120:738-742, 1964.
9. Pasnau, R.O. Therapy of ulcerative colitis in children: A combined pediatric-psychiatric-surgical approach. *Psychosom.*, 5:137-143, 1964.

CHAPTER 11

A Review: Psychiatric Aspects of Contraception, Abortion, and Sterilization

CRAIG FISCHER

> But alas, no such humble friendship how-
> evei iomantic, could give her the sense that
> we completely shared her thoughts; the
> nature of them made it hard for anyone
> to understand; and her sorrow was very
> lonely.
>
> Virginia Woolf,
> *Moments of Being*

Increased psychiatric involvement in family-planning and issues of fertility regulation reflects a heightened appreciation of the need for population stabilization as well as clinical concern for the individual's health and well-being. The psychiatrist has much to offer, not only by providing traditional consultation, but also by utilizing his training and experience to assist others in the provision of services. The liaison psychiatrist can help assure that the complex psychological, cultural, and social issues accompanying fertility-regulating decisions are adequately dealt with by both patients and staff.[1] This chapter will review the research pertinent to the psychological aspects of contraceptive use and unplanned pregnancy, induced abortion, and elective sterilization. It will then discuss the principles of psychiatric consultation and liaison in a family-planning clinic. Many important topics which are not as prominent in psychiatric consultative practice, such as the psychology of family size determination or contraceptive choice, will not be discussed.

135

The ready availability of effective family planning has numerous beneficial effects on mental and physical health,[2-4] and the adverse effects of excessive population have been frequently demonstrated. Large family size results in a higher infant and maternal mortality rate. There is an inverse relation between family size and IQ for all socioeconomic groups. Adequate spacing of children is beneficial in preserving the physical, emotional, and economic resources of the parents so that each child can be given adequate nurturing.

It is estimated that before the recent liberalization of abortion laws, one million illegal abortions, many of which resulted in sepsis or other complications, were performed annually in the United States. Since the change in abortion laws, the death rate from abortion has dropped dramatically. Illegitimate birth has been noted to have profound and usually adverse effects on both mother and child,[5] and the ready availability of contraception, and particularly abortion, has tended to lower the illegitimacy rate.

There is, nevertheless, no real evidence that planned children do better than unplanned children, although the psychological handicap to an unwanted child is generally accepted by most clinicians on the basis of numerous case histories. The relation between unplanned pregnancies and unwanted children, however, is complex. Clearly many unplanned pregnancies result in entirely wanted children, although the few available studies tend to confirm the disadvantaged position of the unwanted child. Battered children and babies dying of crib death have a significantly higher incidence of unwantedness.[6] Forssman and Thuwe[7] compared 120 children born after therapeutic abortion was denied to a control group born at the same time. At follow-up up to 20 years later, the "unwanted" children had utilized psychiatric services and public assistance more often, had done poorer academically, and showed more antisocial and criminal behavior. Unfortunately, the control group was not well matched for social class and other demographic variables. Another study,[8] performed in Czechoslovakia with a seven-to-nine-year follow-up and a better control group, showed a similar, although not as dramatic, disadvantage for "unwanted" children. Males in particular had poorer health, poorer grades, and more difficulty with peer relationships; they also appeared to be at greater risk for juvenile delinquency. These studies investigated only the effect on the unwanted child. The effect of an unwanted birth on the parents must also be considered, although this has rarely been evaluated.

Family-planning services also assist in meeting a variety of other social needs: counseling for genetic disease, identifying and treating sexual dysfunction, increasing knowledge of one's body, physical examination, and screening for venereal disease. It thus seems clear that the ready availability of family-planning services has a definite role in the prevention of physical and mental disease and in the promotion of a better quality of life.

Maximally effective contraception and fertility regulation is said to follow from informing patients and making services accessible. Recently, however, there has been a growing recognition that more is involved than just logistics and education. Despite widespread knowledge and availability of birth-prevention methods in the United States, rational pregnancy and birth planning does not prevail. Contraceptive effectiveness is not simply a matter of technology; it is also subject to a variety of psychological, cultural, and social influences. Regardless of the method and regardless of its simplicity, safety, availability, or low cost, it appears that many people who state they do not desire pregnancy will not employ contraception or will use it incorrectly. For some, the very effectiveness of a method may make it unacceptable.

Despite the obvious need for psychiatric input in family-planning, however, such involvement has been limited. Psychiatrists have been called in primarily to resolve troubling issues for the primary physician. Before 1973, most legal induced abortions were performed under the guise of psychiatric indication. Because psychiatric consultation was often mandatory for the abortion seeker, needless administrative and psychological barriers and a considerable waste of resources resulted. The Group for the Advancement of Psychiatry[9] has summarized this problem in the introduction to its report on abortion.

> During the past two decades there has been an increasing tendency to invoke and involve the psychiatrist as the arbiter at critical points of conflict between existing social policy and individual dissent and disagreement; abortion is one such instance of this tendency. Psychiatrists, in our opinion, do have a relevant contribution to make to a resolution of the abortion dilemma; but their contribution is limited. When the psychiatrist serves as the deus ex machina of the conflicted social system, he may ease the immediate stress without clarifying or resolving the underlying divisiveness of the community. The unfortunate consequence of this is that society places undue responsibility upon the individual psychiatrist and at the same time shuns its own responsibility to face squarely the issues which have led to such divisiveness. Because of these considerations and because the regulation of access to abortion is, in fact, the product of religious, moral, ethical, socioeconomic, political and legal considerations, psychiatric factors must be examined in relation to these broader perspectives.

Unfortunately, the problem persists. In 1976, an amendment to the Medicaid law threatened to again require such psychiatric justification for abortions, and young nulliparous women requesting permanent sterilization are often routinely referred for psychiatric consultation.

The controversy surrounding family planning is also reflected in the psychiatric literature. Until recently the research has been sparse. Tietze has stated that "the relationship between man's psyche and his reproductive behavior is one of the least explored aspects of disciplines concerned with human population."[10] He cites a bibliography[11] on fertility control for the period 1950-1965 listing over 2,000 references, of which only five percent dealt with psychological or psychiatric matters. Much of the literature that does exist is dominated by speculation and personal opinion.

PSYCHIATRIC ASPECTS OF CONTRACEPTIVE
USE AND NONUSE

In 1970, when family-planning services were at least reasonably accessible, over one-half of the recent births to *married couples* were reported to be unplanned. Fifteen percent of the births were said to have been "never wanted."[12] It has been estimated that over 70 percent of all "unplanned" pregnancies occur when no contraception is used at the time of conception. Bauman and Wilson's survey[13] of college women revealed that only one-third of the sexually active women regularly used contraception, despite the knowledge and availability of various birth-control methods and no conscious desire to become pregnant. Close to one million abortions are performed yearly in the United States, most of which can be assumed to be for unintended pregnancies. Bracken et al.[14] found that only 20 percent of women seeking therapeutic abortion were using contraception at the time of conception and over 50 percent had not used any contraception for the past year. Nearly all demonstrated adequate knowledge of, and access to, contraception and denied any conscious intent to become pregnant. Most stated that they did not believe they would become pregnant even though they were sexually active. Smith[15] essentially confirmed these results: 70 percent of his samples were using either no contraception or a clearly ineffective method at the time of conception, and 40 percent had never used contraception. It is clear then that contraceptive behavior is often discrepant from seemingly rational, conscious intent.

Obviously, a large number of intrapsychic, interpersonal, cultural, and sociological factors are responsible for contraceptive misuse or nonuse despite availability. Unfortunately, little objective evidence is available. Bauman and Wilson[13] surveyed sexually active college women for their reasons for nonuse of contraception. They frequently reported that intercourse was not expected (38 percent), that sex "should be spontaneous" (33 percent), and that obtaining contraception was too embarrassing (16 percent).

Brody and others have argued that emotionally healthy women are more likely to achieve contraceptive success. Success generally reflects the ability to achieve mastery and autonomy in general and requires the capacity to plan and the conviction that one has the power to control one's life. In studies in Jamaica, Brody and his colleagues[16,17] found that failure to achieve self-regulation of fertility was associated with ambivalence about sex, difficulty in asserting oneself in a heterosexual relationship, and the presence of minimal overlapping roles with one's mate. They also discovered a high correlation with poor communication between the patient and her mother and/or the patient and her spouse.

Siassi's[18] study of the use of oral contraceptives in Iran demonstrates the importance of interpersonal and cultural influence. No apparent legal, moral, religious, or financial barriers existed to their use. Ninety-three percent of women continued to use the pills for at least six months if their husbands dispensed the pills, compared to only 12 percent who self-dispensed. In the United States, Bracken et al.[14] found that women with multiple abortions were less likely to have their partner involved in contraceptive decision making.

Beyond these findings, however, most reports have been largely speculative, with theories based on anecdotal accounts or a small number of unstructured interviews of women seeking induced abortion. Many authors have attempted to identify specific personality constellations, but they appear to be biased by personal opinion or a small, homogeneous sample. It should be obvious that contraceptive misuse has complex multiple determinants. Different motives are no doubt active in the unintended pregnancy of a 16-year-old primagravida and her boyfriend in their first sexual encounter as opposed to a 40-year-old married woman and her husband who have six children. Schaffer and Pine[19] have argued that the developmental issues normally active at any particular age are likely to determine the motives for fertility control and how the pregnancy is experienced. Thus, the adolescent is likely to be dealing with issues of identity and separation from home, while the older woman may be reacting to the approaching loss of her reproductive abilities. These cautions should be considered in reviewing some of the more widely promulgated theories, most of which apply primarily to the younger, unmarried woman.

Sandberg[20] and Sandberg and Jacobs[21] have listed a variety of possible reasons for unintended pregnancy. Denial of both the possibility of pregnancy and the occurrence of intercourse is frequent, as in the woman who claims, "I just don't understand how it happened." Love, usually accompanied by romantic fantasies, leads to self-sacrifice and risk taking. Guilt can block use of contraception and lead to a desire to be punished. To use contraception is often seen as an intention to have sex, which interferes with the denial. Power struggles and hostility within the relationship can affect contraceptive use; for example, contraception may be equated with submission. Sexual-identity problems may cause either men or women to desire to prove their fertility and thereby demonstrate their masculinity or femininity.

A frequently cited psychoanalytic theory proposes that a woman acts out incestuous fantasies toward her father in her relationships with a man. Contraception is avoided because pregnancy is desired in fulfillment of the fantasies. At the same time, incest and pregnancy are forbidden and guilt inducing. An abortion thus serves to get rid of the pregnancy, punish the woman, and belittle the father for his oedipal rejection of her.

Another popular theory involves the woman's unconscious desire for pregnancy in order to maintain a precarious identification with her mother in an attempt to resolve conflicts over feminine identity. She may also have an unconscious desire to have a child vicariously for her mother and identify with the child in desiring dependent care from her mother.[19] Such pregnancies may occur about the time a girl leaves her parents' home and often arise from con-flicts based on feelings of prior maternal deprivation. Kane et al.[22] found that patients seeking abortion were more likely than controls to have lost one or both parents before the age of 18. Similarly, unintended pregnancy has been observed frequently to occur in anticipation of, or immediately following, an interpersonal loss, such as rejection by a boyfriend, leaving the parents' home, deterioration of a marriage, or even the loss of a fetus through induced abortion.

PSYCHIATRIC ASPECTS OF ABORTION

In the past decade legal induced abortion has become a significant aspect of family-planning. In the United States, one abortion is performed for every four live births.[12] Legal barriers to abortion have largely disappeared following the 1973 Supreme Court decisions, although political battles are still active. The moral and religious issues, which center primarily on determining when life begins and on the right of a woman to control her own body, remain unsettled.

Much of the traditional medical opposition to induced abortion emphasized the risk to the abortion seeker. How much of this argument was a rationaliza-tion for moral opposition is difficult to tell. Certainly, before the advent of modern surgical techniques, sepsis and hemorrhage were significant risks of induced abortion, as of course they were for most other surgical procedures. In the last 30 years, however, abortion performed by a competent surgeon under usual hospital conditions (rare for illegal abortions) has not created a substantial medical risk. Surgical technique has improved so that most abortions can now be performed with little inconvenience, less risk than a tonsillectomy, and only one-tenth the maternal mortality of a full-term delivery.[12]

As it became clearer that abortion did not present a substantial medical risk, attention turned to the supposed psychiatric risk. Before 1953, the literature on the psychological sequelae of abortion was filled with dire warnings of adverse effects. (Curiously, by 1950, one-half of the legal abortions performed in the United States were justified by psychiatric indications, as were nearly all by 1973.) Stated conclusions were not substantiated by the data presented, but these unwarranted conclusions were quoted and perpetuated in later articles. For example, in 1936 Taussig[23] reported on three cases of psychosis following abortion in Russia; however, only one of the women had actually been seen by the author or was even reported in detail, and she was psychotic before the abortion. Yet his paper was frequently cited in support of arguments against abortion.[24] Gradually more adequately designed studies appeared, although the results often remained contradictory.

A rather stereotyped view of women often dominated the literature. In, 1963, for example, Fogel[25] reported that "every woman, whatever her age, her background or sexuality, has a trauma at destroying a pregnancy. This is a part of her own life. She destroys a pregnancy, she is destroying herself." It was also argued, again by a man, that abortion is a violation of woman's nature "as giver, nurturer, and protector of life" and is sure to result in "loss of identity."[26] The psychoanalytic literature is similarly filled with speculations of unconscious guilt, although actual symptoms are rarely presented. In pointing out the lack of evidence for substantial guilt in abortion patients, Friedman et al.[27] note that "a woman's final state of mind is not dictated solely by her unconscious."

In the past two decades, there have been numerous attempts to investigate more systematically the effects of abortion on women. Design and methodological difficulties, however, are abundant, including the lack of prospective design and of an appropriate control group, confounding from poor sampling, vague or variable outcome criteria, an inadequate follow-up interval, and failure to consider the influence of setting. There are essentially no truly prospective studies. At best, subjects have been assessed just prior to abortion with a comparison made to their state sometime following. Such studies fail to differentiate the effect of having an abortion from the effect of being pregnant and may tell us only how stressful the period of pregnancy is before abortion. More important, since such studies rarely consider the subject's emotional state before pregnancy, the findings are very difficult to interpret. When the antepartum state is assessed, it is approached retrospectively, usually during the stressful period preceding abortion, and consequently distortion is almost certain. Admittedly, it would be very difficult to conduct a truly prospective study; it may even be irrelevant. And considerable confusion exists as to the pertinent research questions. Although comparison with the antepartum state may give us a better understanding of the entire process, the decision whether to justify or discourage abortion on psychiatric grounds does not require it.

Confusion about research questions also makes choosing an appropriate control group difficult. Comparisons could be made, for instance, with women forced to carry an unwanted pregnancy to term because abortion was refused, with all women carrying a pregnancy to term, or with nonpregnant women undergoing similar surgical stress. Perhaps because of this difficulty, very few studies have used any control group or even addressed the issue. Evans et al.[28] showed similar rates of regret among adolescents choosing to terminate pregnancy by abortion and those choosing to marry or adopt out. The rate of postpartum psychosis is about one to two per thousand term deliveries, and about 0.2-0.4 per thousand induced abortions.[12] However, the obvious sampling differences between groups in these studies make the results rather tentative.

Variable outcome criteria add to the difficulty in interpreting the research findings. Outcome has been assessed from guilt hypothesized in the course of psychoanalytic treatment, subjective reports by the patient of relief or regret, observations of depression or anxiety by an interviewer, changes in written psychological test scores, requests for postabortion psychiatric treatment, and the presence of psychiatric illness or hospitalization. The opportunity for bias is clear, and the results of different studies are difficult to compare.

Lack of attention to sampling techniques adds further confusion to the results. Frequently subjects who have had varying abortive procedures or other concurrent surgery are lumped together. Women who present for a second trimester abortion, concurrent sterilization, or hysterectomy are no doubt psychologically different as a group from women requesting simple first trimester abortion, and the procedures must also exert differing stresses.

Another significant confounding influence is that of the social and institutional milieu in which abortions are performed and studied. If abortion is generally viewed as a traumatic experience that is weakly justified but basically immoral, adverse reactions would not be surprising. The attitudes of the culture, the legal system, family and friends, and the health care providers all must influence outcome. The imposition of barriers to abortion, such as the need to feign mental distress in order to satisfy psychiatric indications, increases the stressfulness of the process and conveys an unfavorable attitude toward abortion.

Cultural views regarding the role of women may also be influential. If women see themselves primarily as mothers, conflict about pregnancy and a sense of loss following abortion seem more likely. As women become more valued in other roles, the decision whether to abort may become less conflicted. All of these influences limit the value of past studies on abortion. However, if present trends toward public acceptance of abortion and alternative roles for women continue, the findings of past studies can be considered as estimates of the worst effects of abortion.

Although the methodological problems cited make definite conclusions impossible, general agreement has been reached on some of the research questions. A few studies will illustrate the typical findings. Ekblad[29] performed one of the first systematic studies of abortion outcome. He questioned 479 Swedish women up to two and a half years after abortions performed for "psychiatric indications." He found that 88 percent had either minimal or no regret. Only one percent had developed psychiatric symptoms sufficient to impair their ability to work, and all of these had had prior psychiatric disturbance. He concluded that induced abortion carried only a minimal risk of psychiatric sequelae and that the greater the psychiatric indication, the greater the risk. These conclusions have generally been confirmed by others. Levene and Rigney[30] found that of 56 patients, five consulted a psychiatrist within a few months following abortion, and two of these had had prior psychiatric treatment. None of their subjects required psychiatric hospitalization. Barnes et al.[31] similarly reported that nine out of 99 patients saw a psychiatrist in the year following the abortion. Two of these patients required psychiatric hospitalization; both had previously been in mental institutions.

A much more extensive study was reported by the Joint Program for the

Study of Abortion,[12] involving nearly 73,000 abortions, with variable but usually short-term follow-up. Only 16 patients were known to have developed significant psychiatric complications, five of whom became depressed after developing major medical complications. Two suicides occurred, one in a patient with extensive prior and concurrent psychiatric problems and the other in a patient who had gone through the procedure while misdiagnosed as pregnant. She killed herself before she could be informed of the error.

Although the development of new major psychiatric disease following induced abortion is rare, more subtle psychological effects commonly occur. Several studies indicate that the highest prevalence of symptoms and disturbance occurs in the period just before the abortion, with significant subsequent improvement in mental state. Several authors report a brief period of mild post-abortion depression, guilt, or sense of loss in some women, but this does not seem to occur universally. Perhaps more typical are reports of relief and improved functioning.

A recent report by Payne et al.[32] confirms these findings. Although hampered by lack of a control group and reliance on patient reports for some of the data, it is a significant advance in design and execution. The authors hypothesized a multivariate model, following the affects of anxiety, anger, depression, guilt, and shame in 84 patients from before the abortion until six months after, against 24 independent variables. Various assessment techniques were used, including interviews and several objective tests. The results confirmed that an unwanted pregnancy has complex determinants, involving socioeconomic and other demographic variables, the patient's personality and mental health characteristics, and the quality of her interpersonal relationships, as well as her attitude toward the pregnancy. These variables often exerted a selective effect on the affects. In general, the levels of all five affects were highest just before the abortion, fell dramatically in one day, and rose very slightly over the next six months. Feelings of loss, sadness, or depression were experienced by only a few women following the procedure. If the assessments are valid, these findings confirm that abortion rarely causes significant psychological trauma. They further suggest that it is the unwanted pregnancy that is stressful and the abortion relieves this stress. The authors suggest a crisis model in which the pregnancy generates conflict and upsets homeostasis, forcing the development of new adaptive patterns to seek resolution. Abortion is one element in the solution. The process by which the crisis is resolved can lead to maturation or regression, depending on how the individual handles the conflict.

Some of the study's more specific findings are also noteworthy, particularly since they help predict those women who will have trouble dealing with the conflicts of unwanted pregnancy and abortion. Women with a history of mental illness had higher levels of anxiety and anger and a longer elevation of depression and anxiety, suggesting weaker coping mechanisms. Similar problems were apparent in women with no prior deliveries. Those with an "unstable, conflictual relationship" with husband or lover or interpersonal relationships "fixated at an immature level" and those with a history of poor relationships with their mothers were likely to show signs of distress. Religious or cultural attitudes against abortion or sexuality also unfavorably affected outcome, as did marked ambivalence, indecision, and passivity in the process of obtaining the abortion. Women who reported using the rhythm method, contraceptive foam, or no method of birth control showed more guilt and shame than those using a diaphragm, an intrauterine device, or oral contraceptives. Users of less effective contraceptive methods seem more likely to be conflicted about their procreative and sexual activity. Most of these predictors of outcome have been previously suggested from anecdotal evidence.[27,33,34]

Special consideration has been given in the literature to induced abortion in the second trimester of pregnancy. Such abortions carry a significantly greater medical risk and are much more expensive. The procedure presents an opportunity for psychological trauma because the intact fetus, which may occasionally show movements, is often seen by the patient. However, in 1973, 17 percent of abortions were postponed until the second trimester.[12] Obstacles within the health care delivery system may account for up to 25 percent of these delays,[35] but in general women seeking second trimester abortions form a group distinct from abortion seekers in general. They tend to be younger, more often single and nulliparous, and are less likely to have ever used contraception. They appear to be more invested in the pregnancy and tend to speak of a "baby" rather than "fetus," although this finding might reflect the more advanced stage of the pregnancy rather than a characteristic of the woman.[36-39] The psychological outcome of these patients has not been systematically investigated. However, poorer outcome, which is reported anecdotally, would be expected because of their generally more immature coping styles, their increased attachment to the fetus, their greater ambivalence, and the greater trauma of the procedure itself.

In summary, despite considerable confusion due to poor methodology and some bias, tentative conclusions are possible regarding the emotional effect of induced abortion. Major psychiatric sequelae are unusual and occur mainly in those patients with a history of mental illness. Although some women feel mildly depressed or remorseful for a few days following the procedure, most probably respond with little other than relief from the discomfort of an unwanted pregnancy. Certain women, such as those who are more conflicted about the pregnancy, abortion, contraception, procreation, or sexuality appear to have more difficulty. The ease with which a woman deals with these conflicts tends to be correlated with her general coping ability. Those with greater ego strength do better, but even those with limited ego strength are usually able to handle the crisis without apparent adverse effect.

PSYCHIATRIC ASPECTS OF STERILIZATION

Over seven million Americans—16 percent of all married couples—have undergone surgery for the purpose of sterilization. Sterilization is the most common method of fertility control in the United States for married couples over 30 years old.[3] Very little is known, however, about the psychological aspects of such surgery. Miller[40] has suggested that there are three main research questions. First, what are the psychological antecedents—that is, what are the characteristics and motivations of women or couples who seek sterilization? Second, how is the decision made? (Unfortunately, this question has not been investigated, although theoretical models have been suggested.) And finally, what is the effect or psychological outcome?

Little systematic research has been conducted into the motivation for voluntary sterilization. The decision to sterilize is usually viewed as healthy and goes unquestioned. Sterilization seekers are seen as generally stable, confident, independent, sexually adjusted, and anxiety-free people who have a relatively strong desire to avoid further pregnancy and doubt their ability to use other contraceptive methods successfully.[40,41] Although this description seems reasonable, it awaits objective confirmation. Additional unanswered questions concern characteristics of the couple, especially as to which member will undergo the surgery, and of women requesting extreme sterilizing procedures such as a hysterectomy.

Considerable attention has been directed recently to one group of patients, young nulliparous women. (Psychiatric involvement in this area resulted primarily because such women were often routinely referred for psychiatric consultation. As with abortion, psychiatrists were asked to intervene when the primary physician became uncomfortable with allowing a patient to decide her own fate.) Kaltreider[42] compared young nulliparous sterilization seekers to a control group of women who wanted no children, but used conventional contraception. She found that for both groups a combination of intrapsychic and feminist/ gender role issues created the desire to remain childless. Population-control issues had minimal influence. The women in the control group were more ambivalent about childbearing and appeared to want to retain their options. The sterilization seekers were more fearful of the responsibility and loss of freedom accompanying parenthood and were particularly fearful of being bad mothers or of being emotionally changed by a child. Many feared becoming like their own mothers, whom they saw as cold and rejecting. Sixty percent of those seeking sterilization stated they could not stand children, compared to none of the controls. Few had ever thought of themselves as mothers—for example in childhood or adolescent fantasy. Kaltreider concluded that these women's decision to be sterilized was seemingly well reasoned, although psychologically overdetermined.

Lindenmayer[43] studied a number of patients referred for consultation. On the basis of interviews, he found three major motivating dynamics. The fear of responsibility, often resulting from maternal demands for perfection, was prominent. Repressed dependency needs emerged as fear of having someone dependent on them and as conflicts around dependency on men. Finally, many displayed a fear of impulsivity. They felt they could not trust themselves to use conventional contraception properly and had to resort to the more radical control of permanent sterilization.

Nearly all of the published psychiatric research on sterilization deals with outcome. Much of it, however, is difficult to interpret and currently irrelevant. As with the corresponding abortion literature, a better understanding can be obtained from a brief historical review of attitudes, indications, and surgical technique. As recently as 1955, even significant multiparity was not considered an indication or justification for tubal ligation.[44] During the late 1950s and 1960s, when most of the reported studies were performed, multiparity, as defined by the "120 rule," was sufficient. That is, sterilization would be performed if the product of a woman's age and parity was at least 120. Only in this decade has sterilization become truly voluntary. Since most of the outcome research was performed under the old indications, it assessed a population which may no longer be typical. Medical attitudes clearly affect a patient's experience, again limiting the value of older studies. Also, the surgery itself has become much simpler, cheaper, safer, less painful, and less debilitating, thus eliminating some possible causes of poor outcome. Sterilizations performed for "medical" indications, which are associated with more regret, are much less frequent.

The typical outcome study has been a retrospective questionnaire or interview survey, usually asking about regret or satisfaction with the procedures. The weaknesses of these studies have been reviewed by Schwyhart and Kutner[45] and Miller[40] and are similar to those discussed for abortion. Conclusions are often not substantiated by the data. Almost all the designs are retrospective and thus highly sensitive to distortion. A patient may incorrectly attribute any number of changes in his or her life to the operation. Rarely are control groups used. Significant independent variables are often ignored, such as indication, physician and social attitude, counseling (if any), the type of procedure performed, and any concurrent operations. For example, sterilization accompanied by abortion has a much higher regret rate than sterilization alone; yet many studies are confounded by such cases and do not correct for them in their analysis. Sampling techniques have been haphazard and fail to consider these variables. Follow-up periods may be variable. Most studies have a high subject attrition rate. Schwyhart and Kutner[45] showed an inverse relation between the regret rate found by a study and its attrition rate, suggesting that regret may be significantly underestimated.

Outcome criteria have often been vague and difficult to interpret. Rates of "regret" or "satisfaction" are presented without further definition. Regret may easily occur for a variety of reasons, which have rarely been differentially studied, such as the inability to reproduce, problems related to complications of the surgery itself, poor marital or sexual adjustment, or the appearance of symptoms such as guilt or depression. Similarly, terms such as "adverse psychological effects" may range from the presence of minor transient symptoms to the need for psychiatric hospitalization. Only rarely have objective measures of outcome been used or any attempts made at cross-validation. Barglow and Eisner[46] found a four percent regret rate by questionnaire, but a 15 percent rate by interview. Basil[47] reported that 99 percent of vasectomized men reported satisfaction, although as many as 30 percent had developed emotional problems. Finally, the assessment of outcome has been superficial. No attention has been given to possible effects on such things as self-concept, body image, and the nature of social, family, and sexual interactions.

Estimates of general dissatisfaction or regret following voluntary tubal sterilization range from one to 18 percent, but if the problem of subject attrition is considered, it could be as high as 25 percent. Thompson and Baird[48] found a five percent overall regret rate, which rose to eight percent if the procedure occurred in the postpartum period and to 24 percent if sterilization was for medical indications. Sexual problems, generally a lessening of libido, occur in two to 25 percent and marital problems in six to 14 percent. Following tubal ligation, seven to 45 percent of women report menstrual changes, which may be psychologically mediated. When psychiatric symptoms are directly assessed, the results are conflicting. Anywhere from none to over one-third of patients are said to develop new psychiatric symptoms, primarily depression. However, nine out of ten women judged to be depressed or "neurotic" before surgery are improved by the procedure.

Cox and Crozier[49] attempted to uncover correlates of dissatisfaction. They found that women reported feeling regret if they also experienced a worsening of their sex life, emotional problems following the surgery, postoperative dysfunctional bleeding or dysmenorrhea, if they were of high parity, or if the surgery was for medical indications. However, regret was not correlated with preoperative emotional or menstrual problems, subsequent remarriage by the patient, death of a child, or the patient's age. Schwyhart and Kutner's[45] reanalysis of reported studies showed that parity had a small but significant effect. Patients with four or more children had a regret rate of 3.2 percent, while those with less than four had a rate of 7.1 percent. This difference is small enough to have only minor clinical relevance. Furthermore, parity per se may not be the significant variable. Many clinicians instead argue that regret occurs if the desire to mother more children is frustrated, regardless of the number of children already borne. This argument, though untested, would suggest that a nulliparous woman who has never wanted children is at less risk than a grand multiparous who seeks to end her reproductive career for economic reasons, for example. The data from medically indicated sterilizations support this argument.

Miller[40] has pointed out that the literature has a rather negative bias, since it generally assesses regret, dissatisfaction, and deterioration in function. Rarely is consideration given to the benefits of sterilization, such as freedom from fear of pregnancy and greater economic and emotional resources to devote to already existing children. Furthermore, the absence of controlled studies makes comparison of sterilization to its alternatives impossible. We do not know how many women, struggling with an unwanted pregnancy or with the risks of oral contraceptives, regret that they were not previously sterilized.

THE ROLE OF THE CONSULTATION-LIAISON PSYCHIATRIST

The psychiatric consultant cannot and should not decide who should be given access to procedures such as abortion or sterilization. Not only would such a role clearly violate a patient's right of self-determination, but it would also require predictive skills that no one possesses. However, the psychiatrist can still provide some important direction in family-planning services. Lipowski[50] has defined the purpose of the psychiatric consultant as assisting in the achievement and maintenance of the best patient care and the avoidance of maladaptive behavior. These goals can be attained in the family-planning clinic through a variety of interventions: providing traditional direct consultation, assisting the staff in the identification of patients who require consultation or other special interventions, educating the providers to be sensitive to the emotional and psychosocial aspects of their patients and to handle these issues appropriately, assisting the staff in managing their own feelings in response to troubling ethical issues, and performing clinical research into the many still unanswered questions.

Psychiatric consultation in a family-planning clinic is rarely sought except for patients seeking abortion or sterilization. Various explanations are possible. Patients seeking other services may well be psychologically healthier and are certainly being seen at a less stressful time. Psychiatric consultation no doubt also seems less urgent because fertility regulating measures other than abortion and sterilization do not present as troublesome moral and ethical dilemmas for the staff.

Like many such clinics, the UCLA Family Planning Clinic relies heavily on often highly skilled, though nonprofessional, counselors. These counselors provide the primary contact with the patient; the physicians conduct examinations and perform the surgical procedures. A woman requesting abortion or sterilization is seen at length by a counselor, who takes a history, describes the procedure, discusses the decision, and guides her through the system, including, for example, holding her hand during the abortion. The counselor is generally the only staff person who directly attends to the patient's emotional needs.

The counselor's role with patients seeking abortion includes facilitating the decision-making process, lessening the burden of acute stress, preventing adverse sequelae, forestalling recurrent maladaptive behavior such as repeated unwanted pregnancy, promoting emotional growth, and identifying concurrent psychiatric and psychosocial problems. The counselor may use one of two basic approaches, which, although they have similar assumptions, may have very different implications for counseling. The first may be called the motivational approach; it is based on the tenet of dynamic psychiatry that argues a person will benefit from understanding the causes of his or her behavior. If a patient can understand why she became pregnant (with the usually correct assumption that the pregnancy was not "accidental") and why she now wants an abortion, she will be better able to make a rational decision. Having addressed the conflicts and made a free choice, the patient should then be able to undergo the procedure without adverse reaction or regret. Furthermore, her insight should prevent her from engaging in similar maladaptive behavior in the future.[51]

In practice, this approach has several severe limitations. Such insight is virtually impossible to obtain in this setting. A rapid decision must be made in an atmosphere and within a time period hardly conducive to contemplative introspection. Furthermore, it may not even be desirable. The patient is not in continuing psychotherapy, in which she would be able to incorporate the insight in a constructive manner. With the rather limited time available for counseling, or even consultation, such probing for unconscious motivation is more likely to be fruitless or even detrimental and can clearly interfere with other interventions. Most abortion patients are simply unwilling or unable to engage in these efforts, and many are resentful at the suggestion of their responsibility for causing the pregnancy. For others, such inquiries, left incomplete because of the situational constraints, reinforce the guilt from which they are already suffering.

The alternative approach is based on a crisis model.[32,52,53] Although it does not deny the importance of unconscious conflicts, it argues that maximum benefit does not require their uncovering. Instead, the focus is placed on the process by which the crisis of the pregnancy and abortion is handled. Pregnancy often occurs in the struggle around a developmental conflict. With proper management, its termination can help elucidate the conflict and promote growth. For example, adolescent pregnancy is theorized to occur often out of the girl's ambivalence regarding dependency on her parents. The patient may be testing her ability to conceive and identify with her mother, seeking to retain intimate contact with her parents, and also attempting to free herself from her parents and the identity constraints they place on her. By being allowed to take responsibility for her pregnancy and abortion, the patient is aided toward separating from her family and establishing an adult identity. In general, the crisis around an unwanted pregnancy can be seen as an opportunity to develop new adaptive patterns. Payne et al.[32] conclude that "the opportunity to choose or reject abortion and the opportunity to play an active role in resolving this personal crisis promotes successful adjustment and maturation." Free choice is essential, as is strenuously combating a patient's regressive movements toward passivity and increased dependency.

The most effective counseling uses aspects of both approaches. Each patient must be counseled and evaluated in the context of her unique life situation, with attention to her individual intrapsychic and interpersonal milieus. The initial focus of the interview is to encourage the open expression of the feelings attached to the pregnancy and anticipated abortion. Many patients defend themselves with rationalization and intellectualization: "I'm single and would have to work, so it wouldn't be fair to the child." Virtually every patient has some ambivalence, usually quite conscious, which deserves expression in order to lessen subsequent regret, guilt, and sense of loss. Often this requires acknowledgment by the counselor that ambivalence and negative feelings are common. Motivation for and against the abortion is discussed, with attention to any possible coercive influences in the patient's environment. Alternatives are investigated and can be reviewed in detail. Assessment is made of the patient's present coping mechanisms and how she has dealt with similar crises in the past. Motivations behind the pregnancy are rarely explored in depth; however, the counselor may inquire whether the pregnancy is "intended," to give the patient an opening to this area. If the pregnancy is clearly part of an obvious maladaptive pattern, the area will be explored more profoundly. The proposed procedure itself is described, and the possibilities of pain, discomfort, and anxiety are considered. The discussion serves to dispel many misconceptions and is generally reassuring.

Nearly all of the abortions performed at our clinic utilize sedation and a local anesthetic. However, some women specifically request general anesthesia. Our general impression is that these women tend to avoid dealing with their negative feelings about the abortion and thus prefer to remain "unaware" of it. This impression awaits confirmation, however, as does any indication that some women do better with general versus local anesthesia.

The counseling also includes a discussion of contraception and provides an opportunity to evaluate the woman's long-term fertility-related decisions. Throughout the counseling, strong emphasis is placed on the patient's responsibility for the decision making specifically and for her behavior in general.

The counseling frequently reveals significant concurrent problems, which may or may not be related to the pregnancy. Unwanted pregnancy often occurs in the midst of difficulties with a husband or boyfriend. Much of the counseling could be more effectively conducted with the couple than the individual patient. However, our efforts to involve the partner have rarely been successful, despite clear evidence that the couple's problems are influencing the pregnancy and abortion decisions. The counselor also frequently encounters psychopathology that predates the pregnancy, as well as often overwhelming socioeconomic problems.

In our clinic, approximately one-fourth of the patients seeking abortion are referred to a mental health worker. Most of the referrals, however, are not for consultation, but rather for treatment of long-standing minor emotional difficulties or sexual dysfunction. Consultation should be sought, however, for patients who appear to be at higher risk for an adverse reaction, in the presence of acute or severe psychopathology, in cases of multiple induced abortions, and when capacity to consent is questioned. Except where capacity may be impaired, the consultation does not determine whether the patient should be allowed to abort. This decision rests with the patient and the primary physician. If the gynecologist believes that a competent patient, having been informed about the procedure's risks and alternatives, has the capacity to determine her own fate, then the decision rests entirely with the woman.

Certain patients, however, are incompetent to make a reasoned decision about the pregnancy and abortion because of mental retardation, organic brain disease, psychosis, or other mental illness. In order to give an informed consent, a person must be able to understand the information presented regarding the proposed procedure, its risks and alternatives and be capable of using that information to make a decision. She should be able to appreciate the consequences of the anticipated intervention and be able to weigh these in the context of her individual life situation. As the California Supreme Court warned in a case granting minors the right to consent to abortion, the ability of some "competent" individuals, especially young adolescents, to meet the latter standard is questionable since this process requires rather mature cognitive skills and the ability to conceptualize at least a rudimentary life plan.

In most medical practice, competency issues can be handled in a more direct manner. Elective procedures can be deferred until a patient becomes competent or a guardian is appointed. More urgent surgery can be performed either on an emergency basis or following a rapid court determination. Abortion, however, can rarely be said to be medically urgent. Our culture is biased against abortion in that we do not require competency or consent to become pregnant or give birth. Also, unlike most other surgical issues, a decision about abortion is not as clearly slanted toward one alternative: consent is not so much a weighing of risks as a choice between carrying or not carrying a pregnancy, and medical expertise contributes little to that choice. The incompetent pregnant woman thus creates a dilemma. At present, the legal procedures necessary to have a temporary guardian appointed can rarely be completed before the option to abort expires. Yet to deny a patient an abortion because she is incompetent forces her to carry a pregnancy she may not want; she is denied medical care because of her mental state.

Another group who should be referred for consultation are those who present a high risk for adverse psychological sequelae. A history of mental illness, especially suicidal behavior or postpartum psychosis, deserves careful evaluation. Patients with severe ambivalence about the abortion or those unable to reach a decision are especially troublesome. They may take a very passive approach and try to lure the counselor or physician into deciding for them. They will often reveal that abortion is basically abhorrent to them, but they feel they are being forced by circumstances. Recently, one such patient opened her counseling session with the statement, "I have come here to kill my baby." With others, it is clear that the decision has not really been theirs. Frequently, the family, spouse, boyfriend, or physician will coerce the patient, particularly if she feels very dependent on them. These patients should be convinced that the decision must be made by them, that no one can make it for them. Often, suggesting a delay for a week or two allows the patient to consider her decision in a less stressful atmosphere, while being assured that she can still have an abortion if she so desires. The consultant, in supporting the patient's right to decide her own fate, shields her from outside pressures. Most patients are then able to resolve their ambivalence and overcome their passivity.

Also referred for immediate consultation are patients who otherwise appear to be having significant difficulty dealing with the abortion or pregnancy. These include women who evidence severe anxiety, depression, or psychosis; those with excessive denial of feelings; and those who are experiencing extreme interpersonal difficulties. Patients who are medically ill may also need support to help them cope with the acute stress. Patients who are being aborted for medical indications are generally much more attached to the pregnancy and therefore likely to feel a greater loss following abortion. The recent study of Payne et al.[32] also suggests that patients who are single or nulliparous, have had a poor relationship with their mother, or show generally immature interpersonal relationships are at a higher risk and deserve special attention. Certainly these patients should be counseled more carefully, although routine referral does not seem warranted.

A final group who deserve consultation are women who have required multiple induced abortions. Many of these patients appear to be using sexuality in a self-destructive or immature manner and are likely to have serious conflicts about their sexual and reproductive identities. An attempt to uncover these conflicts and explore the maladaptive behavior patterns can prevent repeated unwanted pregnancies.

For many of the patients for whom referral is indicated, the consultation need not be performed before the abortion. Although prior consultation is certainly preferred, it often does not pertain to the decision. For most, the major value appears to be in helping the patient deal with her reaction to the pregnancy and abortion and resolve her crisis in a beneficial, maturing manner. Brief therapy along a crisis-intervention model is useful and should often include the partner of an ongoing relationship. Careful follow-up should be conducted. Scheduling a routine visit for medical follow-up provides an opportunity for another contact with the counselor, who can lend further support as well as assess any adverse reaction requiring psychiatric attention. Patients who evoke particular concern are scheduled for earlier follow-up visits.

The principles of counseling women requesting tubal sterilization are similar to those for patients seeking abortion. The task is not to determine who should or should not be sterilized, but rather to assist the patient in making a truly informed decision. It is essential that she have a clear understanding of what the procedure will accomplish and that any unrealistic expectations be dispelled. Some women, for example, see sterilization as a cure for their pelvic pain, poor marriage, or inability to have orgasm. Although any of these changes could occur, they should not be the motivation. The anecdotes of patients who later regret sterilization are filled with such false expectations. Similarly, a decision for sterilization that arises as an attempt to resolve an acute crisis is probably also ill-advised. Such irrational motivations should be pointed out and thoroughly explored. To detect these motives, the patient must be questioned about the process by which she reached her decision. An assessment of her sexual adjustment and marital stability is also important. The stability of the decision over a period of time suggests good motivation, and our experience supports prior findings that if a waiting period is required prior to surgery, a lower rate of regret is obtained.[54] Because of crowded surgical schedules, elective sterilization is not performed until several months after the initial request. We have found that a significant number of women decide against surgery during that period. Patients who appear to have difficulty maintaining life goals should be particularly cautioned.

The counselor must confirm that the patient understands the impact, meaning, and consequences of the operation, in particular its irreversibility. A device often used to assess this is to ask the patient if she would want additional children if a child died or if she remarried. Although sterilized women usually do not have regret after such events, the question often uncovers ambivalence that needs further consideration. It also aids the patient with one of the tasks of her decision-making process, that is, to fantasize about the outcome. Another area that should be discussed is contraceptive history, particularly to assure that the patient is not choosing sterilization because of ignorance of temporary methods. Patients who express concern about the outcome should be counseled carefully. Fears such as loss of femininity or sexual responsiveness usually reflect ambivalence. Any obvious psychopathology should raise concern, and inquiring about past psychiatric history can be revealing.

The counseling procedure described assures that patients are well informed and well motivated and that most have made very reasonable decisions. However, an occasional patient will require psychiatric consultation. Referral should be made whenever motivation is suspect or more than mild ambivalence is detected, when there is evidence of coercive influence, when significant psychopathology or a history of serious mental illness is noted, or if capacity to consent is questioned. Any sign of unfulfilled maternal desire, regardless of parity, also calls for consultation.

Although some clinicians suggest routine psychiatric referral for young or nulliparous women, we have not found this to be indicated. There is no evidence that such women have a poorer outcome. They should generally be more carefully counseled, but we need not assume that their decision is poorly reasoned. Our experience with these patients, however, does confirm that of others who have found that the desire for sterilization is often based on neurotic influences. For example, because of their own relationships with their mothers, many doubt their ability to be a good mother. Yet sterilization may still be the best course. Although neurotically derived, this self-concept is unlikely to change. The decision may thus be very realistic.[41]

LIAISON FUNCTIONS

Few areas of medicine attract controversy as readily as family-planning. The provision of fertility-regulating services consistently raises issues of moral, religious, legal, and social import and underscores conflict between individual and societal rights. For example, the provision of contraception to minors is becoming an increasingly common practice, reflecting a concern for the problem of unwanted pregnancy in minors, an increasing acceptance of teenage sexual activity, as well as a general trend in medicine toward self-determination. However, those who react with outrage point to a deterioration of the perogative of the parent, a disintegration of the role of the family, an invitation to promiscuous sexuality, and a general decline in the morals of society.

The physician dealing with family-planning is placed in a novel situation. Although medical education gives attention to the prevention of disease and the promotion of health, most medical practice is concerned with curing or alleviating disease. But where is the "disease" in the woman seeking tubal ligation because she does not want to have children? Individual self-determination has not traditionally been valued in medicine. Why should a doctor take a "life" in performing an abortion on a woman who feels a child would interfere with her career, when all his training and values have been to the contrary? These difficulties with fertility-related decisions and behavior affect both the patient and the professional providers and increase the importance of psychiatric input. The patient must deal with these conflicts not only intrapsychically, but also in relation to the attitudes and values of his or her family, friends, and social milieu. Rational decision making in such a charged atmosphere often requires the assistance of staff sensitive to these conflicts.

As in other settings, the liaison psychiatrist in a family-planning clinic serves to improve patient care by maintaining a comprehensive approach, educating staff to be attentive to psychosocial issues, and mediating possibly harmful conflicts among staff members and between staff and patients. Pasnau[55] has pointed out the special problems encountered in liaison with an obstetrics and gynecology service, and these are greatly magnified in family-planning. There is a great need for attention to emotional issues in dealing with problems so closely associated with a patient's sexual and reproductive functions. Gynecologists, however, have rarely been prepared by their training to deal with the psychosocial aspects of their patients' problems. Many display considerable difficulty in understanding or dealing with these issues.[55] Although gynecologists who choose to work in family-planning generally are more attuned to the emotional needs of their patients, they still vary considerably in their interest and sensitivity.

One of the liaison psychiatrist's major contributions is to be a visible and vocal reminder of the importance of psychosocial issues. Counselors report that a psychiatrist serves to validate their role and values. At times they feel at odds with the medical staff, since they tend to see themselves as much more identified with the patients' interests. The physicians, of course, usually see their role as primary. This conflict naturally may generate anger and resentment that interferes with optimum patient care. The medical system may intimidate the counselors, so that tensions remain submerged. The psychiatrist, however, is seen as an ally of the counselors as well as the physician, and his presence may cause a shift in the perceived power structure that allows the conflicts to be more readily discussed and resolved.

Conflicts also arise within individual staff members, and the psychiatrist can often assist in their resolution. Procedures such as abortion can be experienced as antithetical to the purpose of medical practice. Family-planning continually tends to raise disturbing ethical and moral issues with which the staff must deal. McDermott and Char[56] reported that following the repeal of abortion restrictions in Hawaii, the nursing personnel who attended the consequent abortions universally experienced a transient state of anxiety and depression, despite conscious attitudes supporting abortion. Kane et al.[57] similarly found that staff behavior indicated much emotional turmoil. They reported that the physicians tended to rationalize the abortions as benefiting society. Most of the abortions were performed for supposed "psychiatric indications," and the physicians generally stated that they opposed abortion "on demand." Their denial that the indications were merely legal justifications demonstrates their conflict. Nearly all the physicians stated they would prefer not to do abortions if someone else would instead.

The liaison psychiatrist also has an important educational function. Both physicians and counselors can benefit from instruction in such areas as interviewing skills, the recognition of psychopathology, the identification of patients who are at risk for adverse psychological reactions, the appreciation of psychodynamics and interpersonal process, and the psychology of fertility regulation. Recommendations regarding the institutional setting, such as the importance of separating obstetrical and abortion patients and personnel, can also be beneficial. Finally, the liaison psychiatrist can assist with much-needed clinical research. Areas seriously needing investigation include determining the benefit, if any, of various types of counseling; defining the more subtle effects of such procedures as abortion or sterilization on self-image, sexuality, and marital and family relationships; and gaining increased understanding of the factors influencing contraceptive choice and use. In performing these functions, the liaison psychiatrist contributes to the provision of humane and effective family-planning services.

REFERENCES

1. Brody, E.B. Editorial. The psychiatrist and family planning. *Am. J. Psychiat.*, 130: 1173-1174, 1973.
2. Group for the Advancement of Psychiatry, Committee on Preventive Psychiatry. *Humane Reproduction*, Report No. 86. New York:GAP, 1973.
3. Hatcher, R.A., et al. *Contraceptive Technology 1976-77.* New York:Irvington Publishers, 1976.
4. Lebensohn, Z.M. Legal abortion as a positive mental health measure in family planning. *Compr. Psychiat.*, 14:95-98, 1973.
5. Furstenberg, F. The social consequences of teenage parenthood. *Fam. Plan. Perspec.*, 8:148-164, 1976.
6. Raven, C. Testimony in favor of abortion reform, hearing before the Michigan State House Committee on Social Services. *Woman Physician*, 26:584-586, 1971.
7. Forssman, H., and Thuwe, I. One hundred and twenty children born after application for therapeutic abortion refused. *Acta Psychiat. Scand.*, 42:70-87, 1966.
8. Dytrych, Z., et al. Children born to women denied abortion. *Fam. Plan. Dig.*, 3:10, November, 1974.
9. Group for the Advancement of Psychiatry, Committee on Psychiatry and Law. *The Right to Abortion: A Psychiatric View*, Report No. 75. New York:GAP, 1969.
10. Lebensohn, Z.M. Abortion, psychiatry and the quality of life. *Am. J. Psychiat.*, 128: 946-951, 1972.
11. Tietze, C. Bibliography of Fertility Control, 1950-1965, Publication No. 23. New York, National Committee on Maternal Health, 1965.
12. Institute of Medicine. *Legalized Abortion and the Public Health.* Washington, D.C.: National Academy of Sciences, 1975.
13. Bauman, K.E., and Wilson, R.R. Contraceptive practices of white unmarried university students: The significance of four years at one university. *Am. J. Obstet. Gynecol.*, 118:190-194, 1974.
14. Bracken, M.B., et al. Contraceptive practice among New York abortion patients. *Am. J. Obstet. Gynecol.*, 114:967-977, 1972.
15. Smith, E.M. A follow-up study of women who request abortion. *Am. J. Orthopsychiat.*, 43:574-585, 1973.
16. Brody, E.B. Psychocultural aspects of contraceptive behavior in Jamaica. *J. Nerv. Ment. Dis.*, 159:108-119, 1974.
17. Brody, E.B., Ottey, F., and La Grande, J. Couple communication in the contraceptive decision making of Jamaican women. *J. Nerv. Ment. Dis.*, 159:407-412, 1974.
18. Siassi, I. The psychiatrist's role in family planning. *Am. J. Psychiat.*, 129:80-85, 1972.
19. Schaffer, C., and Pine, F. Pregnancy, abortion, and the developmental tasks of adolescence. *J. Am. Acad. Child Psychiat.*, 11:511-536, 1972.
20. Sandberg, E.C. Psychological aspects of contraception. In: *Comprehensive Textbook of Psychiatry*, 2nd Ed., ed. A.M. Freedman, H.I. Kaplan, and B.J. Sadock. Baltimore: Williams & Wilkins, 1975, pp. 1487-1496.
21. Sandberg, E.C., and Jacobs, R.I. Psychology of the misuse and rejection of contraception. *Am. J. Obstet. Gynecol.*, 110:227-242, 1971.

22. Kane, F., et al. Motivational factors in abortion patients. *Am. J. Psychiat.*, 130:290-293, 1973.

23. Taussig, F.J., *Abortion, Spontaneous & Induced*. St. Louis: C.V. Mosby, 1936, as quoted from Simon and Senturia, Ref. 24.

24. Simon, N.M., and Senturia, A.G. Psychiatric sequelae of abortion. *Arch. Gen. Psychiat.*, 15:378-389, 1966.

25. Martin, C.D. Psychological problems of abortion for the unwed teenage girl. *Genetic Psychology Monographs*, 88:23-110, 1973.

26. Jonas, C.H. More victims than one. *Way*, 23:40, 1967.

27. Friedman, C.M., Greenspan, R., and Mittleman, F. The decision-making process and the outcome of therapeutic abortion. *Am. J. Psychiat.*, 131:1332-1337, 1974.

28. Evans, J.R., Selstand, G., and Welcher, W.H. Teenagers: Fertility control behavior and attitudes before and after abortion, childbearing or negative pregnancy test. *Fam. Plan. Perspec.*, 8:192-200, 1976.

29. Ekblad, M. Induced abortion on psychiatric grounds. *Acta Psychiat. Neurol. Scand.*, 99 (Suppl.):1-238, 1955.

30. Levene, H., and Rigney, F. Law, preventive psychiatry and therapeutic abortion. *J. Nerv. Ment. Dis.*, 151:51-59, 1970.

31. Barnes, A., et al. Therapeutic abortion: Medical and social sequels. *Ann. Intern. Med.*, 75:881-886, 1971.

32. Payne, E.C., et al. Outcome following therapeutic abortion. *Arch. Gen. Psychiat.*, 33:725-733, 1976.

33. Marmer, S.S., Pasnau, R.O., and Cushner, I.M. Is psychiatric consultation in abortion obsolete? *Int. J. Psychiat. Med.*, 5:201-209, 1974.

34. Pasnau, R.O. Psychiatric complications of therapeutic abortion. *Obstet. Gynecol.*, 40:252-256, 1972.

35. Koronyi, T., et al. Reasons for delayed abortion: Results of 100 interviews. *Am. J. Obstet. Gynecol.*, 117:299-311, 1973.

36. Bracken, M.B., and Swigar, M.E. Factors associated with delay in seeking induced abortions. *Am. J. Obstet. Gynecol.*, 113:301-309, 1972.

37. Kaltreider, N.B. Psychological factors in mid-trimester abortion. *Psychiat. Med.*, 4:129-134, Spring 1973.

38. Kaltreider, N.B. Emotional patterns related to delay in decision to seek abortion. *Cal. Med.*, 118:23-27, 1973.

39. Mallory, G.B., et al. Factors responsible for delay in obtaining interruption of pregnancy. *Obstet. Gynecol.*, 40:556-562, 1972.

40. Miller, W.B. Psychosocial aspects of contraceptive sterilization. Presented at Conference on Research on the Behavioral Aspects of Surgical Contraception, National Institute for Child Health and Human Development, Betheseda, Md., June 18-19, 1973.

41. Miller, W.B. Assessing patients' motives for requesting sterilization. *Med. Aspects Human Sex.*, 9:99-100, 1975.

42. Kaltreider, N.B. In: Voluntary sterilization: The role of the psychiatrist. Panel at Annual Meeting of the American Psychiatric Association, May 8, 1975.

43. Lindenmayer, J. In: Voluntary sterilization: The role of the psychiatrist. Panel at Annual Meeting of the American Psychiatric Association, May 8, 1975.

44. Prystowsky, H., and Eastman, N.J. Puerperal tubal sterilization: Report of 1,830 cases. *JAMA*, 158:463-467, 1955.

45. Schwyhart, W.R., and Kutner, S.J. A reanalysis of female reactions to contraceptive sterilization. *J. Nerv. Ment. Dis.*, 156:354-370, 1973.

46. Barglow, P., and Eisner, M. An evaluation of tubal ligation in Switzerland. *Am. J. Obstet. Gynecol.*, 95:1083-1094, 1966.

47. Basil, R.E. Reported in: *Clin. Psychiat. News*, 3:8, August, 1975.
48. Thompson, B., and Baird, D. Followup of 186 sterilized women. *Lancet*, 1:1023-1027, 1968.
49. Cox, M.D., and Crozier, I.M. Female sterilization: Long-term follow-up with particular reference to regret (Abs.). *J. Reprod. Fertil.*, 35:624-625, 1973.
50. Lipowski, Z.J. Consultation-liaison psychiatry: Past, present and future. In: *Consultation-Liaison Psychiatry*, ed. R.O. Pasnau. New York: Grune & Stratton, 1975, pp. 1-28.
51. Friedman, C.M. Making abortion consultation therapeutic. *Am. J. Psychiat.*, 130:1257-1261, 1973.
52. Glasser, M.L., and Pasnau, R.O. The unwanted pregnancy in adolescence. *J. Fam. Prac.*, 2:91-94, April, 1975.
53. Perez-Reyes, M.G., and Falk, R. Follow-up after therapeutic abortion in early adolescence. *Arch. Gen. Psychiat.*, 28:120-126, 1973.
54. Adams, T.W. Female sterilization. *Am. J. Obstet. Gynecol.*, 89:395-401, 1964.
55. Pasnau, R.O. Psychiatry and obstetrics-gynecology: Report of a five-year experience in psychiatric liaison. In: *Consultation-Liaison Psychiatry*, ed. R.O. Pasnau. New York:Grune & Stratton, 1975, pp. 135-147.
56. McDermott, J.F., and Char, E.F. Abortion repeal in Hawaii. *Am. J. Orthopsychiat.*, 41:620-626, 1971.
57. Kane, F.J., et al. Emotional reactions in abortion services personnel. *Arch. Gen. Psychiat.*, 28:409-411, 1973.

CHAPTER 12

The Traction Intolerance Syndrome: Psychiatric Complications of Femoral Fractures in Young Adults

NICHOLAS H. PUTNAM
JOEL YAGER

When I meet the morning beam
Or lay me down at night to dream,
I hear my bones within me say,
"Another night, another day."

"Wanderers eastward, wanderers west,
Know you why you cannot rest?
'Tis that every mother's son
Travails with a skeleton.
—A.E. Housman,
The Immortal Part

Surprisingly little has appeared in the recent literature regarding psychiatric problems encountered on an orthopedic service. We have found, however, that common difficulties arise in relation to patients' temporary loss of mobility due to prolonged traction. In particular, young adult patients with fractures of the femur treated with traction experience a high incidence of behavioral and emotional complications. We have referred to this as the "Traction Intolerance Syndrome." This syndrome presents significant difficulties for patients and profes-

159

sional staff and frequently prompts requests for psychiatric consultation and co-management during hospitalization.

Although common sense suggests that accidents are chance events, the consulting psychiatrist on an orthopedic service soon realizes that this is often not the case; the fracture population is probably not a random sample of the general population. Certain types of persons may be more likely to have accidents resulting in fractures, and these persons are likely to react to their hospitalization in characteristic ways. Insurance companies attribute an "accident habit" to these patients, and Freud[1] felt such individuals possess a "traumatophilic diathesis." In her classic work Dunbar[2] reviewed studies suggesting that personality type (in addition to dangerous environment and "chance") was an important determinant of accidents.

Dunbar reported that fracture patients showed few neurotic traits, but did "manifest a jerky, restless type of tension . . . and showed a tendency to hurl themselves into some form of ill-considered activity in situations of particular emotional stress;" she further observed that as a group they displayed little interest in intellectual values or verbalization. Her experience led her to generalize that fracture patients tend to have accidents at points in their lives when their hostility is aroused or when pressure from authority becomes too great. In her view, such patients initially react to an accident by feeling guilty and may feel destructive toward themselves or others; these feelings, however, are rapidly repressed, and patients then become preoccupied with the injury itself.

Thus, similar personality characteristics may contribute both to accident proneness and to the likelihood of psychiatrically troubled recovery. In this regard, fractures of the femur present special problems. While internal surgical fixation is usually employed for older patients with femoral fracture to avoid prolonged traction and the medical and surgical complications common in that age group, prolonged traction is considered the treatment of choice in young persons where the risk of morbidity secondary to immobility is small. Our experience, however, has been that psychiatric morbidity is quite high in young persons with fractured femurs who must undergo prolonged skeletal traction. Femoral fractures in young adults are almost always the result of trauma, and although Dunbar observed that accident-prone patients tend either to actively modify or to escape from their situations rather than keep their anger "bottled up and boiling inside," the physical constraints of traction prevent patients from using these customary characterological defenses. Dunbar also noted that: "By avoiding any marked submission or domination in vocational or social roles, (fracture patients) usually managed to minimize or avoid serious conflicts with authority." In the situation of prolonged skeletal traction, however, the role of patient is unavoidable, and conflicts with authority become inevitable as the patient attempts to negotiate the satisfaction of his many needs.

TRACTION INTOLERANCE SYNDROME

To verify our impression that psychiatric complications are frequent among young patients with fracture of the femur treated with traction, we reviewed all charts of patients aged 16 to 45 years with the diagnosis of fractured femur admitted to the UCLA Orthopedic Service during 1975. Traction Intolerance Syndrome was defined as any behavioral and/or emotional reaction related to skeletal traction severe enough to require psychiatric consultation and/or the use of major psychiatric medication for prolonged periods in the absence of pre-existing major psychiatric illness.

Of the patients in this age group who underwent traction for a period of greater than three weeks, five out of nine fulfilled the criteria for Traction Intolerance Syndrome. More striking, however, was the fact that *all* of the patients who developed Traction Intolerance Syndrome were between 16 and 26 years of age, and *all* of the patients in that age group with fractured femurs who underwent traction for a period of at least three weeks developed severe traction intolerance. Thus, in our series, traction intolerance in late adolescence and early adult life was 100 percent.

The accidents leading to the fractures frequently resulted from reckless driving in automobiles or motorcycles, occasionally under the influence of alcohol or drugs. Past histories of fighting, legal difficulties, and various degrees of substance abuse were not uncommon.

The syndrome was manifested by various patient behaviors: manipulation or removal of traction apparatus; angry threats or attacks against the hospital staff; unauthorized self-medication with alcohol, marijuana, or other self-obtained medication; manipulative behavior surrounding attempts to increase the amount of prescribed pain medication over levels deemed reasonable by the treating staff; depressed mood with sullenness, withdrawal, and feelings of hopelessness; and emotional lability and childlike behavior, including tearfulness, pouting, and obstinate (and sometimes dangerous) noncooperation.

When we first planned to study the psychological reactions of young adults to prolonged traction, we expected to encounter a wide range of coping styles and degrees of psychological disability. One previously described case seemed to respond to minimal intervention:[3]

A patient was suffering from a fractured leg which would not knit. He was afraid his family was suffering while he was in the hospital. This anxiety caused him to lack appetite, thus nutrition was impaired, and therefore the fracture failed to knit. After the patient had been assured that his family was well cared for and happy, he stopped worrying, ate heartily, and his broken bones began to knit [p.649].

We were surprised, however, to find that all our patients were far more trouble-some from the standpoint of the relationship between patient and physician. The following cases are illustrative.

Case 1

A 20-year-old black male sustained a compound comminuted supracondylar fracture of his left femur when, while working as a parking-lot attendant, he pul-led a car into a narrow parking space with his left leg hanging out of the open door. The patient was placed in skeletal traction and on the fourth postoperative day began to complain that his pain medication was ineffective. On the fifth postoperative day, the physician's note read "multiple functional and social complaints." On the eleventh postoperative day, it was noted that "patient per-sists in moving weights and untying knots of traction apparatus."

The following day the physician's note read "more complaints—keeps moving traction, taking weights off ropes, and tying traction apparatus to one another." The patient was receiving morphine, 10 mg. with Vistaril, 50 mg. IM q. 4 h.; Thorazine, 10 mg. p.o. t.i.d.; Dalmane, 30 mg. p.o. q.h.s.; and Valium, 5 mg. p.o. b.i.d. In view of the seriousness of the patient's fracture and the importance of proper treatment, a psychiatric consultation was requested.

The patient gave a history of previous involvement in several accidents and fights, but denied drug abuse or legal difficulties. He said he was not interested in drugs, violence, or "any kind of trouble with the hospital staff." However, he admitted manipulating his traction apparatus and asking visitors to remove weights from it and spent considerable time complaining of the severe pain, the ineffectiveness of the medications prescribed, and his physicians' failure to understand his need for greater pain relief. The liaison psychiatrist recommended that the dosage of Thorazine be increased and began to see the patient several times a week to develop a supportive relationship. The patient agreed to try to omit one dose of pain medication for each 24-hour period, and his need for a greater amount of information and support from the house staff was pointed out to his physician.

Two days following the psychiatric consultation, the traction was readjusted by the orthopedists, without the knowledge of the liaison psychiatrist and with-out any prior discussion with the patient. At this point the patient physically threatened a member of the house staff. He was seen by the chief resident, who noted the patient's desire to file a formal complaint against the hospital and requested further help from the consultant.

As the weeks of traction wore on, the patient became increasingly infantile and demanding. He spoke in a whining tone, complaining of pain and lack of concern on the part of the house staff and of lack of care on the part of his family. He continued to manipulate his traction, although the entire staff, including the psychiatrist, emphasized the possible dire consequences of such interference. One month following the initial psychiatric consultation, the patient was still in traction and complaining of increasing pain at the site of his pin. The patient was seen by the senior orthopedic resident, who noted that the patient's problems included "possible narcotic addiction" and discontinued the patient's Tylenol with codeine, the analgesic he was then receiving. At that time the patient was on Thorazine, 50 mg t.i.d., and 100 mg. q.h.s.; Valium, 5 mg. t.i.d.; Atarax, 50 mg. t.i.d.; and Chloral hydrate, 1 gm. q.h.s. With continued visits by the psychiatrist, however, the patient ceased to threaten the house staff and his attitude improved, partially in response to a new roommate and responsibility for some of his own bandage care. Occupational therapy was instituted and proved helpful; medication was gradually reduced. After approximately 50 days of skeletal traction, the surgical house staff agreed that his mood had begun to improve, and after approximately ten weeks in traction, the patient was placed in a long leg cast and discharged.

Case 2

The patient was a 20-year-old, single white male who sustained a compound fracture of the distal third of the left femur, the middle of the tibia and fibula, and the left os calcis as a result of a motorcycle accident. The severe injury to his left leg was treated with prolonged traction, and five weeks after injury, a below-the-knee amputation was performed because of persistent infection that failed to respond to intensive antibiotic treatment.

Skeletal traction was begun shortly after the amputation. Within a short period of time, the patient began to express increasing anger toward the hospital staff, and three weeks following the amputation the orthopedic staff noted that he "demonstrated virtually no capacity to effectively deal with either pain or stress." He demanded increasing amounts of pain medication, while at the same time he manipulated the traction in such a way as to subvert treatment. He refused to cooperate with nurses in his care and expressed considerable anger toward the staff. Intensive efforts by nursing personnel, including a nursing student who worked nearly full time with the patient, were unsuccessful in obtaining his cooperation for back care to prevent bed sores. His anger culminated in an episode in which he threw an alcohol bottle at a nurse. A psychiatric consultation was requested because the patient's poor cooperation impeded treatment.

Psychiatric evaluation revealed that the patient was preoccupied with the pain of the healing fracture. Strikingly, the patient showed little reaction to his amputation. He was mildly depressed, but mainly appeared angry and constantly complained about pain. Queried about his feelings regarding the amputation, the patient stated, "That really doesn't bother me . . . what really bothers me is the traction pressing in my crotch." He asked repeatedly whether the psychiatrist would be able to obtain more pain medication for him.

The patient had changed his life style over the several years preceding his accident when, according to his mother, he began "spending time with the wrong kind of people." The patient saw a psychiatrist for one previous visit in relation to minor drug abuse. It was the consultant's impression that the patient had major personality problems which predated his accident.

One week after the initial consultation, an emergency psychiatric consultation was called when the staff's manipulation of the traction apparatus caused him to complain of severe pain. The consultant recommended that Thorazine, 50 mg. p.o. or 25 mg. IM q. 4 h. p.r.n. for severe agitation be added to his medication and that the staff not withhold pain medication that would normally be given to a more cooperative patient. The surgical house staff and psychiatric consultant differed in this regard: the surgical house staff felt that 14 weeks of medication put the patient at risk for narcotic addiction. On the other hand, the liaison psychiatrist suggested that 14 weeks of medication might have resulted in an increased tolerance and that therefore further pain medication should not be withheld during periods of traction manipulation. It was decided to give the patient additional pain medication.

Although the fractured bones were noted to be in fair alignment, the surgical house staff questioned whether the patient could psychologically tolerate two more months of traction necessary for adequate healing to take place. Psychiatric consultation was again requested as part of a review to consider the possibility of surgical internal fixation. Although internal fixation would have greatly reduced the patient's hospital course, it also carried a five to ten percent risk of further infection and possibly higher amputation. The decision was made to continue traction and forgo surgery, and frequent psychiatric visits continued. A medication regimen that included Mellaril, 25 mg. b.i.d. and 50 mg. q.h.s.; Chloral hydrate, 500 mg q.h.s.; and Valium, 10 mg. t.i.d., was initiated. This combination appeared to have a significant calming effect on the patient without producing excessive sedation. His response was good, and he was ultimately discharged without further surgery.

Case 3

After being run off the freeway on his motorcycle, this 26-year-old white male orthopedic technician sustained a right femoral fracture, a fractured right humerus, and a right upper extremity nerve palsy to the deltoid, latissimus dorsi, and infraspinatus muscles. He was treated with skeletal traction. One month following admission a request for psychiatric consultation was precipitated by the patient's telling a nurse that he might have to use a knife or a gun to show the doctors how angry he was, and indeed, a knife was found in his closet. His anger was particularly provoked by an incident in which his traction slipped.

He felt that no one was interested in his opinion on his care in spite of his background as an orthopedic technician. He also felt overwhelmed by a variety of personal problems and noted that he was unable to do much about these while in traction. The main theme of the consultation was his despair over being in a position of dependency. He stated that he took great pride in being "a man of action," and although he preferred to solve his problems with words, he was not above violence. He denied a criminal record, but admitted to the "recreational" use of various drugs. While in the army he had once been seen by a psychiatrist because of "authority problems" and used that relationship to obtain an early discharge. He was eager to talk, friendly, and requested additional visits with the psychiatrist.

The consultant saw the patient three times a week in individual sessions. During these sessions, the patient ventilated feelings of helplessness, was occasionally tearful, and spent considerable time discussing prior situations that had elicited similar feelings. Valium, 10 mg. q. 4 to 6 hours, was prescribed, and the consultant strongly recommended that the attending physicians make brief daily personal contact, even if limited to a few minutes.

The patient occasionally acted out by consuming alcohol brought to him by his friends. In addition, toward the end of his second month in traction, he began to refuse venipuncture necessary for regulation of anticoagulant medication. After this man's need to have control over some aspect of his treatment was pointed out to him, and the importance of a proper dose of anticoagulant was explained, his cooperation improved.

With continued psychotherapy, the patient made no more threats against the staff. As the weeks in traction wore on, the patient began to have increasing anxiety regarding his impending marriage and fewer concerns about his prolonged traction. Subsequent psychotherapy dealt with family issues, and one session included his fiancée. The remainder of his course was uneventful, and at discharge he stated that he had benefited greatly from his contact with the psychiatrist.

Case 4

Although males in this age group are more likely to sustain injuries resulting in prolonged traction, the only female in our group of patients to sustain such an injury and undergo prolonged traction also developed the Traction Intolerance Syndrome. She was a 25-year-old white female referred to the psychiatrist by the attending physician because of multiple complaints of pain "related to psychological processes, mainly." After one month of treatment the attending physicians debated the merits of continued traction versus pinning. The orthopedists felt that continued traction would be undesirable "because of the patient's hysterical personality." However, although psychiatric consultation was requested, the patient was transferred to a nursing care facility before the consultation could be carried out.

PATHOGENESIS

It is our impression that factors contributing to the pathogenesis of the Traction Intolerance Syndrome lie within the patient, his family, and the treatment setting.

Patient Factors

As discussed above, certain personality types may be more likely to share common patterns of reaction to their plight. The physical constraints of traction prevent patients from using their usual coping behaviors, such as active modification or avoidance of unpleasant situations. Authority conflicts frequently occur in the course of patients' attempts to obtain satisfaction of their needs, including pain relief.

Patients with Traction Intolerance Syndrome typically demonstrate the cognitive coping style Lipowski[4] refers to as *minimization.* They ignore, deny, or rationalize the personal significance of their fractures. Along with minimization these patients adopt the behavioral style of *avoidance.* Lipowski feels such behavior, consisting of "active attempts to get away from the exigencies of illness," is "often observed among individuals for whom acceptance of the sick role signifies a severe threat to their self-image as independent, masculine or invulnerable." Patients with traction intolerance actively modify or avoid their treatment by removing parts of the traction apparatus, or when placed in a cast, they may engage in weight-bearing activities before being advised to do so. Such patients also actively seek a premature end to traction, often requesting internal fixation despite its greater risks, which they minimize or deny. The commonly observed "fight or flight" attitude appears as excessive hostility and/or excessive helplessness and dependency. Although the fracture itself may not be consciously experienced as serious by the patient, displaced anger may be directed toward the traction apparatus and attending staff. Patients with traction intolerance have a difficult time finding a middle ground that Chodoff[5] calls "insightful acceptance" of their predicament.

Family Factors

While the patient is in the hospital, ongoing interactions between the patient, his family, and other important figures may be important determinants of the patient's illness behavior. Overtly or covertly, intentionally or unintentionally, these important figures may induce or provoke maladaptive behavior on the part of the patient, such as excessive regression or, conversely, hypermasculine denial. Such figures may contribute to the patient's conflicts by constantly discussing how the patient's absence and inability to perform usual role functions—as breadwinner, emotional support giver, lover, and so on—create hardships for those who depend on him, and they may imply that other substitutes will have to be found. At times, family or friends may provide the patient with illicit drugs or alcohol. Family members whose lives are complicated by the patient's injury and prolonged absence may at some level hold the patient responsible for the accident. One patient's hospital course was complicated by his family's relative indifference to his predicament; they eventually spent his disability check on recreational activities while he remained tied to the traction apparatus.

Staff Factors

The staff caring for such patients may also contribute to the occurrence of traction intolerance. While surgical house staff may prefer active interventions that can bring about dramatic and rapid cure, the treatment of choice for young patients with severely fractured femurs does not include such active intervention, and the patient's course is often long and troublesome for all concerned. As these patients become more demanding, the surgical staff may become increasingly frustrated or lose interest and spend progressively less time with the patient, contributing to the likelihood of mutual misunderstanding and hostility. The surgeon's relationship to the patient may begin to revolve around the prescription of analgesics, the periodic and sometimes painful adjustment of the traction apparatus, and discussions of "how much longer" the patient's traction will last. As will be further discussed, when physicians are suspicious of patients' attempts to control their own treatment—for example, in dictating doses of medication and tranquilizers—they may inadvertently undertreat patients with these medications. The nursing staff may mediate between the patient and physician, and often it is the nursing staff that encourages the physician to request psychiatric consultation for the patient.

TREATMENT

The consulting psychiatrist can contribute in several different ways to the management of the Traction Intolerance Syndrome. As Miller[6] points out, psychiatric intervention can occur on biological, psychological, and social levels.

Biological Intervention

The psychiatrist can advise the surgical house staff on the proper use of analgesic and psychotropic medications. Marks and Sachar[7] have shown that undertreatment of medical inpatients with narcotic analgesics is common, and our experience suggests that this is true on the orthopedic service. Golden,[8] writing about the problems surgeons face in dealing with chronic pain in their patients, notes that physicians are extremely uneasy about prescribing narcotics to patients who demand them. The physician's fears of contributing to a tendency toward addiction often seem to overwhelm all other considerations, including the presence of severe pain over a period of weeks. This holds despite the fact that few patients who become addicted in the course of medical treatment remain addicted when the pain is eased or cured. In cases of Traction Intolerance Syndrome, we have observed analgesics being withheld because the orthopedic staff feared that the patient might become addicted. Often, however, especially during the manipulation of the fracture site to obtain a better alignment, the patient may need a larger than usual dose of analgesic. Phenothiazines should be prescribed cautiously. However, they are quite useful with extremely agitated patients and should be given in adequate doses. Phenothiazines can also be an important component in pain management. By combining phenothiazines and analgesics for pain control and allowing the patient to manipulate the dose of the phenothiazine within a safe range, the house staff can give the patient some autonomy over medication while weaning him from analgesics. For example, the dose of analgesic may be kept constant, while the patient is allowed to decide if he wants an h.s. dose of Thorazine, or Thorazine 25 to 50 mg. p.o. q. two, four, or six hours. Benzodiazepines can at times be substituted for phenothiazines, and other classes of medications such as the ataractics can also be used.

Psychological Intervention

On the psychological level, the liaison psychiatrist has much to offer. The orthopedic staff is often unable to spend the amount of time with the patient necessary for optimal psychological support, and most patients with Traction Intolerance Syndrome are eager to talk about their condition. Stein et al.[9] point out that syndromes of psychological reactions to physical injury lend themselves particularly well to brief psychotherapy and note that the therapist should pay attention to common themes in the patient's reactions to illness. These themes occur frequently in traction patients. The first theme utilizes denial as a primary defense ("minimization"). In many femoral fracture patients, despite repeated explanations, the seriousness of the injury is denied or minimized. A major fracture, with possible complications of chronic infection and amputation, may be felt to be merely another "broken bone." The patient may then complain loudly about the rigors of the treatment. Often it falls to the psychiatrist to introduce reality to the patient's denial. The patient may gradually be able to become more aware of the extent of his injury and that insight may lead to better acceptance of the necessities of treatment.

The patient in prolonged traction resents the insult to his physical integrity and often displaces his angry feelings onto his own family or the treating staff. This quickly arouses negative counterfeelings and disrupts the supportive relationships the patient desperately needs. By making appropriate connection between the injury and the patient's experiences of emotional disturbance, the psychiatrist can direct the patient toward a more appropriate expression of his feelings.

Finally, the patient in prolonged skeletal traction may have *cognitive* misconceptions about important aspects of his injury and treatment. By reviewing some of the basic principles of orthopedics and discussing and correcting the patient's misconceptions, the liaison psychiatrist may help the patient become less resistant to procedures which are often quite awesome and mysterious. Some patients on anticoagulant therapy have no idea why it is necessary frequently to draw early morning blood samples while the anticoagulant dosage is being adjusted. One of our patients occasionally "cheeked" his anticoagulant medication to "fool" the house staff, a dangerous practice which he discontinued when the psychiatric consultant advised him of the perils of receiving too much or too little anticoagulant. (It is interesting to note that the patients often confide their antics only to the psychiatrist.)

A full and open discussion with the patient of the facts of his condition, often including viewing the x-rays, can be very helpful, but must be done with discretion and with the close cooperation of the orthopedist. Naturally, the surgical house staff themselves are in an ideal position to clarify misconceptions held by the patient, and the liaison psychiatrist should in every instance encourage them to do so. However, this kind of communication often does not take place, partly because of time constraints on the house staff and partly because the physician-patient relationship can become so disturbed that clear exchange of information cannot take place.

Social Intervention

On the social level, the consulting psychiatrist can influence both the family and the hospital staff.

Family Intervention

Conjoint family meetings with the patient and family may provide the consultant with an opportunity to observe, assess, and intervene in pathogenic transactions that abet the syndrome. The family's misconceptions about the nature of the injury and course of treatment may be corrected and the family given an opportunity to have its questions answered. Aspects of the patient's condition may then be seen as appropriately serious by the family, and this may reduce some of the pressure on the patient. Also, interviews with family members apart from the patient and social service attention to ongoing life problems outside the hospital may help ease tension between the patient and family and in turn diminish the patient conflicts that generate the syndrome. Such work with patient and family may naturally continue after discharge from the hospital.

Staff Intervention

By the time the psychiatrist is called to see the patient, the patient may have alienated many of the hospital personnel. A discussion with the medical and nursing staff of the relevant dynamics of the case can result in their reapproaching the patient and incorporating renewed concern for his emotional well-being into the overall care plan.

The patient-physician dyad is frequently disturbed in such situations, and the consultation request may primarily reflect the orthopedist's anger and frustration with the patient. Occasionally, the patient may be told, "I think you'd better have a talk with a psychiatrist," in an admonishing tone that conveys displeasure, moral judgment, and the need for behavior control. The psychiatrist needs to hear the patient's ideas about why the referral was made and then realistically label the request for help as an act of concern for the patient by the orthopedist. If nurses, physical and occupational therapists, and volunteers can spend time with the patients suffering from traction intolerance, the psychiatrist is greatly aided in his task.

Finally, our finding that psychiatric morbidity in young persons undergoing skeletal traction for treatment of fractured femurs is high (100 percent in our series) should be underscored. This observation, if corroborated at other medical centers, may have implications for the use of skeletal traction in the young adult age group. As the Traction Intolerance Syndrome becomes better understood, the liaison psychiatrist may be able to help the orthopedic surgeon weigh the psychological and medical risk factors in a given case so that the best treatment decision concerning either prolonged traction or internal surgical fixation can be made.

REFERENCES

1. Freud, S. Quoted in Dunbar, F. *Psychosomatic Diagnosis.* New York:Hoeber, 1943.
2. Dunbar, F. *Psychosomatic Diagnosis.* New York: Hoeber, 1943.
3. A Case History of R. Cabot's. Quoted in Dunbar, F. *Emotions and Bodily Changes.* New York:Columbia University Press, 1954.
4. Lipowsky, Z.J. Physical illness, the individual, and the coping process. *Psychiat. Med.,* 1:91-102, 1970.
5. Chodoff, P. Understanding and management of the chronically ill patient. *Am. Prac.,* 14:136-144, 1962.
6. Miller, W. Psychiatric consultation. Part I. A general systems approach. *Psychiat. Med.,* 4:135-145, 1973.

7. Marks, R., and Sachar, E. Undertreatment of medical patients with narcotic analgesics. *Ann. Intern. Med.,* 78:173-188, 1971.
8. Golden, J. The surgeon and the psychiatrist: Special problems in psychiatric liaison. In: *Consultation-Liaison Psychiatry,* ed. R.O. Pasnau. New York:Grune & Stratton, 1975, pp. 123-133.
9. Stein, E.H., et al. Brief psychotherapy of psychiatric reactions to physical illness. *Am. J. Psychiat.,* 125:1040-1047, 1969.

This article is printed with revisions by permission of the Baywood Publishing Company. A slightly altered version of this material appears in Volume 8 Number 2 of the International Journal of Psychiatry in Medicine.

CHAPTER 13

Endocrines In or And Depression

JEFFERY N. WILKINS

> Both men and ships live in an unstable element.
>
> Joseph Conrad,
> *The Mirror of the Sea*

The primary objective of this chapter is to discuss the relationship between thyroid hormone and endogenouslike depression in man. Unless otherwise indicated, the term *depression* will refer to endogenouslike depression, which is characterized by feelings of guilt, hopelessness, helplessness, agitation, worry, somatic preoccupation, and vegetative signs, none of which is attributable to some life experience. A case history of a patient with hypothyroidism and clinical depression will be presented; this will be preceded by a consideration of four questions which will serve to review the literature on thyroid hormone, note the role of endocrines in depression, and help define a pathophysiological mechanism to understand the development of depression in patients with hypothyroidism. This chapter will also underscore the importance of a close working relationship between the medical and psychiatric services.

Question One. What is known about the central nervous system (CNS) need for thyroid hormone, and pathophysiologically how could inadequate brain tissue levels of thyroid hormone play a role in the etiology or manifestation of depression?

Question Two. What is the significance of the subjective memory complaints and new learning deficits in hypothyroid patients? Can these subjective complaints be explained by depression?

We shall discuss questions one and two together. Hypothyroidism in the adult has been reported to disrupt mental function and sometimes produce clinical depression.[1-3] Pathophysiological mechanisms for these symptoms are as yet unclear, and most of the research on the CNS need for thyroid hormone has centered on studies of the maturing brain and cretinism. In the immature brain, thyroid hormone has its predominant effect on microsomal protein synthesis, as shown in work with intact animals[4] and in vitro;[5] these effects are not demonstrable in mature brains. On the basis of studies on immature brains, Sokoloff and his colleagues at the National Institute of Mental Health believe that thyroid hormone controls microsomal protein synthesis through direct effects on the mitochondrion[6] in generating RNA translation, increase in nuclear RNA polymerase activity, enhanced synthesis of ribosomal RNA, and eventually in a rise in the number of functional ribosomes in the cell.[7]

It is conceivable that in the mature brain, thyroid hormone has an effect on protein synthesis, but not as great an effect as in the immature brain. Such influence may not be measurable by conventional techniques; yet over a prolonged period of time inadequate tissue levels of thyroid hormone may produce deleterious effects on brain function. Chronically compromised CNS protein synthesis may alter the amounts of available neurotransmitters at the interneuronal synapse, resulting in clinical depression; this hypothesis is congruent with the catecholamine and indeoleamine theories[8] of depression.

Even more likely is that interference with CNS-RNA-controlled protein synthesis could result in impairment of memory consolidation. Data on protein synthesis and memory come from studies using protein-synthesis blockers and RNA precursor uptake. Cohen and Barondes[9] have reported that acetoxycycloheximide, a protein-synthesis blocker that does not interfere with intercerebral electrical activity, significantly impairs long-term memory in the rat. Further, Zemp et al.[10] report an increase in the incorporation of radioactive uridine into RNA in the brains (specifically the diencephalon, hippocampus, and parts of the basal ganglia) of trained mice versus control mice; no increase was found in other tissues such as the liver or kidney.

In keeping with this hypothesis, Whybrow and Hurwitz[11] describe significant effects of hypothyroidism on affect and cognition. In seven patients with confirmed hypothyroidism and ten with hyperthyroidism, they measured responses on a variety of psychometric tests, including performance tests. They used the Clyde Mood Scale, Porteus Maze Test, Trailmaking Test of Reitan, Minnesota Multiphasic Personality Inventory (MMPI), and Brief Psychiatric Rating Scale (BRPS), in addition to clinical interviews. They found that hypothyroid patients predominantly manifested marked depression of mood. Both hyper- and hypothyroid patients manifested disturbances of recent memory. The disturbance in cognition as measured by the Trailmaking Test of Reitan was more profound in the hypothyroid group. Six of the seven hypothyroid patients noticed deterioration of recent memory and difficulty in concentration. Their results fell within the range considered by Reitan to be evidence of brain damage. With establishment of euthyroidism the hyperthyroid patients returned to normal cognitive functioning; however, the hypothyroid patients had a residual cognitive deficit.

It should be noted, though, that euthyroid patients with endogenouslike depression may also manifest impaired memory. Walton[12] has reported that depressed patients achieved lower scores on the Wechsler Memory Test, and most recently, Steinberg and Jarvik[13] report on a study of memory function in 26 endogenously depressed patients versus 26 matched controls. Before medication the depressed patients had a significantly decreased mean score for immediate reproduction and mean computed registration score on all of the memory tests used.

Therefore, hypothyroidism appears to significantly alter cognitive functioning; depression may adversely affect memory, but further study is warranted here. If hypothyroidism and depression coexist, as in the case study, the cognitive impairments due to hypothyroidism will likely predominate and continue to exist long after establishment of chemical euthyroidism.

Question Three. Currently, how are (a) thyrotropin-releasing hormone (TRH) and (b) combined administration of triiodothyronine (T_3) and tricyclic antidepressant medications used in the treatment of depression?

The hypothalamic thyroid axis involves the action of the tripeptide TRH on the anterior pituitary, which releases thyroid-stimulating hormone (TSH), which in turn effects the release of thyroxine (T_4) and T_3 from the thyroid gland. Following the laboratory synthesis of TRH, there were initial encouraging reports[14,15] in its clinical utilization for treatment of depression. However, subsequent controlled studies by a variety of investigators failed to substantiate these earlier claims. Most recently, Hollister et al.[16] have reported that some depressed patients have a blunted TSH response to TRH, and this finding may eventually be of some diagnostic value.

Whybrow et al.[17] have reported on the synergistic effect of T_3 or TSH plus imipramine or amitriptyline in relieving depression. In 1969 Prange et al. began their work with T_3 and antidepressants in selected patients using the Hamilton Rating Scale for Depression and Self-Rating Depression Scale for evaluation purposes. In two studies[18] they treated female patients with endogenous depression and females with heterogenous depression, respectively. In both studies the group receiving T_3 plus imipramine achieved remission in approximately half the time required for the patients receiving placebo plus imipramine.

Hence, in treating endogenous depression, concurrent use of T_3 and tricyclics may hold clinical promise. TRH has not borne out earlier expectations.

Question Four. What consistent endocrine changes have been found in patients with depression?

To answer question four, it is necessary to understand alterations in hormone secretion patterns as reflections of disrupted CNS-mediated biological rhythms. Hormone release from the anterior pituitary and adrenal cortex is largely controlled through CNS-endocrine gland axes acting predominantly through hypothalamic releasing and inhibiting peptides. In man, andrenocorticotrophic hormone (ACTH) follows a circadian diurnal pattern of release; growth hormone (HGH) is largely released during sleep stages III and IV; prolactin, follicle-stimulating hormone (FSH), and luteinizing hormone (LH) also appear to follow circadian patterns. The hypothalamus plays an integral role in the instinctive behaviors of eating, drinking, aggression, and sexuality. Symptoms such as sleep disturbance, anorexia, and loss of sexual drive in endogenous depression are likely due to disruption of hypothalamic mechanisms; such disruptions should be reflected in altered patterns of hormone release.

The most extensively studied endocrine axis in endogenous depression is the hypothalamic-pituitary-adrenalcortical (HPA) axis. Studies have focused on cortisol metabolism, tissue levels of cortisol, the regulatory mechanisms of cortisol secretion, and the cortisol response to dexamethasone.

A consistent finding reported by many clinical investigators is the elevated production rate of cortisol in almost all patients suffering from depression.[19] In a recent study[20] of six depressed patients, the mean cortisol production rate was 30.1 mg./day, which fell to a mean of 19.7 mg./day on recovery; eight control subjects, on the other hand, had a mean production rate of 17.2 mg./day.

From a variety of findings, including elevated plasma-free and total cortisol, normal plasma corticosteroid-binding globulin (CBG) capacity, elevated cerebrospinal fluid cortisol, and elevated urinary-free cortisol excretion, it appears that depressed patients show a significant increase in tissue and CNS levels of active cortisol. It is interesting to compare such increases with the more extreme elevation in Cushing's disease, in which depression is a common clinical event.

The finding of inadequate suppression of cortisol by dexamethasone in a high percentage of depressed patients may eventually serve as an aid in diagnosis and prognosis of clinical depression.[21] The suppression response is generally evaluated by measuring the 9:00 A.M. plasma cortisol following dexamethasone administration the previous midnight. Recently, Carroll et al.[22] have reported that when cortisol levels were measured every 20 minutes for 24 hours following dexamethasone administration, 19 of 28 depressed patients with definite histories of recurrent episodes had at least one abnormal cortisol value.

Langer et al.[23] have recently reported on human growth hormone (HGH) response to a single intravenous administration of amphetamine sulfate (0.1 mg./kg.) in control subjects and in patients diagnosed as having reactive depression, endogenous depression, schizophrenia, and chronic alcoholism. All of the patients were tested during overt manifestations of their disease. Peak levels of HGH were obtained between 30 and 60 minutes following the intravenous amphetamine injection. Compared with the control subjects, endogenously depressed patients released significantly less HGH ($p < .01$) and patients with depression significantly more HGH ($p < 0.5$). Human growth hormone response to intravenous amphetamine in the patients with schizophrenia and chronic alcoholism did not significantly differ from the control subjects.

Considering both hypothyroidism and depression, it should be noted that diminished growth hormone secretion can result from hypothyroidism alone. Hypothyroid patients have been found to have depressed growth hormone release;[24] and pituitary and in vitro studies of rats with induced hypothyroidism demonstrate marked reductions of synthesis and release of growth hormone.[25]

In sum, the loss of the normal diurnal pattern of the HPA axis and the diminished output of growth hormone to amphetamine challenge may reflect a hypothalamic disturbance in depression. As studies progress, altered circadian secretory patterns of growth hormone, prolactin, ACTH, and possibly LH and FSH are likely to be found in patients with depression.

CASE REPORT

The following case history describes clinical hypothyroidism and depression and considers their etiology.

V.S. was a 69-year-old, right-handed, white, male truck loader and driver of Mediterranean descent, with a chief complaint of a two-year history of profound progressive muscular weakness and cramps and intermittent pressure (not headache) in the occipital-cervical region of the skull associated with dizziness and "cloudy" sensorium. About ten years ago the patient experienced the insidious onset of extremity and low-back muscular "aches" which worsened with exercise. Accompanying the pain was progressive weakness, which led to decreased physical ability at work and around the home. His private physician treated him episodically for these symptoms with calcium injections; the patient continued his work as a truck loader and driver.

Four years ago the patient noted difficulty with memory, primarily for recent events. About a year later V.S. described a sudden onset of numbness along his right thigh lasting three or four months. In addition, he experienced low-back pain and dragging of his left foot. V.S. was referred to a neurosurgeon, who diagnosed chronic low-back pain, dysesthesias secondary to neuralgia paresthetica, left-foot drop, and a memory deficit for placement of objects and planned activities. An EMG was found to be abnormal with diffuse positive sharp waves, fibrillation potentials, and neuropathic polyphasic potentials, especially throughout the right leg.

Progressive muscular weakness continued until the patient required other workers to help load his truck, though he continued to work by "pushing himself." In addition, at this time he noted the onset of "spells" of pressure originating in the left upper cervical region and extending into the left side of his skull.

He described an occasional clouding of his sensorium and vision and slowing and slurring of his speech. These spells occurred almost always on rising and lasted from five minutes to hours. He denied any aura, seizure phenomena, or amnesia.

V.S. admitted cold intolerance at this time, drying and coarseness of his skin, and loss of body hair, though these were not of major concern to him. One year ago he developed chronic early morning awakening. During these times he would "worry" about his physical condition and brood that he might have a fatal disease. In addition, he described guilt about not being able to perform well at work or at home; he began to wonder if his wife or boss thought him to be lazy. He developed anorexia and episodic constipation, and his weight dropped from 190 to 160 pounds during this year, with a significant loss of muscle bulk.

Finally, V.S. accrued a month's vacation and left work, feeling he could no longer function. His physician, concerned about the possibility of a brain tumor, arranged for an EMI scan, which was negative. At this point, the patient presented to the Veterans Administration Hospital.

He was initially evaluated medically and subsequently transferred to the psychiatric facility because of marked depression; there he received a two-week course of increasing doses of amitriptyline to 200 mgs. q.d. Because of his peripheral neurological findings and continued complaints of head pressure, Neurology was asked to evaluate him.

Medical and Family History

V.S. had no history of serious illnesses or hospitalizations. He denied familial endocrinopathies. He reported no allergies, took no medications, drank two to three ounces of hard liquor a day, and smoked a pack of cigarettes daily. His father had died in a mental hospital of tertiary syphilis when V.S. was in his late twenties.

Physical Examination

Height 5'11", weight 159 lbs. Temperature 98°F, pulse 80, blood pressure 120/80, and respirations 15. V.S. appeared his stated age, with slowness and slight slurring of speech and depressed facies. His skin was dry with no evidence of perspiration; he was balding over the top of his head. The left lobe of the thyroid was palpable and estimated at 25 grams with no nodules or bruits. The remainder of the examination, except for the neurological, was unremarkable.

Neurologically, he was slow to respond; the deep tendon reflexes were diminished and slightly asymmetric; no ankle jerks were present; plantar reflexes were down bilaterally. He had weak intrinsic hand muscles, and his left foot was weak to dorsiflexion. V.S. had difficulty rising from a sitting position and poor balance. There was bilateral muscle wasting of the bicep, tricep, deltoid and quadricep muscle groups.

He looked depressed and sad, was fully oriented with a clear sensorium, but was slow to respond. There was no evidence of a thought disorder; speech patterns and content were normal. There were no delusions or hallucinations, though he did focus on somatic complaints and dread of a fatal disease. Insight, judgment, general knowledge, and recent and remote memory were grossly intact, though he complained of poor recall for recent events.

Psychometrics

The patient was administered the Wechsler Adult Intelligence Scale, the Wechsler Memory Scale, the Minnesota Multiphasic Personality Inventory, the Graham-Kendall, and the Halstead-Reitan Neuropsychological Test Battery and Semmes-Teuber Spatial Orientation Test.

MMPI: The 278 profile was consistent with extreme depression. In addition to subjective unhappiness, the patient's response pattern indicated psychomotor retardation, somatic concerns, mental dullness, brooding, and apathy. He believed that many of his personal assets and abilities were diminishing and that he was unable to do anything about these losses. Despite these findings, his reality testing and psychological supports were apparently intact.

WAIS: The results indicated a disparity between the Verbal score of 124 and the Performance score of 104, with the Full Scale result being 116. On the Verbal tests, the patient demonstrated an ability to comprehend, conceptualize, generalize, and manipulate verbal material quite well. His memory was above average for his age, but slightly below his other verbal abilities. On the Performance tasks, all of which were in the average range, the patient was less able to synthesize or to unite the components of a task into a coherent whole. His ability to learn new material also appeared to be impaired in comparison with other cognitive abilities.

Wechsler Memory Scale: The patient achieved an average overall score on the WMS. His memory for visual material was adequate or good, but there was a very slight tendency to perseverate, which is sometimes an indicator of organic dysfunction. His memory for logical verbal material presented as a short story was quite poor, which was consistent with his inability to deal with material that is best organized into a whole. He showed some ability for new learning, but not nearly what would be expected from a person of his intelligence.

Graham-Kendall: The Graham-Kendall was slightly abnormal, again raising some question of a brain lesion. Like the memory scale, it showed a very slight tendency to perseverate. Also, as he had on the WAIS, he approached the task in an analytical, piece-by-piece manner, instead of conceptualizing it as an integrated entity.

Halstead-Reitan Neuropsychological Test Battery; Semmes-Teuber Spatial Orientation Test: No aphasia, agnosia, or motor incoordination were noted. Conceptual ability and spatial orientation were poor but marginally acceptable.

He displayed an interesting deficit: when he was blindfolded his preferred-hand (right) performance was very poor; his left-hand performance was adequate; with both hands his performance completely deteriorated. The information gained by his left hand was apparently not communicated to the right.

In summary, the psychometric data revealed a profound disturbance of affect and more subtle cognitive defects. The MMPI showed profound depression associated with feelings of loss and fear of incompetency. On Performance tasks he demonstrated a tendency to perseverate and inability to unite the components of a task into a coherent whole. His memory and new learning skills were compromised compared to his overall verbal abilities, and he further demonstrated right to left task deficit.

Hospital Course and Current Treatment

The diagnosis of hypothyroidism was established by the Neurology Service, and thyroid replacement was instituted. In addition, he was treated with weekly psychotherapy and amitriptyline to 300 mgs. h.s., with rapid alleviation of vegetative symptoms; subjective and objective improvement of mood did not occur as quickly.

The most salient aspects of this patient's history, physical findings, and laboratory are summarized in a problem-oriented manner.

Problem 1: Two-Year History of Head Pressure and Dizzy Spells

Three years prior to admission, the patient had a normal EEG; skull films and EMI were negative at the time of admission. Subsequent brain scan, EEG, and CSF studies during the hospital admission were within normal limits. *Impression:* Symptoms secondary to hypothyroidism; no space-occupying lesion or other CNS disturbance noted.

Problem 2: Three-Year History of Left-Foot Drop and Distal Motor Weakness

The physical examination corroborated the patient's complaints. The EMG was abnormal with positive sharp waves with fibrillation in the lower extremities. Nerve conduction tests demonstrated some distal denervation. A muscle biopsy of the right gastrocnemius demonstrated myopathic changes, both chronic and active. Serum ANA and rheumatoid factor were negative, an ESR was 46, and CPK was slightly elevated. The patient was evaluated by Rheumatology and it was not felt that he demonstrated polymyositis. *Impression:* Myopathy, either secondary to hypothyroidism or idiopathic.

Problem 3: Chemical Hypothyroidism

T_3 radio-uptake (RU) was 31, T_4 less than 1, free thyroid index (FTI) less than 4. He was initially put on Cytomel, 5 mcgs. t.i.d., which was changed to Synthroid, 0.05 mgs. q.d. One month later, his thyroid functions showed a T_3 RU of 32, T_4 of 2.6, and FTI of 2.0. The patient, however, noted no change in his symptomatology. His thyroid replacement was eventually increased when he became an outpatient, and his most recent thyroid function values were T_4 10.0, T_3 110.6, TSH 3.2. He had antithyroglobulin antibodies positive at 1:6400 and thyroid microsomal antibodies positive at 1:6400.

Despite his euthyroid status, the patient continued to complain of muscle weakness and lack of energy and drive; yet there were obvious changes toward normal in his voice, speech, skin, hair, and available energy, and his major muscle groups test at normal strength. *Impression:* Hypothyroidism, presumably due to autoimmune destruction (Hashimoto's disease?).

Problem 4: One-Year History of Vegetative Symptoms,
Rumination, and Guilt

The patient gave a one-year history of early morning awakening with rumination, feelings of guilt, hopelessness, helplessness, anorexia with a 30-pound weight loss, and episodic constipation, which eventually became continual. The patient showed grave concern over having an undiagnosed fatal disease. It may be significant that when the patient was 12 years old, his father was removed from the home with what he then fantasied was an undiagnosed, fatal disease. As noted under Problem 3, he continued to manifest somatic complaints. Clinical judgment dictated treatment with antidepressant medication, in addition to thyroid hormone replacement therapy. *Impression:* Endogenouslike depression associated with hypothyroidism.

Problem 5: Subjective Memory Complaints and New Learning Deficit

The patient complained of increasing memory difficulties beginning four years prior to admission. He had partial memory and learning deficits on psychometric testing. *Impression:* Mild residual CNS deficit from hypothyroidism.

Summary

Organizing all of the clinical data on this patient under one diagnostic classification is difficult. Chronic tissue thyroid hormone deficiency may account for his lack of energy, muscle weakness and subsequent myopathy, cognitive deficits, and eventual manifestations of endogenouslike depression. Idiopathic myopathy and endogenous depression related, but not secondary, to hypothyroidism cannot be ruled out.

It is conceivable, though doubtful, that these illnesses were unrelated. Most likely, the hypothyroidism "predisposed" this patient to depression, and this predisposition can be viewed both from a biological and psychodynamic standpoint. Recalling the introductory discussion, one may postulate a theoretical chemical explanation: V.S.'s hypothyroid state resulted in altered CNS functioning due to chronically compromised mitrochondrial energy transport and microsomal protein-synthesis machinery, possibly resulting in decreased availability of neurotransmitters. The depression then manifested itself when a critical disturbance of intraneuronal and interneuronal functioning was reached. The vegetative symptoms of early morning awakening, anorexia, weight loss, and constipation followed the disrupted CNS function.

One cannot, however, overlook the effects of V.S.'s illness on his self-concept. Weakness, fatigability, dizziness, and declining mental acuity jeopardized his image as a man, a breadwinner, and head of the household. The "ego damage" sustained may certainly have been enough to intensify the vegetative and cognitive symptoms and perpetuate a cycle of biologically based depression.

HORMONES AND DEPRESSION: FUTURE CLINICAL RESEARCH

Exciting work is in progress on the relation between hormones and affect. Rubin et al.[26] and Weitzman[27] are studying 24-hour hormone-release patterns in normals and such studies are now being applied to endogenously depressed patients. It is conceivable that particular secretion patterns of growth hormone, prolactin, ACTH, follicle-stimulating hormone, and luteinizing hormone may prove to be valuable diagnostic and prognostic aids. For example, a specific release pattern might have high correlation with an excellent response to antidepressant drug therapy.

The recent discovery of the endorphins, endogenous peptides with opiate-like activity in the pituitary and other parts of the brain, opens up a new area of research in depression and other disorders. These peptides could very well play a role in the state of "feeling good" versus "feeling bad." There is speculation that the endorphins may be involved in maintaining "normal behavior," with the corollary that any disruption of endorphin balance would lead to "abnormal behavior."[28] Studies in this area are likely to focus on (a) blood and cerebrospinal fluid levels of the endorphins correlated to psychiatric clinical state and (b) effects of opiate blockers, such as naloxone, which also block the actions of the endorphins.

In the introduction to "Project for a Scientific Psychology," Freud[29] wrote: "The intention is to furnish a psychology that shall be a natural science; that is, to represent mental processes as quantitatively determined states of specifiable material particles." Only through a determined liaison between clinical psychiatry and research shall we come closer to that goal.

Acknowledgement

The author wishes to thank Drs. D. Schwartz, G. Katz, A. Edwards, J. Way, F. Risch and Ms. S. Crantz for their help.

REFERENCES

1. Asher, R. Myxoedematous madness. *Br. Med. J.,* 2:555-562, 1969.
2. Libow, L.A., and Durrell, J. Clinical studies on the relationship between psychosis and the regulation of thyroid gland activity. *Psychosom. Med.,* 28:377-382, 1965.
3. Whybrow, P.C., Prange, A.J., Jr., and Treadway, C.R. Mental changes accompanying thyroid gland dysfunction. *Arch. Gen. Psychiat.,* 120:48-63, 1969.
4. Geel, S., Valcuna, T., and Timiras, P.S. Effect of neonatal hypothyroidism and of thyroxine on L-$[^{14}C]$ leucine incorporation in protein in vivo and the relationship to ionic levels in the developing brain of the rat. *Brain Res.,* 4:143-150, 1967.
5. Schenck, L., Ford, D.H., and Rhines, R. The uptake of S^{35} -L-methionine into the brains of euthyroid and hyperthyroid rats. *Acta Neurol. Scan.,* 40:285-290, 1965.
6. Klee, C.B., and Sokoloff, L. Mitochondrial differences in mature and immature brain: Influence in rate of amino acid incorporation into protein and responses to thyroxine. *J. Neurochem.,* 11:709-716, 1964.
7. Sokoloff, L., Robert, P.A., Januska, M.M., and Kline, J.E. Mechanisms of stimulations of protein synthesis by thyroid hormones in vivo. *Proc. Natl. Acad. Sci.,* 60:652-659, 1968.
8. Baldessarini, R.J. The basis for amine hypotheses in affective disorders. *Arch. Gen. Psychiat.,* 32:1087-1093, 1975.
9. Cohen, H.D., and Barondes, S.H. Acetoxycycloheximide effect on learning and memory of a light-dark discrimination. *Nature,* 218:271-272, 1969.
10. Zemp, J.W., Adair, L.B., Wilson, J.E., and Glassman, E. The effect of training on the incorporation of radioactive precursors into RNA of brain. In: *Molecular Approaches to Learning and Memory,* ed. W.L. Byrne. New York:Academic Press, 1970, pp. 41-51.
11. Whybrow, P.C., and Hurwitz, T. Psychological disturbances associated with endocrine disease and hormone therapy. In: *Hormones, Behavior and Psychopathology,* ed. E. Sachar. New York:Raven Press, 1976, pp. 125-143.
12. Walton, D. The diagnostic and predictive accuracy of the Wechsler Memory Scale in psychiatric patients over sixty-five. *J. Ment. Sci.,* 104:1111-1116, 1958.
13. Steinberg, D.E., and Jarvik, M.E. Memory function in depression. *Arch. Gen. Psychiat.,* 33:219-224, 1976.
14. Kastin, A.J., Ehrensing, R.H., Schalch, D.S., et al. Improvement in mental depression with decreased thyrotropin response after administration of thyrotropin-releasing hormone. *Lancet,* 2:740-742, 1972.
15. Prange, A.J., Jr., Lara, P.P., Wilson, I.C., et al. Effects of thyrotropin-releasing hormone in depression. *Lancet,* 2:999-1002, 1972.
16. Hollister, L.E., Davis, K.L., and Berger, P.A. Pituitary response to thyrotropin-releasing hormone in depression. *Arch. Gen. Psychiat.,* 33:1393-1396, 1976.
17. Whybrow, P.C., Prange, A.J., Jr., McClane, T.K., Rabon, A.M., and Lipton, M.A. Thyroid-hormone enhancement of imipramine in non-retarded depression. *New Eng. J. Med.,* 282:1063-1067, 1970.
18. Prange, A.J., Jr., Wilson, I.C., Breese, G.R., and Lipton, M.A. Hormonal alteration of imipramine response: A review. In: *Hormones, Behavior, and Psychopathology,* ed. E.J. Sachar. New York:Raven Press, 1976, pp. 41-67.
19. Gibbons, J.L. The secretion rate of corticosterone in depressive illness. *J. Psychosom. Res.,* 10:263-266, 1966.
20. Sachar, E.J., Hellmann, L., Roffwarg, H., et al. Disrupted 24 hour patterns of cortisol secretion in psychotic depression. *Arch. Gen. Psychiat.,* 28:19-24, 1973.
21. Carroll, B.J., Curtin, G.C., and Mendels, J. Neuroendocrine regulation in depression. *Arch. Gen. Psychiat.,* 33:1051-1058, 1976.

22. Carroll, B.J., and Mendels, J. Neuroendocrine regulation in affective disorders. In: *Hormones, Behavior, and Psychopathology*, ed. E.G. Sacher. New York:Raven Press, 1976, pp. 193-224.

23. Langer, G., Heinze, G., Reim, R., and Matussek, N. Reduced growth hormone responses to amphetamine in "endogenous" depressive patients. *Arch. Gen. Psychiat.*, 33:1471-1475, 1976.

24. Brauman, H., Smets, P., and Corvilain, J. Comparitive study of growth hormone response to hypoglycemia in normal subjects and in patients with primary myxedema or hyperthyroidism before and after treatment. *J. Clin. Endocrin. Met.*, 36:1162-1174, 1973.

25. Wilkins, J.N., Mayer, S.E., and Vanderlaan, W.P. The effects of hypothyroidism and 2,4-dinitrophenol on growth hormone synthesis. *Endocrinol.*, 95:1249-1267, 1974.

26. Rubin, T.R., Poland, R.E., Rubin, L.E., and Gouin, P.R. The neuroendocrinology of human sleep. *Life Sci.*, 14:1041-1052, 1974.

27. Weitzman, E.D. Neuroendocrine pattern of secretion during the sleep-wake cycle of man. *Prog. Brain Res.*, 42:93, 1975.

28. Bloom, F.E., and Guillemin, R. Endorphins: Profound behavioral effects in rats suggest new etiological factors in mental illness. *Science*, 194:630-632, 1976.

29. Freud, S. Project for a scientific psychology (1895). In: *The Standard Edition of the Complete Psychological Works of Sigmund Freud*, 1:295-343, ed. J. Strachey. London: Hogarth Press, 1966.

CHAPTER 14

Consultation to Neurology: Brain, Behavior, and Patient Care

WALTER KAYE
S. CHARLES SCHULZ

> Integration has been traced at work in two great, and in some
> respects counterpart, systems of the organism. The physico-
> chemical (or for short physical) produced a unified machine
> from what without it would be merely a collocation of com-
> mensal organs. The psychical, creates from psychical data a
> percipient, thinking and endeavouring mental individual ... they
> are largely complemental and life brings them co-operatively
> together at innumerable points ... the formal dichotomy of the
> individual, which our description practised for the sake of analy-
> sis, results in artefacts such as are not in Nature.
>
> —Sir Charles Sherrington,
> *The Integrative Action of the Nervous System*

The preceding chapters have explored a variety of responses to stress and
illness and underscored the fact that each patient's reactions are unique and
must be understood in a highly personalized fashion. Whereas the preceding
chapters describe behavioral responses to life stress or serious illness, the psychiatric consultant to a Neurological Service has the additional task of dealing with
the brain as an organ. As Geschwind[1] remarks, "Many lesions of the brain
directly affect the parts of the nervous system that are involved in emotional
behavior and may cause primary behavior disorders."

In the past we have witnessed a tendency for neuropsychiatric consultants to
"overpsychologize" in their evaluation of patients. This can be a serious mistake,
as discussed by Benson and Blumer:[2]

The abnormal behaviors traditionally called psychiatric disease can result from abnormalities in three separate spheres: the organism itself, the environment influencing the organism, and physical disease affecting the organism. To say that psychiatric disease often results from trouble in two or even all three of these spheres is merely to state the obvious. Yet, in the contemporary practice of psychiatry, the importance of one of these factors, environmental influence, has been placed so high as to totally eclipse the other two. This is particularly true in America where a combination of behaviorist psychological and Freudian influenced psychodynamic theories have strongly dominated psychiatric thinking. Consequently, many psychiatrists tend to overlook both the genetic factors and the presence of physical disease when evaluating their patients. The emphasis on psychodynamic patterns has been so strong that the existence of specific psychiatric, and particularly neuropsychiatric, syndromes has often been overlooked. This same bias has led to an erroneous belief that the organic mental syndromes are intractable and can be safely ignored [p. xv].

Beyond this concern there is also the danger of strict compartmentalization. Smythies[3] points out: "One can be certain that all reductionistic attempts to explain 'mind' in terms of brain chemistry (only), or any combination of these will fail. The facts of conscious experience are irreducible and must enter in their own right as basic irreducible elements into any comprehensive account of the mind." Lipkin[4] also addresses the danger of dichotomization in his paper, "Functional or Organic? A Pointless Question." He states: "Since almost all illness has both psychological and physical components in the clinical picture, the question becomes rather whether how much of the presenting picture is determined by the patient's psychological problems and how much by the structural changes." Lipkin proposes a multifaceted evaluation schema based on etiology, anatomy, pathophysiology, and functional estimation. We found this approach especially helpful in understanding patients with neurological disorders, as there is more and more research linking specific brain function, behavior, and psychiatric disturbance.

It is important for the neuropsychiatric consultant to familiarize himself with recent work that elucidates the connection betweeen the structure and chemistry of the brain and behavior. For example, Slater and Beard[5] suggest that there is a schizophreniform psychosis secondary to temporal lobe epilepsy. They describe the phenomenology of the disorder, explore family histories, and offer a neuroanatomical hypothesis. Stevens[6] similarly reviews the anatomical relation between temporal lobe epilepsy and schizophrenia and concludes that faulty function of the limbic striatum may influence emotional and behavioral patterns. There are also numerous studies delineating the neurochemical basis of psychiatric disorders. The reader may be familiar with Snyder's[7] writings concerning the role of dopamine in schizophrenia. Akiskal and McKinney[8] review studies of biogenic amines and affective disorders and point to decreases in biogenic amines in depression. They conclude, however, with an integrated model suggesting that not only chemical, but genetic, constitutional, and cognitive aspects of the individual need to be considered in any model of depression.

The danger of dichotomizing is to assume that if a problem has an organic base, then a medication or procedure is all that is indicated. Conversely, if a symptom is believed to be purely psychogenic, important organic treatments may be ignored. Surridge,[9] for example, cautions against simply grouping patients with multiple sclerosis who develop psychopathology as "emotionally labile." He has found that sophisticated psychological testing will yield important information which bears on psychiatric management. Surridge notes that multiple sclerosis patients with depression appear to have a depressed affective charge as a consequence of disabling disease, but these patients do not have the organic findings of diminished intelligence and memory seen in those who present with elation.

This chapter will illustrate how we evaluated and treated three neuropsychiatric cases—in each instance we were mindful of how changes in brain structure and chemistry might influence a patient's condition; we were also sensitive to behavior that could be considered secondary to dynamic difficulties. We will discuss a patient with a presumed biochemical brain disorder—Gilles de la Tourette Syndrome, a patient with multiple brain injuries, and a young man with a probable structural brain abnormality leading to episodic dyscontrol.

CASE 1

J.R. was a 27-year-old white male with onset of Gilles de la Tourette Syndrome at age 14. He had been married for seven years and had been rather successfully employed as a real estate agent for five years. Throughout his marriage his wife had been only marginally tolerant of his facial twitching, explosive outbursts, and bizarre, stereotyped movements. She had finally insisted that unless he were treated with Haloperidol, a medication that diminishes Tourette symptoms,[10] she would leave him. The patient had been treated with Haloperidol seven years before, but at that time developed an agitated depression which he insisted was due to the drug; he was opposed to reinstituting it. He was, however, even more frightened of his wife's leaving because he felt that he could "never find another woman who would marry a man with Tourette's." Consequently, he finally consented to treatment.

After a month's treatment he was taking 8 mg. of Haloperidol daily with some relief of tics, but began to experience depression, dysphoria, difficulty in concentrating, loss of self-confidence, and considerable guilt. He discontinued the Haloperidol, the Tourette's symptoms returned, and his agitated depression continued.

By the time he came to the Neuropsychiatric Outpatient Clinic at UCLA he was unable to work because of anxiety and agitation, had lost ten pounds, and was experiencing severe sleep impairment. He presented ruminative thoughts of hopelessness and worthlessness and begged for reassurance. He was staying home all day, unable to concentrate on any task and continually pacing and obsessing. In the late evenings his depression and agitation would usually lessen. He had not had any income for months, placing him in very real financial difficulty.

He was sure his wife was going to leave him now, not only because of his continuing tics, but also because he was depressed and "a burden to her." She did little to support him and frequently stated he was "impossible to live with." She even left him several times, but returned because the separation made her husband even more agitated and hopeless.

There was no history of Tourette's in J.R.'s family. However, the patient's mother had experienced two episodes of severe agitated depression in the past ten years, both requiring hospitalization, medication, and electroconvulsive therapy. J.R.'s life-long coping style at times of stress and rejection was angry withdrawal. He reported that in childhood particularly, his tics prompted ridicule. He had become extremely sensitive to the slightest hint of criticism and reacted in a defensive and petulant manner. Since any minor criticism was seen as complete rejection, he had been unable to establish a stable, mature relationship with anyone. J.R.'s self-image and self-confidence at the best of times were poor.

In diagnosing and treating J.R., the authors used Benson and Blumer's tripartite model of psychiatric illness. The actual assignment of various symptoms to each category is somewhat arbitrary and open to argument. We would consider J.R.'s basic character style of anger and defensiveness as the "abnormality in the organism itself;" the severe marital and financial stress were anxiety-provoking issues or "the environment influencing the organism;" the Tourette's Syndrome and the endogenous depression were seen as the "physical disease affecting the organism."

Gilles de la Tourette's Syndrome was once considered a purely "functional" disease. There is now convincing evidence that it has an organic basis, but the locus of pathology remains unknown. Van Woert and associates[11] have summarized the pharmacologic and cerebrospinal fluid studies that support the hypothesis that Tourette symptoms are related to dopaminergic hyperactivity in the central nervous system.

Schildkraut[12] believes that functional levels of catecholamines control affective disorders and that depression may be a deficiency and mania an excess in catecholamines. Other studies, however, indicate that affective disorders are an area of considerable complexity and that the balance of catecholamines plays an important, but still unclear role.[13,14] There is the possibility that Haloperidol may have precipitated J.R.'s endogenous depression; we await clarification of the multiple biochemical and pharmacological implications of such treatment.

We first concentrated on treating the agitated depression with sequential trials of various medications—Elavil, Tofranil, Mellaril, and Lithium were prescribed with no significant relief of symptoms. However, Parnate, an MAO inhibitor, proved effective, and J.R. became calm, rational, and optimistic. He stopped the drug after one month and his agitated depression returned; re-institution of the Parnate again relieved his depressive symptoms.

We felt that J.R.'s environmental and characterological problems could best be treated by weekly supportive psychotherapy. Empathy and understanding are an integral part of any psychopharmacological intervention. The opportunity to ventilate feelings and talk to a physician who offers a sense of stability and consistency is essential, especially while waiting for a medication to take effect. Furthermore, patients with anxiety, depression, or psychosis often feel unable to make simple decisions and choices. A directive approach gives them the struc-ture they are unable to provide for themselves.

J.R.'s wife was also seen. She expressed much ambivalence about leaving him. She was "embarrassed by his tics," but nevertheless desired that their relation-ship continue. She was an anxious, histrionic woman who felt guilty about forc-ing her husband to take the medication, but was unable to cope with his agita-tion and obsessions. She was assured that several different treatment modalities were yet to be explored and agreed to cooperate with us. This stabilized J.R.'s environment and diminished his anxiety until the Parnate became effective.

It was thus our experience that a trusting therapeutic relationship, continuous evaluation of symptoms and medications, and support and reassurance maxi-mized the possibility of a good outcome. It is our view that it is essential to work in a number of different spheres concurrently.

CASE 2

The psychiatric consultant is often asked to see a patient with permanent brain damage if the patient exhibits an extreme behavioral disorder. Brain damage may impair multiple facets of brain function and personality: there may be concentration difficulties, memory loss, decrease in ability to compare and abstract stimuli, and inappropriate affective responses. The patient himself may recognize affective and cognitive changes; he may experience a decrease in self-esteem and become irritable, anxious, or depressed. Interactions with rela-tives may be very stressful for the patient when these persons are not supportive or create expectations the patient cannot meet. The psychiatrist can often pro-vide a valuable service in helping the patient and his significant others under-stand and deal with these difficulties.

W.T., a 59-year-old white male, had been a successful author. He particularly prided himself on his independence, self-reliance, and self-control. He had be-come expert at various sports such as skiing, scuba diving, and airplane flying. He had great charm and wit and many friends.

Approximately one year prior to our evaluation he underwent vascular sur-gery and during the procedure suffered multiple emboli to the brain. He remained in a delirious-amnesic state for the next six months. His neurological and psychiatric sequelae were multiple, including moderate left hemiparesis, right ocular blindness, mild dysarthria, and pseudobulbar palsy with emotional incontinence-uncontrolled laughing or crying. He found it difficult to concentrate and was unable to write. In addition, there were a number of severe situational problems, including marital, financial, and legal difficulties. He experienced anxiety, depression, and suicidal thinking. He fatigued easily and slept poorly, spending most of his day in bed.

There are a number of neurological and psychological consequences of brain damage that vary according to the location, severity, and type of lesion. Lipowski[15] has summarized this area beautifully in "Organic Brain Syndromes: Overview and Classification." However, psychiatric literature has generally tended to neglect the treatment of the social and emotional reactions of a patient who retains a sense of self-awareness with mild to moderate nonspecific brain dysfunction. A few authors, among them Fowler[16] Najenson et al., [17] and Plutzsky,[18] have written on the practical treatment of brain-impaired patients, and Post[19] has described psychiatric intervention in dementia.

Luria's[20] concept of mental processes may suggest a useful model for treating patients with irreversible brain disease. He describes mental processes as resulting from the participation of groups of brain structures working in concert, each of which makes its own particular contribution to the organization of this functional system. He distinguishes three principal functional units of the brain whose participation is necessary for any type of mental activity: a subcortical unit for regulating arousal or awakening; a posterior cortical unit for obtaining, processing, and storing information arriving from the outside world; and a frontal cortical unit for programming, regulating, and verifying mental activity.

A theoretical scenario of information processing would be as follows: a snake crawls into one's line of vision. To be aware of this fact, one must first be operating at a certain level of arousal—one must be awake. As one scans the snake, one receives and analyzes the information against past memories of objects that are thin, long, legless, and slithery. Along with this past memory of "snake" are associated messages such as "danger" and "fear." At this point one formulates a plan of dealing with this problem (running) and verifies that the body is, in fact, going quickly in the opposite direction. Concomitantly, there is a certain level of increased arousal to help process information and certain metabolic and hormonal processes to help deal with danger.

This is very much the process we go through countless times each day as we scan the environment; check the information against past memories and affects; formulate, carry out, and verify our behavior; and regulate internal processes. We sometimes have to concentrate on one object to the exclusion of others. We may become angry or upset, but because we are in a social situation in which we know it is not appropriate to express our feelings, we control our responses. We perform other associated and complex activities such as selecting from an abundance of information, holding a number of percepts in our mind, and carrying out a behavior.

From this model we can derive one way of understanding the person with nonspecific mild dementia. While such a person may still be capable of processing information, he has limitations: (1) He may be slower in recognizing stimuli. There may be a greater amount of "noise" or false messages because he may at times wrongly identify a stimulus. (2) There may be a limited ability to concentrate, to hold and compare as many bits of information as before. (3) He may have difficulty retaining memories, especially of recent experiences. (4) Because of diminished concentration and ability to internalize and compare bits of information, he may have difficulty planning a course of action. He may then rely more on simple stereotypes of past, overlearned memories. (5) There may be, in a sense, less of a reserve of brain function. He may become easily fatigued and consequently make more errors. (6) He may have difficulty properly modulating and directing strong emotional responses. He may be unable to internalize highly charged emotional situations and respond with an abstract, socially acceptable, nonphysical response. Rather, he may react in a more primitive, concrete, physical way, such as with rage or crying.

Normally, as a person matures, he explores his abilities and develops a comfortable concept of capabilities and limitations. A sudden catastrophic event, such as a shower of emboli to the brain, can produce a dramatic decrease in capacity and consequently in self-image. Depression in reaction to loss of capabilities, anxiety and guilt over burdening one's family, the fear of being neglected, and any number of reactions to poor health and old age may also beset the patient with brain damage. The psychological symptoms are often amenable to treatment and must not be overlooked simply because they occur in the context of brain injury. A therapeutic intervention is intended to help the patient determine the real limits of his altered capabilities. This, of course, may be difficult to explore in an office and may require the assistance of the family, nurses, occupational therapists, and the social work staff. It may be necessary to run through a typical day with the patient or actually observe his routine to help him develop confidence in carrying out daily tasks.

Patients often react to brain dysfunction with premorbid characteristic personality patterns; for example, they may deny or overreact. Since these are difficult styles to change, the consultant may use them to advantage. There may at times be some benefit in allowing the patient to deny disease processes, if denial does not significantly impair functioning. Overreacting, anxious patients will need extra support, reassurance, and anti-anxiety medications. Some patients who appear able to incorporate higher-order feedback may benefit from exploring exactly what loss of function they have suffered so that they may form a new self-image based on new but limited potential.

All patients require a thorough evaluation so that a tailor-made program of rehabilitation can be instituted which maximizes their sense of usefulness. It may be helpful to alert the family to predictable changes in behavior. These include: memory and concentration difficulties, problems with impulse control, labile affective responses, easy fatigability, and difficulty in conceptualizing new plans. These alterations may become particularly evident if brain-damaged persons are emotionally stressed or placed in new and unfamiliar environments.

It must be remembered that there is some plasticity in the ability of the brain to compensate for deficits. With time, some return of function may appear. Consequently, with patience and support, an individual may gradually improve and become more self-sufficient.

It must also be kept in mind that the concept of success in these patients is relative. A return to a former level of function may be unlikely, but various degrees of self-reliance and adjustment are possible. W.T. was seen in weekly sessions for six months, usually alone, but occasionally with relatives. Initially, he ventilated great anger and depression over his situation. In return, he was given the message that his was a normal and realistic response. He discussed his impaired self-image, his inability to pursue his hobbies, and his fears that he would be abandoned by his family. W.T.'s misgivings were openly discussed with the family. Positive coping behaviors were reinforced. A daily routine was devised encouraging gradual return to realistic activity. In time W.T.'s improvement reached a plateau, but we continued to see him and his family on a regular basis to help solve problems as they arose.

CASE 3

The complexity and confusion existing between behavior and brain function is well illustrated by patients with episodic disorders. Some of these patients have behavior patterns that are clearly ictal while others manifest certain difficulties between seizures. Careful study of patients with epilepsy or, as in the case presented here, of those with episodic dyscontrol, may teach us much about the intricate relation between brain structure, emotions, and behavior. In the case that follows, the multifaceted approach described in the previous cases was absolutely necessary.

J.L., a 22-year-old single white male was brought to the Neurology Clinic by his mother for evaluation of "temper outbursts." The patient's chief complaints were that he "lost touch with reality," which on further questioning meant perceptual changes such as derealization, memory lapses for recent events, and rage episodes. The patient stated that his parents had been divorced when he was three and that his mother had remarried when he was nine. J.L. reported getting along poorly with his stepfather. At one time, when his stepfather beat J.L.'s mother, he hit his father over the head with a hammer and stabbed him in the chest. This was the most horrifying of a number of upsetting family experiences. J.L. remembered these experiences vividly, but they were different from the "rages" he experienced beginning at age 13 or 14. These were characterized by the sudden onset of yelling and screaming and then throwing things. During the episodes he often felt stunned or "not all there," and as the episode ended, he would experience an angry feeling and not know why.

Just prior to the evaluation, J.L. had separated from a girlfriend of long-standing and was both depressed and angry. This certainly was a stress leading to an increasing number of episodes before hospitalization.

Evaluation on the Neurology Ward revealed a normal EEG, including naso-pharyngeal leads, but a lumbar puncture did show seven mononuclear cells in his cerebrospinal fluid. All cultures and chemical studies of the cerebrospinal fluid were normal. No lesions were seen on EMI scan. The EMI scan did show slightly enlarged ventricles, but this was interpreted as not clinically significant. Psychological testing revealed an above average IQ and intact long-term memory, but recall and delayed memory were mildly impaired. The diagnostic conclusion was consistent with limbic system dysfunction and episodic dyscontrol. J.L. was treated with Dilantin and phenobarbital which were successful in decreasing the number of rage episodes. He was then hospitalized psychiatrically for two weeks to analyze and attempt to alleviate his feelings of depression and anger concerning his recent separation from his girlfriend. Further psychotherapy was recommended, but he elected to move to another state to obtain employment. Follow-up one year later revealed no evidence of neurological deterioration, but J.L. did have violent episodes when he failed to take his medications.

This case is typical of episodic dyscontrol, a disorder first described in Mark and Ervin's[21] book, *Violence and the Brain*. Monroe outlines the characteristics of this disorder in the second edition of the *American Handbook of Psychiatry*[22] and in his own book.[23] According to Monroe's classification, J.L. evidenced a blend of seizure dyscontrol and instinctual dyscontrol. Seizure dyscontrol is seen as "the more primitive dyscontrol act and is characterized by intense indiscriminate affects, chaotic and uncoordinated motor patterns and indiscriminate selection of the object acted on." Instinctual dyscontrol is defined as "a higher level of dyscontrol act in which the affects are more clearly differentiated. The motor pattern, although lacking in subtlety is nonetheless efficient and coordinated." J.L. himself reported, and this was observed by others, that he was well coordinated during his attacks. Also, these episodes were of indeterminate length and did not involve loss of responsiveness to others.

In Walker's[24] article, "Murder or Epilepsy," criteria for ictal events associated with violence are outlined: (1) The patient is subject to bona fide epilepsy. (2) Spontaneous attacks are similar to those occurring at the scene of the crime. (3) The period of lost awareness is commensurate with the type of seizure. (4) The degree of unconsciousness is consistent with the seizure disorder. (5) The type of EEG is consistent with clinical features. (6) The circumstances of the crime are compatible with the lack of awareness (such as no motive).

By these criteria for a violent ictal event, J.L. did not suffer from classical seizure episodes. Unlike patients with purely instinctual dyscontrol, he described a dreamy state, or standing outside of himself during episodes, and for the last episode described nervous irritability leading up to the rage. We would borrow Monroe's use of the word "epileptoid," defined as "periods of circumscribed excessive neuronal discharge in the central nervous system." It succinctly describes J.L.'s behavior.

Mark and Ervin[21] approach the phenomenon in a somewhat different fashion. They would include this patient in the group described as having dyscontrol syndrome. Their definition of this syndrome is based on a study of a large number of violent patients who had a number of symptoms in common: (1) a history of physical assaults, (2) pathological intoxication, (3) a history of impulsive sexual behavior, and (4) a history of many traffic violations. They note that one-half of the patients studied had seizure phenomena, but only a few had classic temporal lobe epilepsy. A number of the patients they studied had normal EEG's. In essence, Mark and Ervin feel the dyscontrol syndrome is a result of a brain abnormality, most probably in the limbic system, which sometimes can be ameliorated by anticonvulsants such as Dilantin.

In this case, it is important to note the importance of performing sophisticated Luria-based psychological testing which includes a detailed test of intelligence, memory, and perception. This permits the assessment of the functional integrity of various brain structures with more precision and certainty than is possible with superficial psychological testing or conventional mental status examinations.

As a result of diagnosing J.L.'s behavior problem as episodic dyscontrol and not a purely characterological disturbance, an important part of his treatment plan could be formulated which included anticonvulsants. These medications diminished the frequency of his episodic states until he voluntarily stopped them. The other aspect of J.L.'s treatment consisted of psychotherapy while on the Neurology Ward and later on the Inpatient Psychiatry Service. The work consisted of an exploration of personal events, both past and present. J.L. did become less depressed about his recent separation as this was worked through. Even though the significance of his neurological diagnosis was thoroughly explained, we worked together to understand the significance of events preceding rage episodes with the understanding that high levels of stress often precipitated these uncontrollable episodic states.

Thus, it is evident that patients with similar behavioral problems are extremely difficult to strictly categorize, particularly because we really know so little about the location-relation of brain pathology that causes this spectrum of episodic disorders. Simply dismissing such problems as character disorders ignores the neurophysiologic research that clarifies some episodic outbursts of rage. We feel medication can be valuable in decreasing the frequency of episodes and that psychotherapy can be useful in helping these patients learn about themselves, the multiple components of their behavior, and how they relate to other people.

SUMMARY

In the past the psychiatric consultant's role has been that of a somewhat isolated specialist who usually saw patients with a medical and coincidentally psychiatric problem. This book discusses many ways that the psychiatrist has expanded that role. The neuropsychiatric consultant's work takes him one step further—he must deal with the added dimension of treating patients who present brain abnormalities interrelated with psychiatric difficulty.

We have shown that these problems may have a biochemical underpinning, as in the case of Gilles de la Tourette Syndrome, or structural lesions, as in the case of episodic dyscontrol. We have detailed how we evaluated these patients so that the appropriate treatment could be directed to each facet of their difficulty. In this task we were aided both by new diagnostic equipment such as the EMI scan, sophisticated psychological testing, and exciting research which is bringing "brain and behavior" closer together.

We are at the threshold of understanding the neurochemical and electrophysiological basis of behavior. Yet in our quest to comprehend how the brain processes information and how disease disturbs function we should never forget Miller's[25] words: "It is a very limited concept of medicine that strives to understand disease, but not the needs of sick people."

REFERENCES

1. Geschwind, N. The borderland of neurology and psychiatry: Some common misconceptions. In: *Psychiatric Aspects of Neurological Disease,* ed. D. Benson and D. Blumer. New York:Grune & Stratton, pp. 1-9, 1975.
2. Benson, D., and Blumer, D. (Eds.). *Psychiatric Aspects of Neurological Disease.* New York:Grune & Stratton, pp. xv-xvi, 1975.
3. Smythies, J. Psychiatry and neurosciences. *Psychol. Med.,* 3:267-269, 1973.
4. Lipkin, M. Functional or organic? A pointless question. *Ann. Intern. Med.,* 71(5): 1013-1017, 1969.
5. Slater, E., and Beard, A. The schizophrenia-like psychosis of epilepsy. *Br. J. Psychiat.,* 109:95-150, 1963.
6. Stevens, J. Psychomotor epilepsy and schizophrenia: A common anatomy? In: *Epilepsy, Its Phenomenon in Man,* ed. A. Brazier. New York:Academic Press, pp. 189-214, 1973.
7. Snyder, S. Drugs, neurotransmitters and schizophrenia. *Science,* 184:1243-53, 1974.
8. Akiskal, H., and McKinney, W. Overview of recent research in depression. *Arch. Gen. Psychiat.,* 32(3):285-305, 1975.
9. Surridge, D. An investigation into some psychiatric aspects of multiple sclerosis. *Br. J. Psychiat.,* 115:749-764, 1969.
10. Shapiro, K., et al. Treatment of Tourette's Syndrome. *Arch. Gen. Psychiat.,* 28:92-97, 1973.
11. Van Woert, M.H. et al. Gilles de la Tourette's Syndrome: Biochemical approaches. In: *Basal Ganglia,* ed. M.D. Yahr. New York:Raven Press, pp. 251-260, 1976.
12. Schildkraut, J. A catecholamine hypothesis of affective disorders. *Am. J. Psychiat.,*

122:509-522, 1965.

13. Goodwin, F. L-dopa, catecholamines and behavior: A clinical and biochemical study in depressed patients. *Biol. Psychiat.,* 2:341-366, 1970.

14. Shopsin, B. Catecholamines and affective disorders revised: A critical assessment. *J. Nerv. Ment. Dis.,* 158:369-383, 1974.

15. Lipowski, Z.J. Organic brain syndromes: Overview and classification. In: *Psychiatric Apsects of Neurological Disease,* ed. D. Benson and D. Blumer. New York:Grune & Stratton, pp. 11-35, 1975.

16. Fowler, R.S. Adapting care for the brain-damaged patient. *Am. J. Nursing,* 72:1932-1935, 2056-2059, 1972.

17. Najenson, T., et al. Rehabilitation after severe head injury. *Scand. J. Rehab. Med.,* 6:5-14, 1974.

18. Plutzsky, N. Principles of psychiatric management of chronic brain syndromes. *Geriatrics,* 29:120-127, 1974.

19. Post, F. Dementia, depression and pseudo-dementia. In: *Psychiatric Aspects of Neurological Disease,* ed. D. Benson and D. Blumer. New York:Grune & Stratton, pp. 99-120, 1975.

21. Mark, V., and Ervin, F. *Violence and the Brain.* New York:Harper & Row, 1970.

22. Monroe, R. Episodic behavioral disorders: An unclassified syndrome. *American Handbook of Psychiatry,* 2nd Ed. New York:Basic Books, 1974.

23. Monroe, R. *Episodic Behavioral Disorders.* Cambridge: Harvard University Press, 1970.

24. Walker, E.A. Murder or epilepsy. *J. Nerv. Ment. Dis.,* 133:430-436, 1961.

25. Miller, H. Fifty years after Flexner. *Lancet,* 2:647-654, 1966.

Index